Textual and Theatrical Shakespeare

STUDIES IN
THEATRE HISTORY
AND CULTURE
Edited by
Thomas Postlewait

Textual and Theatrical Shakespeare

Questions of Evidence

Edited by Edward Pechter

University of Iowa Press

Iowa City

University of Iowa Press, Iowa City 52242

Copyright © 1996 by the University of Iowa Press

All rights reserved

Printed in the United States of America

DESIGN BY OMEGA CLAY

Printed on acid-free paper

Library of Congress Cataloging-in-Publication Data

Textual and theatrical Shakespeare: questions of evidence /
    edited by Edward Pechter.
        p.   cm.—(Studies in theatre history and culture)
    Includes bibliographical references and index.
    ISBN 0-87745-545-7
    1. Shakespeare, William, 1564–1616—Dramatic
production.   2. Shakespeare, William, 1564–1616—
Criticism, textual.   3. Shakespeare, William, 1564–1616—
Stage history.   I. Pechter, Edward, 1941– . II. Series.
PR3091.T49   1995
792.9′2—dc20   95-50872
                                                   CIP

01 00 99 98 97 96 C 5 4 3 2 1

Contents

Preface

Textual and Theatrical Shakespeare: Questions of Evidence is a collection of essays by ten critics who approach Shakespeare's plays from a variety of positions—literary and textual commentary, performance criticism, social history, cultural theory, and theatre history. The contributors reflect and reflect upon the different kinds of evidence available to us from Shakespeare's various incarnations as historical subject and as "our contemporary," as well as from Shakespeare's amphibious occupation of both "the stage and the study."

This book had its origins in the work of a group of McGill Shakespeareans, under circumstances described in the statement of the director, John Ripley, just below. I am grateful to the group, including Patrick Nielson and Denis Salter as well as the four whose essays are included here, for inviting me to join with them in their work and to undertake this book and for helping me in all the stages leading to its realization. My thanks go also to Sarah Stanton for some shrewd editorial advice early on and to Thomas Postlewait, whose generous intelligence is reflected throughout.

EDWARD PECHTER

A number of the essays in this volume were originally delivered in the course of a year-long colloquium on the topic "Shakespeare in Performance: The Nature of Evidence," sponsored by the McGill University Shakespeare in the Theatre Research Group. The Group's research is made possible by the generosity of the Fonds pour la Formation de Chercheurs et l'Aide à la Recherche of the Ministère de l'Education of the Gouvernement du Québec, for which we express our warmest appreciation. We are indebted to those who contributed invited essays; to our research assistants, Iona Brindle, Marcel Dacoste, Felicity Enayat, Michael Morgan Holmes, and Jessica Slights; and to the Department of English, McGill University.

JOHN RIPLEY

Textual and Theatrical Shakespeare

1

Textual and Theatrical Shakespeare: Questions of Evidence

Edward Pechter

In 1977, writing in *The Shakespeare Revolution*, J. L. Styan declared that "some of the more fruitful research of recent years has been in the history of performance, reconstructed through prompt-books and contemporary reports. Such work recognized directions for future Shakespeare studies, and brought practice and criticism into a healthier alliance for the benefit of both the stage and the study" (6). In concluding that the mutually beneficial alliance between "practice and criticism" was an accomplished fact, Styan now seems overly optimistic. To be sure, theatrical performance has been thoroughly legitimized as an approach to Shakespeare; the fact that Shakespeare wrote for the stage is now routinely acknowledged as a relevant consideration, some-times even as the necessary starting point for all interpretation. Room is made to include academic criticism in Royal Shakespeare Company (RSC) and comparable programs and a substantial space reserved in the major Shakespeare journals for commentary on recent productions. At the same time, however, the relationship between "the stage and the study" remains problematic. The inhabitants of these different domains— "the wide-eyed spectator" and "the slit-eyed reader," as Harry Berger calls them—are different; perhaps not to the extent of a mutual incom-prehension and hostility (as in Berger's deliberately jocular exaggera-tion), but large gaps remain between the commentary centered either in the theatrical performance of Shakespeare's plays or in the literary and cultural analysis of Shakespeare's texts. Why these gaps exist, how we can close them, or indeed whether we should even be trying to do so— these are the sorts of questions raised by the essays below.

What Styan could not see in 1977 was the imminent transformation of Shakespearean commentary, and of literary and theatrical studies in general, through the dissemination and eventual absorption of new historical and theoretical assumptions. By now, the various claims that have driven this change should be familiar: the beholder's share; the arbitrariness of the sign and textual indeterminacy; gender and social distinctions as influential factors in the production and reception of texts; the contingent rather than necessary distinctions between academic disciplines; and the fluctuating historical determinations of literature (including theatrical production) as a special category of discourse. As a consequence of these beliefs, many Shakespeareans have tended to reconceptualize both the object and the activity of their work in rhetorical and cultural terms. From their perspective, the interpretation of Shakespeare consists not so much in uncovering the meanings already embedded in a more or less stable and self-explanatory text, but in constructing meanings which have themselves been provisionally constructed and reconstructed in socially specific and ideologically motivated ways.

With the widespread adoption of such a perspective, we have a problem determining on what bases to organize and regulate interpretive activity. What can or should count as evidence for the claims we make? These questions about evidence have become a central concern for critics in the humanities (as witness the space devoted to them in our most prestigious journals),[1] and they are particularly complicated questions for Shakespeareans as a consequence of the multiplicity of forms in which Shakespeare is available for our scrutiny: produced historically and reproduced to the present day in both theatrical and literary interpretation (to say nothing of popular culture). If it once seemed easy enough to exchange and combine interpretive resources from literary and theatrical evidence, it now looks as though such a "revolutionary alliance" was made possible only by abstracting both domains from the contingencies of history and interpretive activity (which texts? what is performance?) and by collapsing the distinctions between them. These distinctions, though, matter profoundly. To judge from its root in seeing, evidence consists of ocular proof; but as Berger's wide-eyed specta-

tor and slit-eyed reader suggest, different ways of seeing will see different things—producing different kinds of evidence by differently consti-
tuting the object of perception. The essays in *Textual and Theatrical
Shakespeare* are written out of this perplexing situation and collected as
a way of considering the possibilities available to us, given the constraints of our different Shakespearean interests, for (in Richard Rorty's
phrase) continuing a useful conversation.

In "How Good Does Evidence Have to Be?" Michael Bristol starts the
discussion with a wide-ranging, general consideration of the different
ways evidence functions to structure critical inquiry and justify its
claims. In a "theoretical context," concerned with discovering "regularities, general laws, and causal explanations within a well-specified object
domain," evidence is expected to be disinterested and independent of the
hypothesis it is designed to test. In a "forensic context," however, "oriented to public discussion and debate," evidence is often circumstantial
or "soft" and always in some measure generated out of and toward a set
of interests.[2] Not that as humanists "we have a warrant for indifference
to questions of evidence": though our evidence can never provide us
with "solid and unshakable guarantees about the truth of specific beliefs," it "doesn't have to." It needs to give us only a basis for "preferring socially usable knowledge, whenever we can get it, to rumor, superstition, and wishful thinking."

Two of Bristol's topics are especially pertinent to the essays following
his: the transferability of evidence between different kinds of study and
the rhetorical context for evidence. About the first Bristol provides reas-
surance. "The use of evidence can be extremely helpful when there are
strong disagreements over multiple competing accounts of a difficult
question"—as with the authorship controversy. Most readers will share
Bristol's sense of the appropriate conclusions to draw from the available
evidence (Shakespeare wrote the plays), but then how can we account for
the long history of anti-Stratfordian resistance? Pig-headed bias or original sin may be relevant here (as when not?), but Bristol's analysis of
"particularist research" implies a more interesting explanation. Culling
the archives in order to reconstruct extraordinary lives, particularist researchers skipped over as tedious the details of disputes among anonymous ordinary people. Such details are currently the evidentiary staple
for an *Annales* model of social history, but since this model did not exist
for particularist researchers, the details that might have supported it
were simply invisible: they "did not belong to the category of 'evidence'

because they couldn't answer any question worth asking." The issue (as Hayden White argued years ago) "is the question of precisely what counts as evidence and what does not, how data are to be constituted as evidence" (*Metahistory*, 284). From this perspective, to succeed in mediating let alone resolving differences, evidence must be sharable among parties working out of similar basic assumptions. Otherwise, it will function not to resolve disputes but to reproduce them.

Is evidence transferable between the different literary and theatrical approaches to Shakespeare? It is hard to answer the question in general; it depends on what we mean by "literary" and "theatrical" (and probably by "we"). In considering recent claims that Shakespeare revised his plays, Bristol suggests some grounds for optimism. The revisionist hypothesis substitutes "a bias in favor of the working theatre" for "a bias in favor of . . . the printed book," but it "is not a radical rejection of the standard account." The matter seems more complicated, however, in the case of "the sharpest challenge to the standard account," where "the very notion of authorship" is claimed to be "an ideological fiction." Bristol casts a cool eye on the evidentiary bases for this claim as made by Margreta de Grazia and Peter Stallybrass in a powerfully controversial essay published in a recent *Shakespeare Quarterly*: "the problem here is certainly not with the quantity" of evidentiary support, "no fewer than 115 footnotes in an article of 33 pages," but rather "with the explanatory relationship between the evidence assembled and the hypothesis proposed." If, as Bristol suggests, de Grazia and Stallybrass are seeking "to redeem and vindicate the dignity of those anonymous laborers" who contributed to the printing of the 1623 Folio, there is no logical necessity for "refusing to countenance the idea that individualized creativity has anything whatever to do with the production of textual artifacts."

But then what kind of explanatory relationship is possible here? How can any kind or amount of evidence serve to demonstrate that authorship, or anything else, is an ideological fiction? The question can be thought through in different terms, as one of persuasion rather than demonstration; this brings us to the second topic, the rhetorical context for evidence. As Bristol points out, the persuasive power of evidence "depends ultimately on an appeal to the authority of a community," and the community of *SQ* readers, given their training in the conventions of literary research, may well tend to be convinced by the sheer mass of the scholarly apparatus which de Grazia and Stallybrass produce in support of their argument. Judged as a rhetorical rather than as a strictly logical performance, de Grazia and Stallybrass' argument makes better sense. They are advocating a new kind of disciplinary commitment—to cultural studies, communications technology—and in seeking converts from among Shakespeareans, they must erode the authority that sustains the old discipline. Claims about the death of the author may be undemonstrable, but as the power of this essay to engage readers' beliefs attests, faith can be built on the evidentiary foundations of things unseen.[3]

With Alan Dessen's "Recovering Elizabethan Staging: A Reconsideration of the Evidence," we leave these abstract considerations for an immediately practical engagement with the problem of evidence. Taking off from "the discovery in 1992 of a hitherto unexamined Jacobean printed quarto with playhouse annotations," Dessen addresses himself directly to the question of what such "evidence can establish about what the original playgoers actually saw when they watched a given scene." In reviewing the early texts, he uncovers a wide range of detail richly suggestive as a source for plausible speculative reconstruction. If "establish" is the key word, however, this evidence turns out to be generally disappointing ("no 'Ahas!' or 'Eurekas!' . . . no smoking gun"), and Dessen's essay is a profoundly cautionary tale. Part of the problem is that playhouse annotation in the Renaissance seems to have been a minimalist activity, nothing like the detailed practices of later theatrical bookkeepers. Moreover, even the annotations that we have are laconic. As a form of in-house commentary, they take for granted (and therefore do not need to specify) the very matters we are seeking to clarify. As a consequence, we can sometimes find more detailed descriptions of theatrical performance in Renaissance playtexts apparently derived from nontheatrical origins, though these descriptions may tell us more about the needs and desires of authors, readers, and printers than about the theatrical practices themselves. And finally, whatever evidence we might have that can survive all of this skeptical scrutiny is difficult to generalize. Although it may be able to suggest what some original playgoers actually saw when they watched a given scene, it is doubtful whether we can or should transfer the conclusions we might draw from such evidence to other playgoers at other playhouses watching different plays.[4]

In "Performance-Game and Representation in *Richard III*," Robert Weimann builds upon the formative distinction he developed in earlier work between upstage and downstage positions, *locus* and *platea*, the two different places of medieval performance carried over (conceptually if not physically) onto the stages of Renaissance amphitheatres.[5] The *locus* is the place of representation and history, where we see a monstrous Richard of Gloucester connive and murder his way onto the throne. The *platea* is the place of theatrical performance, where we engage directly with Richard Burbage's brilliant performative efforts in the collaborative venture of producing the play. Though *locus* and *platea* can be (and have been) used to designate the distinctions between a textual and theatrical Shakespeare, Weimann wishes here to locate these differences within theatrical performance itself: "it is not enough to dispense with the text/performance dichotomy; performative action itself needs to be relocated at that crucial point where dramatic language and cultural institution, representation and existence, can be seen to interact."

In emphasizing "interaction," "transaction," "ambidextrous design," and the like, Weimann strongly argues his claim for the "bifold authority" of Shakespeare; but this "principle of multi-consciousness" or "double-eyedness," as he has called it elsewhere,[6] remains slippery as well as richly suggestive. If text-and-performance can be folded into performance, can they not be folded into text as well, with reading also understood as a response to a bifold authority?[7] However this may be, the dialectical nature of performance itself as Weimann describes it is hard to translate exactly into practical terms. Though Richard can be himself alone and then negotiate the distance to a position occupied by Burbage himself alone, is he ever both at the same time?—a "double man," to recall Falstaff's words toting Hotspur's corpse at the end of *1 Henry IV*. Does Richard/Burbage ever occupy his own real property, or is the space between *locus* and *platea* just that—always defined differentially and relationally? Does "that crucial point where dramatic language and cultural institution . . . can be seen to interact" correspond to any physical viewing position inside any actual Renaissance theatre?

This emphasis upon seeing brings us back to—or shows that we have never really left—questions about evidence. At the end of his essay, Dessen smiles in passing at his version of a fantasy all Shakespeareans share—the magical surfacing of a videotaped Globe performance. But even if we had such a tape, or even if we could be transported through space and time to the performance itself, the available evidence would continue (as Dessen is fully aware) to be problematic. We'd have to crack not only the visual codes (to determine the ghost's visibility in *Hamlet*, say, in Dessen's example) but the cultural codes as well (to read the ghost's visibility within the framework of disputed claims about the authority of apparitions—which is to say, within the fragmented religious context of post-Reformation Europe). But as Weimann's essay suggests, even this wouldn't be enough. By emphasizing the immediacy of the theatrical situation—performance as "existence" or "being," as "an irreducible investment, on the part of actual (not fictional) agents, of their mental and visceral energy, their time, skill, competence, and, even, their sociocultural status and interest"—Weimann implies that we would need not only to read but to live inside the cultural codes: get under the skin of the original spectators, occupy a position not only within the distracted Globe but within their distracted globes.

For Weimann, the context for Renaissance theatrical performance is understood in materialist terms. Against a traditional social order defined by inherited status, "the new forces of capitalism" (as he has put it elsewhere), "the emerging relations of economic and cultural exchange, the volatile and increasingly placeless institution of the market must have constituted countervailing energies that . . . profoundly involved the theater" ("Representation and Performance," 508). But just what is the "institution of the market," and on what evidentiary basis do we erect such an explanatory narrative? These are the questions underlying Kathleen McLuskie's contribution, "The Shopping Complex: Materiality and the Renaissance Theatre." Granting that "the connection between early modern and the postmodern market is made easier by the way in which dramatic texts provide powerful poetic and theatrical images which generalize 'the market,'" McLuskie nonetheless cautions that "these satisfyingly coherent connections . . . need to be put under some critical pressure before they can be accepted as equally satisfactory evidence of the historical circumstances of early modern theatrical production."

McLuskie describes commercial activity both as a subject treated by the plays (the market in the theatre) and as the circumstances within which the plays were produced (the market for the theatre). In the case of commerce as a dramatic subject, she emphasizes unevenness and diversity. Commerce could be inflected generically into very different tonalities and meanings: the connection between sex and shopping, for instance, could produce "a narrative of tragic betrayal" or "a set of bawdy jokes." Commerce itself could be played for delight in a burgeoning world of pleasurable innovations as well as for anxious fears about a loss of traditional community. So too with commerce as an institutional situation: McLuskie describes "the instability, the stopping and starting and the bewildering set of temporary and ad hoc alliances among actors, playwrights, and entrepreneurs." To lump all such aspects of Renaissance theatrical enterprise under the rubric of "*the* market" gives a false sense of coherence and stability, projecting backward "the notion of an 'institutionalized' market with its echoes of Louis Althusser's Ideological State Apparatuses" onto a fluid and inchoate collection of tenuously connected or even disconnected arrangements and activities.

In addition to complicating our concepts of the market in and for Renaissance plays, McLuskie wishes to complicate our sense of the relationship between them. Renaissance plays frequently thematized their own market relations as commodities displayed before consumers, but the evidentiary status of these thematizations is by no means clear. In an earlier essay, McLuskie expressed reservations about the mimetic emphasis in some current analyses:

> In our excitement at the discovery that Shakespearean drama was implicated in the real social relations of early modern England, we have perhaps neglected the formal and material circumstances of its operation; the way in which . . . dramatic material is differently inflected according to the rhetorical and dramatic requirements of different stages and audiences [and] the extent to which [Shakespearean drama] is not purely mimetic but is also negotiating with a variety of literary discourses which represent . . . relations outside the parameters of immediate social existence. ("Lawless Desires," 122)

McLuskie develops a similar claim here, partly with reference to *The Knight of the Burning Pestle*. The play can be read mimetically to suggest the decline of certain popular romance genres, at least among private theatre audiences; but the plays sent up by Francis Beaumont continued to thrive, sometimes in the repertoires of the same theatre companies and in front of the same audiences by whom and for whom *The Knight* was itself performed. "It would be dangerous, therefore, to accept the dramatic conflict between Beaumont's Grocer and the boy players" as "evidence of a real divide, either between popular and elite culture or between residual and dominant modes of representation."

Instead of this potentially misleading mimetic analysis, McLuskie proposes a functional or pragmatic interpretive strategy:

> By offering an image of the theatre as purchasable and engaged in a debate with itself over the cultural status of that purchase, these scenes constructed their audience as the consumers of a particularly valued

commodity. The dramatization of market relations, including those in the theatre, translate the economic relations of theatre into cultural relations in which the theatres can trade.

To put this in Weimann's terms, Renaissance plays do not so much represent as perform their own theatricality. To be sure, this analysis is reversible: the "cultural market" is "ultimately dependent . . . on the precise and changing economic relations in which the playtexts were owned." The resulting relationship is at once reciprocal and contradictory (again as in Weimann) and requires a constant revision in the sources we choose for our evidence and the directions in which it is read.

Dessen, Weimann, and McLuskie are concerned with the ways different kinds of evidence authorize and constrain our attempts to retrieve original performances. In the next three essays, the focus shifts to theatre history, the afterlife of Shakespearean texts as adapted for performances in different cultural contexts. John Ripley turns our eyes to *The Ingratitude of a Common-wealth*, Nahum Tate's adaptation of *Coriolanus* first performed in 1682. In view of Tate's reputation as the most egregious of Restoration "manglers" of Shakespeare, *The Ingratitude* might seem to furnish evidence less for understanding *Coriolanus* than for proving Tate's own misprision. According to Ripley, however, Tate's reputation, based on the view that Restoration revisions tried to regularize Shakespeare with reference to neoclassical canons, is itself based on misprision: "Many of the adaptations are as innocent of unity of place or time as Shakespeare's original; scenes of onstage violence are endemic; and the principles of poetic justice are routinely flouted." Making use of Margreta de Grazia's argument about eighteenth-century editing practices, Ripley proposes looking at *The Ingratitude* not as a failure but rather as the achievement of an understanding—though one based on principles and assumptions different from those of the Tate-bashers.

From this perspective, *The Ingratitude* turns out to be "an instructive example of the transformation of a highly fluid Jacobean dramatic text into a stable instrument of Restoration propaganda." A direct Tory intervention in the Exclusion Crisis, Tate's play was nothing if not immediately engaged in contemporary politics. By taking Tate seriously on his own terms, Ripley insists that we acknowledge the "political potential" that Tate must have sensed in his source. With this acknowledgment, the story of Restoration misprision can be understood as part of an ongoing rationalization for refusing *Coriolanus'* political dimension,

both in the theatre (where only Dennis and Brecht "overtly confronted
. . . the play's political vitality") and in "the study" (which "since the
eighteenth century has engaged in what amounts to a critical conspiracy
to displace the play's political concerns with character analysis").

At the same time, however, Tate not only adopted but adapted *Coriolanus*; his "revision was thorough and radical." Hence the shifting subjects and perspectives in *Coriolanus* are stabilized in *The Ingratitude* to
produce a unified effect upon the emotions.

> As the structure is simplified and regularized, the richness and complex-
> ity of the original more insistently reveal themselves. At the moment
> of their disappearance, the interdependence of the disparate foci, their
> capacity to resonate against and reinforce each other, becomes trans-
> parent, revealing how much of the Roman-Volscian narrative and the
> mother-son relationship must be sacrificed to make *Coriolanus*'s polit-
> ical attributes prevail.

This might seem like an argument for *Coriolanus'* political disinterest-
edness after all, even a step toward treating the "Victorian and Edwardian objections to the Restoration adaptors' sacrilege" as justified in
their design "to place Shakespeare's plays beyond history and ideology."
Does Tate's play, then, constitute evidence that the resistance to the political dimension of *Coriolanus* originates in *Coriolanus* itself?

This is not Ripley's point, however. Shakespeare's play is as deeply
political as Tate's, but differently so, as a consequence of the different
conditions of its production. Its open stage encouraged movement in
contrast to the stabilizing frame around the action on the proscenium
stage. Produced within a "functionally ambiguous" or "powerless theatre," *Coriolanus* was not designed (as was Tate's version) for immediate and unequivocal translation into ideological engagement—
something the greater social diversity of Shakespeare's audience would
have rendered very difficult, even if it were not so risky. In "The Shopping Complex," McLuskie emphasizes the cultural reproducibility of
Renaissance drama: as "more easily separable from particular theatrical
and social contexts," it was "more open for its meanings to be reconstructed with the cultural toolkit of a different audience." On the evidence of Tate's play, Ripley makes a similar claim about the staying
power of *Coriolanus*: "to bias *Coriolanus'* overdetermined political vision, to fix its tantalizingly fluid aesthetic, is to diminish it, to deprive it
of the mechanism for self-renewal."

With "The Rhetoric of Evidence: The Narration and Display of Viola and Olivia in the Nineteenth Century," we move from a Restoration version of *Coriolanus* to nineteenth-century versions of *Twelfth Night*. Laurie Osborne examines two bodies of material: accounts of Maria Tree's singing as Viola in an operatic version of the play and illustrations of Olivia's unveiling to Viola in the fifth scene, emphasizing the distance and displacement in both cases of the material from the "aural and visual effects of the performances" they purport to describe. Inevitably, the enactment itself as a "material occurrence" remains "inaccessible": "actual performances are irrecoverable." As a consequence, Osborne proposes, instead of treating such material like a transparent window upon an absent original, to consider it in effect within the rhetorical context suggested by Bristol's discussion of evidence at the beginning: not as instrumental and secondary, the means to knowledge about something other than itself, but rather as the object of study in itself, with its own textual energies and discursive effects.

From this position, Osborne considers William Oxberry's "Memoir of Miss Ann Maria Tree," which, whatever its shortcomings as an account of the actress' vocal performance, provides a rich source of evidence for studying the author's own rhetorical resources and constraints. Though hostile to Tree, Oxberry incorporates favorable accounts of the actress into his memoir, motivated (presumably) by standard rhetorical strategies—refutation (along with proof, the major basis for persuasion) and ethos (by considering negative evidence, he projects a sense of fair-mindedness). Despite Oxberry's efforts to subdue them to his own purposes, however, the earlier accounts resist total incorporation and maintain an independent existence as the source of sympathetic readings of Tree's career. From this Osborne concludes that "our arguments, whatever their own agendas, embody and speak the rhetoric of our evidence" and that "embedded evidence does not necessarily lose its rhetorical force when indented or placed in quotation marks."

One consequence of Osborne's analysis is to reveal the extent to which our understanding is determined by tradition and continuity. Willy-nilly, we discuss Shakespeare's plays within the context of an already-established discussion which reproduces itself even in the midst of our own most strenuously transformative exertions.[8] But Osborne's focus on the rhetorical dimensions of evidence can serve to redeem the regulative function we traditionally ascribe to it as well. Leigh Hunt's interest in Tree's shapely leg, Oxberry's fascination with her scandalous life, and more recently Barbara Melchiori's responsiveness to the lesbian resonances of a poem accompanying a Victorian illustration of Olivia's unveiling—all these may be characterized as displacements from actual performances of *Twelfth Night*. At the same time, however, by reflecting "concerns about female propriety and appearance" and being drawn from "the available discourses of dangerous female behaviors," this material serves "as evidence [for] the cultural negotiations with women's roles in *Twelfth Night* on the nineteenth-century stage"; and unless we conceive of performance as immediate experience—raw sights and sounds unmediated by ideological pressures and interpretive activity—such cultural negotiations are always a constitutive part of theatrical experience (what would we see or hear without them?). From this angle, the "conflicting rhetorical features" of our evidence and the conflicted "traces of performance" within it—the performative and the cognitive properties of our evidence—may be effectively equal if not quite identical to one another.

In "Edwin Booth's *Richard II* and the Divided Nation," Catherine Shaw sets out to explain why basically the same production was accorded such different responses in southern and northern cities in the decade following the American Civil War. She concludes that audiences in the North "rejected the play as out of touch with their own aggressively entrepreneurial energies," whereas Southerners found the play "politically and culturally compatible" with their sense of powerlessness and isolation and with their self-image as "a lost Camelot of landed gentry." Booth's brother assassinated Lincoln and *Richard II* is an assassination play, which reinforces the explanatory power of Shaw's argument. The problem, however, as Shaw readily acknowledges, is that "little or no hard evidence" exists to support this explanation: "no newspaper review, editorial, or political commentary" folds the play into the cultural context in the way she suggests. Shaw deals with this problem by analogy with an assassination attempt on Booth himself, playing Richard II in Chicago. Contemporary responses with only a single exception failed to acknowledge any recognition of the obvious parallel to Lincoln's assassination—as though the memory was simply too painful to confront. In the same way, Shaw suggests, not "bringing out into the open the reasons behind the divided attitudes toward" both Booth and *Richard II* was a way to avoid a traumatic "renewing" of "'war rancors.'" By calling attention to a "significant silence," Shaw's argument suggests that evidence may sometimes be more present in its absence.

The persuasive power of Shaw's essay may depend, however, less on arguments and evidence (including arguments about evidence) than on rhetoric, and in particular on narrative. Shaw begins with an anecdote, the assassination attempt on Booth "late in the evening of April 23, 1879," and the circumstantial detail that characterizes her narration of this event—the exact lines Booth was delivering from Richard's prison soliloquy when "two gunshots," not one, not three, "shattered the silence of the theatre"—is reproduced throughout the essay. These details enrich our sense of Booth himself—his only vote in a federal election (for Lincoln in 1864), his wife's lunacy—and of the theatrical, cultural and political contexts as well: the Macready-Forrest riot, Whitman's ambivalence about Shakespeare, Blaine's exception to the Amnesty Bill. Such details are not always necessarily instrumental to the development of an argument, but each contributes to a sense of densely interconnected circumstances. (That Booth was a target on the evening of *April 23* is a fact whose meaning is impossible to determine, but how can it be without meaning for any Shakespearean?) The power of such details may recall the Geertzian "thick description" to which Bristol refers in the first essay of this anthology, and even more so Bristol's discussion of Alexander Welsh and the persuasive power of narrative accounts in which "circumstantial evidence requires that inferences be made about the likely causes of known effects." In Welsh's terms, Shaw's essay is a "strong representation."

Leanore Lieblein's is the first of three essays that bring the discussion into recent and contemporary theatrical and textual productions of Shakespeare. In all of these essays, there are strong lines of continuity with the questions about evidence raised by earlier contributors working in the modes of historical retrieval. Like Booth's *Richard II* in Shaw's description, the recent Québécois productions Lieblein examines look different under different circumstances. Referring to Michel Garneau's translations of Shakespeare, Lieblein remarks that "traduit en québécois" signified very differently for audiences fifteen years apart: an aggressive challenge to the linguistic dominance symbolized by "le 'grand Will'" in the insecure context of an insurgent nationalism in 1978; the assumption of an achieved authority as "both a 'classical' and an 'international' language" in the confident environment of 1993. The reception by different audiences of *Le Cycle des rois* in 1988 is even more striking. Where francophones saw the histories as evidence of "the greatness, the universality, and the timelessness of Shakespeare," anglophone audiences "experienced them . . . much more ironically" with specific relation to their own diminished cultural position. "A single production," Lieblein concludes, "may find more than one community of reception."

One consequence of Lieblein's analysis is to exert pressure upon a phrase like "a single production" and the implied existence of an authentic original performance underlying the diverse materials that represent it to us. A misleading implication, Lieblein says: "the theatre event as written about is never present, but always elsewhere," and since its traces are available to us only in documentation of a "local, partisan, contingent, and contradictory nature," any attempt "to reconstruct a single 'performance text'" seems futile. Working from a similar position, Laurie Osborne turned her attention to a rhetorical analysis of evidence. Lieblein too acknowledges the rhetorical dimension and our need to be "aware of the ideological and other investments that produced the materials the archives contain"; but her emphasis is elsewhere. Even the most interested document has evidentiary value beyond its own strategy; a press release cannot "'manipulate' an audience . . . without first *seeing* that audience," and "it may be *in* the biases that we find the insights." Above all, Lieblein insists upon the productive variety of the evidentiary materials available to us, "the diversity of viewing positions and agendas that makes such documents a rich source. . . . The more views of a theatre event, the better."

In "'Here Apparent': Photography, History, and the Theatrical Unconscious," Barbara Hodgdon invites us to look at portraits of stars, pictures of actors in rehearsal and performance, and stage tableaux, marshaled for our attention in the form of various commodities—postcards, souvenir programs, dust jackets of academic stage histories. These diverse subjects and contexts cannot easily be subsumed under a unitary concept of knowledge, but Hodgdon's point is precisely to encourage skepticism "about categorizing such photographs as 'evidence.' By bracketing the term, I mean to destabilize its privileged epistemological status: evidence of what? for whom? and in what contexts?" The privileged status depends upon decontamination, reducing the obtrusive interests of photographer and publicity department in order to approximate performance itself. "Such cautionary advice seems eminently sensible," Hodgdon acknowledges, but it risks turning theatrical commentary into "a self-regarding discourse" that operates "exclusively within theatrical culture." Instead of erecting "disciplinary boundaries around

the theatrical still," Hodgdon proposes "a materialist poetics of photographic evidence" as "embedded within a series of authorized and authorizing institutional practices," of "uses which 'dirty' the pictures."

Like Osborne and Lieblein, Hodgdon remarks on the unbridgeable
gap between performance and the evidence by which we try to retrieve
it. "Theatre is a stream of moving images," but "the photographic still
. . . aches with absence even as it stakes out some sort of talismanic claim
on the 'theatrical reality.'" But there are differences from other contributors as well; *aches* is a word that signals Hodgdon's idiosyncratically
personal and confessional investment in her material. "'Here Apparent'"
begins with an autobiographical anecdote: the power of McBean's Burton
to "trap my gaze" reveals "a habit-forming kind of consumership which
blurs the distinction between seeing Burton play Hal (I never did) and
wishing that I had." And it ends with another: looking back at the photograph she chose to illustrate the back cover of a book, she discovers
that, "in spite of paying lip service to documenting theatre," the image
she selected succeeded in "erasing all evidence of the theatrical apparatus." In emphasizing the peculiarities of her interest, the "accident of
knowing that cuts through my experience," Hodgdon's point is not,
however, to affirm the authority of the personal (the latter anecdote, indeed, betrays puzzlement and surprise), still less to celebrate the exclusive singularity of her experience ("private meditation," she tells us,
"bears traces of other, more public reading practices"). Rather, the
anecdotal confessions and in general the Barthesian "writerly" style of
"'Here Apparent'" serve to put pleasure and desire into the question of
evidence. Not that they have been altogether absent; my frequent references to rhetoric implicitly acknowledge the affective motive helping
to drive our pursuits of knowledge. Nonetheless, one consequence of
Hodgdon's suggestive essay is to make us catch a glimpse, behind an aus-
tere phrase like "the rhetorical dimension of evidence," of desire as a
concept that should not necessarily be limited to verbal play. In a recent
piece, commenting on her famous (or infamous) essay "Jane Austen and
the Masturbating Girl," Eve Sedgwick confesses:

> Part of what the performativity of my essay was aimed at, in a context
> where the "question of evidence" seemed all but predetermined as the
> question of evidential truth or credibility, was to de-emphasize the epis-
> temology of evidence and instead stress its erotics—that is, to dramatize

how not only *evidence* is part of the currency of a social and libidinal economy, but equally so is the epistemological stress itself. (136)

Barbara Hodgdon's seductive writing seems to be dramatizing a similar "linkage" of "knowledge/pleasure" (Sedgwick, 133).

"Invisible Bullets, Violet Beards: Reading Actors Reading" juxtaposes Shakespearean actors and academic critics in order "to locate the interface between the interpretive priorities of scholarship and those of the stage." W. B. Worthen finds a superficial similarity but fundamental differences. The actors' idiosyncratic "use of anecdote to situate an unfamiliar discourse (the behavior of Shakespearean roles) in relation to a familiar one (the modern 'self') . . . almost parodies the new historicist penchant for 'episodic, anecdotal, contingent, exotic, abjected, or simply uncanny aspects of the historical record.' " But where this predilection enables actors to familiarize history and affirm the existence of an "integrated, self-present, internalized, psychologically motivated 'character,' " it serves critics rather "as a means of distancing" the past and of resituating "the subject . . . less as an 'identity' or 'self' than as a shifting site where the claims of competing discourses . . . are registered." The result is a sharp contrast between the values actors and critics attach to Shakespearean interpretation:

> If critical reading evokes a hermeneutic of suspicion, the sense that Shakespearean drama negotiates (and is sometimes betrayed by) its densely ideologized theatrical, political, and cultural milieu, reading for the theatre appears to involve a hermeneutic of transcendence, the belief that the values asserted most positively in the play express its core meanings, the meanings that speak equally to Renaissance and modern audiences.

Worthen's essay returns us to the topics with which we began: the differences between theatrically and nontheatrically based commentaries and the possibilities for negotiation between them. Worthen is skeptical about negotiation. He reflects upon the criterion of playability, frequently evoked as "a 'test' that screens out 'meanings' " that are "innately illegitimate, un-Shakespearean"—and rejects it: "There is no way to 'translate' between different modes of producing the text; acting practice and critical practice remain in dialogue precisely because they are incommensurable." *Producing the text* is the key phrase here; it takes us back to the problem under what circumstances evidence helps to decide (in Bristol's words) "strong disagreements over multiple competing accounts of a difficult question." In order for playability to work as a test, critics would have to agree with actors on a concept of the text to stand in a regulatory position above the disagreement; but since the text is differently produced by the parties in dispute (Worthen's quotation marks around " 'Shakespeare' " insist on this point), the evidence, rather than settling the disagreement, simply keeps it going around a different question (not "what does the text say?" but "what is a text?" [Orgel]).

In his concluding words, Worthen holds out the prospect that "contemporary performance practice . . . might respond in its own idiom to the more alienated perspective of contemporary criticism" and that "Shakespeare in the theatre can become . . . involved in our deceptive and slippery rhetoric of self-fashioning." To be sure, the current critical language of constructivism and discontinuous subjectivity seems a natural fit for histrionic idiom; and we might expect the actors to celebrate their freedom as makers of the performance text. From this perspective, it is indeed "surprising" that "actors understand their interpretive practice less as a mode of self-authorized creation than as a mode of fidelity to 'Shakespeare' "; and it may well seem a paradox that they are "interested in what 'Shakespeare' *is* rather than what 'Shakespeare' can be made to *do*." But these commentaries can be read as legitimating and compensatory narratives as well as discourses of self-understanding. From inside a practice that raises potentially unsettling suspicions about fixed identity, the hermeneutics of suspicion may seem *de trop*. For professionals whose work is sporadic and transient, dependent on corporate and government funding and on an appeal to a general audience, a stable Shakespeare embodying universal human values may accommodate a powerful need. In these circumstances, subdued to what they work in like the dyer's hand, the actors' celebratory "hermeneutic of transcendence" might seem overdetermined rather than paradoxical. Importing the "alienated perspective" of cultural critique into the actors' language might enrich their "own idiom" but might also displace it— and perhaps displace them from the practices sustained if not constituted by that idiom.[9]

Like Alan Dessen at the beginning of this collection, Worthen may be construed as telling a cautionary tale, centered upon the constraints that work against bringing "practice and criticism into a healthier alliance for

the benefit of both the stage and the study." Styan's confidence about the
revolutionary achievement of such an alliance was based partly on his
ability to locate the problem within a relatively narrow historical frame.
The twentieth-century theatre historians who were the heroes of his
narrative may indeed have helped to legitimize Shakespeare's theatricality from its questionable status in the nineteenth century; but the gap
between "stage and study" was already an old problem in Lamb and
Coleridge's time, going back as far as the publication of the 1623 Folio
and even earlier, to Ben Jonson's contributions to the preparation of that
volume and to the claims Jonson made in the 1616 Folio by designating
his own plays as "Works" or literary texts.

The problematic relation between Shakespeare's plays as performance
and literary texts could not have been the same problem then as now.
The meanings and values we attach to "the stage and the page" cannot
simply be projected back to Renaissance playhouses, which (as McLuskie
points out) had not achieved any stable institutional form, or to the
early stages of a print culture, within which John Heminge and Henry
Condell's inclusive appeal at the front of the Folio to "the great variety of readers" assumes all kinds of exclusions we no longer take for
granted—not just of the much greater variety of the illiterate, but of
the many book-buyers who simply couldn't have afforded the very substantial price of the volume. Even granting all this, however, we can
nonetheless recognize something very like the problematic contrast we
know between the textual and theatrical embodiments of Shakespeare as
going back to the beginning of things, located in the foundations on
which Shakespearean drama has been constructed for us as an object of
critical interest.

To make matters more complicated, the relation may not be fairly
represented as a single problem and need not be limited to contrasting
categories of text. "The stage vs. the page" seems to be interconnected
with an extensive series of similar contrasts, many of which have been
and will be touched on here: representation and performance; readerly
and writerly texts; closed-fisted logic and open-handed rhetoric; hard
and soft evidence; classical and carnivalesque bodies; science and the
humanities. High and popular culture is yet another related binary, as
Worthen suggests, remarking on the packaging of *The Players of Shakespeare* as "popular and theatrical, not effete and literary." "The intensity
of the 'text vs. performance' skirmishing," he adds, "suggests that the
stakes are mainly ideological." The current construction turns upside

down the standard Renaissance view, in which plays were construed as effeminate and high literary culture represented as manly, like Jonson himself; but such reversibility itself also suggests an ideological force. (One constant factor, interestingly enough, is the relative value attached to the manly and the effeminate—which introduces yet another related set of contrasts to the extensive series I enumerated just above.)

Stage-vs.-page may be understood as a key phrase, on the model of Raymond Williams' "keywords"; the transformations (and continuities) seem like synecdochical histories of culture. We should be skeptical, thus, about any decisive resolution to such differing claims. They simply go back too far, and interconnect too densely, deriving from the long and complex development of our diverse Shakespearean engagements. Since these differences are not just problems to be solved but the formative conditions of our ongoing work, perhaps we shouldn't even wish for their resolution, for what would we do to keep busy in Utopia after achieving the revolution? In any case, we may confidently assume that differences are going to remain among (not to say within) textual and literary scholars, performance critics, social historians, cultural theo-rists, actors, and theatre historians. The traditions out of which we work, our training, the questions we ask, and (the particular concern of this book) the evidence we draw upon to answer these questions, the rhetorical protocols that make our answers persuasive, and the con-stituencies to which our work is directed—all of these are different.

At the same time, we do not have to generalize these differences into an Iron Law of Incommensurable Paradigms: a rigid multidisciplinarity whose constituents, by analogy with multiculturalism, are related *only* by their differences. Chasms may yawn between the actors and critics Worthen talks about, but there are other kinds of actors and critics besides the eminences of the RSC and the new historicism, among whom negotiations would be easier to imagine. Disciplinary limits can-not be erased; but it is increasingly clear that they can come to look ar-bitrary and indefinite, allowing for cross-border shopping (consider Alan Sinfield's adventurous foray at the beginning of *Faultlines* out from cultural critique into the stage history of *Julius Caesar*), and for the "redrawing of boundaries" (in Stephen Greenblatt and Giles Gunn's title words for their MLA report on the current state of literary stud-ies). In the words of mad Ophelia, "we know what we are, but know not what we may be." It is in a similar spirit that the essays in this book have been collected.

NOTES

1. The editors of *Critical Inquiry* devoted sections of three consecutive issues to the problem in 1991 and 1992 and subsequently expanded the discussion into a book (Chandler, Davidson, and Harootunian). The editors of the *PMLA* chose evidence as a special topic for an issue scheduled to appear in 1996.

2. To be sure, opinion is still widespread that scientific norms ought to govern the use of evidence in humanist research—see Frederick Crews, for example.

3. See Fahnestock and Secor for an extremely suggestive discussion of the rhetorical dimension of literary criticism, including its similarities to "faith discourse." For additional controversial discussion of the de Grazia and Stallybrass essay that appeared after Bristol wrote his piece, see Holderness, Loughrey, and Murphy.

4. This difficulty has been developed at length recently by Janette Dillon, commenting on "a new orthodoxy . . . of performance," given to "generaliz[ing] about performance rather than, for example, discussing the specific practices of performers in particular locations" (74, 86). There are arguments with similar implications in Worthen, "Deeper Meanings," especially 446–449, and McLuskie's essay printed below.

5. See *Shakespeare and the Popular Tradition* for the original argument and, more recently, "Bifold Authority," "Representation and Performance," and "Textual Authority."

6. "Representation and Performance," 508. Weimann takes these terms from S. L. Bethell and A. P. Rossiter. Writing earlier, William Empson developed some brilliantly suggestive similar ideas in his chapters on the double plot at the beginning of *Some Versions of Pastoral*.

7. Namely, to a transparent or mimetic language on the one hand, and a playfully "plastic" (Artaud's adjective) and performative language on the other. Hence "performance-game and representation" might then serve to designate a variety of *textual* positions: writerly and readerly, modern and classical, *sjuzhet* and *fabula*, etc.

8. *Language writes man*, to coin a phrase; *a fortiori* theatrical language and theatrical man. Who can see Hamlet or Henry V except against Laurence Olivier's performances? How many spectators during the last quarter-century have detected echoes of the White Box Sally Jacobs designed for Peter Brook's *Dream*, as I did watching Caryl Churchill's *The Skriker* at the National in 1994, though no such echo may have been intended, and though I never even saw Brook's *Dream*? Hodgdon develops this point below, de-

scribing theatrical stills as, consciously or not, "apprenticed to a past," and "visual tradition" as "not only inform[ing] but recuperat[ing] . . . individual talent."

9. To apply this argument to ourselves: the commitment to critique among academics may also be understood as partly compensatory and legitimating discourses specific to the conditions of our work. Unfortunately, this kind of argument has tended to be generated in an unhelpful and mean-spirited way (see Kimball).

2

How Good Does Evidence Have to Be?

Michael D. Bristol

We seek evidence in the hope of diminishing ignorance and also, less grandly, with a view to satisfying our curiosity. Evidence enables us not merely to suspend our disbelief but to overcome it. It is often a piece of evidence that allows us to settle thorny questions and resolve controversies. In the context of scientific research as well as in legal investigations, evidence retains the literal sense of something seen or directly observed, an outward sign or manifestation that furnishes proof and guarantees knowledge. The most familiar way to interpret this concept is through the idea of a physical object or trace, a "clue" such as a hair, a button, or a fingerprint. Written documents form an important class of evidence in this sense. But the notion of evidence takes in a much wider range of situations. The testimony of a respected member of the community or of a witness to an event is an important form of evidence even when no object can be presented for visual inspection. Evidence does not always have the limited sense of an external observation or report, however. There is an additional range of meanings for this term that takes in the idea of our attitudes and our dispositions to believe.

The philosophical doctrine known as "evidentialism" teaches that we are justified in considering a given belief to be knowledge only if that

belief is confirmed by our evidence (Feldman and Conee). Here the notion of "evidence" refers to other, already justified beliefs that support
the maxims or interpretations which I may want to claim as knowledge.
I can say I know something if and only if that something is entailed by
other, already justified beliefs or if I somehow "get" the connection between one belief and another belief. The rigor of this analysis is somewhat deceptive, however. It is quite unclear here just how the epistemic
pump gets primed or how one belief is "connected" to other beliefs.
What's important about evidence in this sense, however, is not that it
could ever provide solid and unshakable guarantees about the truth of
specific beliefs. Evidence can never be that good; fortunately it doesn't
have to be. By choosing the topic of evidence to consider we are only
committed to preferring socially usable knowledge, whenever we can
get it, to rumor, superstition, and wishful thinking.

Veridical Evidence, Circumstantial Evidence, and Wishful Thinking

It will be useful to begin this discussion of the concept of evidence by
distinguishing between theoretical and forensic contexts of inquiry. In a
theoretical context, research aims at the discovery of regularities, general laws, and causal explanations within a well-specified object domain.
In this context evidence is sought for the purpose of confirmation/dis-
confirmation of a general hypothesis. The natural sciences provide the
most important models for theoretical inquiry. To make the case conclusively in favor of confirmation, the evidence for a given hypothesis usually must satisfy very rigorous standards. A suggestive correlation between a set of observation reports and an explanatory hypothesis is
usually not enough to confirm the truth of the explanatory hypothesis.
Nor is it enough to establish that the observation reports in question
should be considered as anything more than potential evidence for the
hypothesis. For the observation reports to count as evidence it must be
shown that they are in fact relevant to the hypothesis, and this requires
that there be an explanatory connection between the truth of the evidence and the truth of the hypothesis.

In a forensic context, by contrast, the task of inquiry is oriented to
public discussion and debate, and therefore it depends ultimately on
an appeal to the authority of a community. That communal authority
may be a broadly based public sphere or forum (the root of the word
forensic), or it may take the form of a jury of one's peers, as in Anglo-

American jurisprudence, or it may be more narrowly embodied in a magistrate, imam, or rabbi, as in other cultural settings. Examples of forensic inquiry might include judicial hearings, parliamentary debates, and literary criticism. In a forensic context evidence is sought for the public adjudication of disputes, usually, though not always, in respect of discrete events. The questions we typically think of in this context are those relating to specific events: what did the president know and when did he know it? However, forensic evidence can also presumably be useful in the discussion of plans and projects (should we concentrate on reducing the debt or should we concentrate on reducing unemployment?) as well as in a selection among several competing historical narratives.

However, although the activity of forensic inquiry is aimed primarily at persuasion rather than rigorous hypothesis confirmation, we should not, I think, be tempted by the thought that it is somehow less dignified or less reliable than theoretical inquiry. The very idea of forensic inquiry presupposes something like an interest in getting at the truth of the matter, and in this sense at least it resembles scientific research. Furthermore, although the natural sciences demand extremely rigorous discovery procedures, the scientific community nevertheless must engage in debate and discussion, using fairly commonplace techniques of persuasion. In both contexts the use of evidence is necessary for establishing the authority of particular arguments. Theoretical inquiry differs from forensic inquiry, however, in the degree of assurance it hopes or expects its evidence to provide.

Suppose I observe that there are drops of water on the floor of the parliament building, around the front door. If I make the inference that it is raining outside, I may be prompted to walk to the window and look at the weather. If it is in fact raining, I can then claim that the water drops that I observed satisfy a very high standard of reliability as evidence of the initial hypothesis. According to Peter Achinstein, when observations meet that high standard of reliability, they qualify as veridical evidence. In the example cited, the water drops would count as veridical evidence if four conditions are satisfied. 1. The water drops have to be potential evidence of raining (i.e., they have to be the sort of drops usually associated with rain). 2. It must in fact be the case that it is raining. 3. It must be possible to generate a chain of inferences that explain the relationship between the hypothesis (it is raining outside) and the observation report (there are water drops on the floor). Such a chain of inferences might include the following well-established beliefs: rain makes people wet, wet people drip, the rate and frequency of water drops on the floors of buildings is proportional to the distance from the entrance, and so on. The last inference is helpful in accounting for the observation of water drops in the lobby and for their absence on the third floor. 4. Other explanations for the drops of water have to be ruled out (for example, that a backbencher spilled his teakettle on the way to his office).

The evidence of the water drops is "hard-wired" into a comprehensive theoretical account or explanation of the relationship between raining, dripping people, and puddles on the floors of buildings. But there are two peculiarities to be noted here. First, veridical evidence that satisfies all of Achinstein's criteria is in a sense completely unnecessary evidence. If I know from direct observation that it is raining, I do not need to look for indirect evidence to support this hypothesis. Another way to say this is to suggest that evidence counts only after the fact of hypothesis confirmation—or in other words evidence is an artifact of theory. Second, it is difficult to see how the requirement for veridical evidence can be met in the important case when the truth of the hypothesis entails unobservable phenomena. It's one thing to satisfy this requirement by sticking your head out the window to see if it's raining, but quite another matter if the hypothesis involves something that can't be confirmed by direct observation, like computer viruses, let's say, or Shakespeare's authorship of the works collected in the First Folio of 1623.

Even the natural sciences often have to contend with unobservable phenomena. In forensic contexts of inquiry veridical evidence of the kind analyzed by Achinstein is seldom available, and in fact the search for this kind of "hard-wired" confirmation of an argument may be quite pointless. Public discussion and policy debate usually will depend on the consideration of circumstantial evidence, where no direct observation of the matters in dispute is possible. Circumstantial evidence has often been described as "soft" or "weak" in contrast with the "hardness" and "strength" of veridical evidence. Invidious comparisons of this kind, however, may be quite misleading. Alexander Welsh has argued that in a forensic context the evidence of things unseen or of what he calls "strong representations" can be extremely powerful. According to Welsh's analysis, the use of circumstantial evidence requires that inferences be made about the likely causes of known effects (Welsh, 7). A strong representation is then a narrative account that can be used to "subordinate the facts to a conclusion that makes a difference one way or another" (Welsh, 9). The requirements of narrative coherence and of explanatory competence suggest that in principle circumstantial evidence very closely approximates the rigorous standards of veridical evidence.

Smith's revolver was found not far from the body of Jackson. Ballistic tests confirm that the bullets that killed Jackson came from Smith's gun. Witnesses report that Smith was seen leaving the building shortly after the estimated time of Smith's death. It was widely known that Smith hated Jackson because Jackson stole some of Smith's ideas for valuable industrial patents. The jury finds Smith guilty of murdering Jackson. The inference that Smith caused Jackson's death is based in part on the presentation of evidence and in part on the jury's background knowledge about the typical causal sequences that lead to violent death. The conclusion that Smith murdered Jackson depends on the jury's ability to make reliable inferences about Smith's intentions, which are not just contingently unobserved like the shot that actually killed Jackson but in principle unobservable.

Although all the evidence in the case is circumstantial, there is nevertheless a strong warrant for accepting the jury's verdict. The hypothesis that Smith killed Jackson is not confirmed by direct observation, but other criteria of the kind proposed by Achinstein are adequately met. The evidence is of a kind usually associated with a verdict of murder, other explanations are ruled out, and it is possible to build a strong chain of inferences that connects the hypothesis with the observation reports. We know, of course, from watching *Murder She Wrote, Perry Mason*, or *Matlock* that in cases of this kind appearances may be profoundly deceiving. Indeed, an entire narrative genre is based on the search for clues that will identify the real killer and exonerate the accused. In order to disconfirm the hypothesis suggested by the evidence, some other, very complicated story must be devised that fully explains all the observation reports and that also supplies additional information identifying the real killer. Alternative narratives can usually be ruled out by the law of parsimony. Even when the evidence is circumstantial, in other words, it may be possible to resolve disputes by considering which of several competing versions requires the fewest auxiliary hypotheses to account for the observation reports. Sometimes, however, there is a separate body of evidence supporting the alternative narrative, and in this case it becomes necessary to decide whether the first body of evidence supports the first hypothesis better than the second body of evidence supports the second hypothesis.

In many contexts of inquiry, the standards of circumstantial evidence are good enough. What really matters in most situations is not the technical distinctions between "hard" and "soft" evidence, but the much more fundamental opposition between evidence and wishful thinking. In order to suggest exactly what is at stake in the concept of evidence, I want to look at an example that will be controversial, if not downright inflammatory. The example I want to discuss here is the Senate confirmation hearings for the appointment of Clarence Thomas to the Supreme Court and its lengthy aftermath of public recrimination. Professor Anita Hill accused Clarence Thomas of sexually harassing her over a period of several months during the time she was his subordinate at the Office of Equal Opportunity, accusations which he vigorously denied. Many people have extremely strong, vivid beliefs on one side or the other on the question of Thomas' guilt or innocence in this matter. The question I want to raise is simply this: Does it *matter* if he did it?

Of course it ought to matter whether Thomas did or did not do the things he has been accused of doing. In the ongoing dispute over this affair, however, it is not really obvious that the participants have a real interest in definitively settling the question. To begin with, there continue to be strongly held and aggressively articulated beliefs on both sides of this controversy. However, although the testimony of witnesses is certainly not lacking in this case, direct and conclusive evidence of the kind that would end public debate does not seem to be available. Instead, since the events in question are unobservable for all practical purpose, strongly held beliefs continue to be based to a considerable degree on whose testimony—Hill's or Thomas'—is thought to be most persuasive. That judgment in turn rests on background beliefs such as the following: 1. Sexual harassment in the workplace is extremely common. The victims of such harassment are often reluctant to come forward, because they are not usually believed. Therefore, we should have a strong bias in favor of believing the victim in such cases. 2. Black men are persecuted for their sexuality, and this persecution often takes the form of accusations of rape or sexual assault. Because these accusations are likely to be motivated by racism and therefore false, we should have a strong bias in favor of believing the claim of innocence by those accused. Now each of these broader historical narratives is itself strongly supported by an extensive body of evidence, and therefore each is in principle relevant to the case at issue here. But in order to decide which of these two historical narratives should be applied in the case of Clarence Thomas, we need to have solid evidence about whether or not the specific allegations made by Anita Hill were true. Or do we?

What if someone absolutely trustworthy (and here you can apply your own standard of trustworthiness) were to come forward and claim to have evidence that would conclusively decide to the satisfaction of just about everyone the issue of what happened in the Hill-Thomas affair, but without telling you which side that conclusive evidence would favor? Keeping in mind your own strong convictions, and the likely social, political, and strategic consequences of an unfavorable result, would you want to risk having the evidence made public? Notwithstanding your faith or the depth of your conviction, I believe that the proper strategic choice here is not to have the evidence disclosed. Although an outright victory is obviously better than any other outcome, the existing situation of interminable discussion and debate might in fact be *better* than taking a chance on ignominious defeat.

The point of the foregoing exercise is to foreground as dramatically as possible the interested character of forensic inquiry and to suggest that conclusive evidence might not in every case be particularly desirable. By asking the question "Does it matter if he did it?" I want to suggest that there may from time to time be circumstances when we are deeply invested in a particular historical narrative, and that this investment may, perhaps with some justification, cause us to become somewhat impatient or even unscrupulous with respect to questions of evidence. Strong beliefs supported only by equally strong and sincere political convictions without reference to their accuracy are probably best characterized as ideological.

Jon Elster has described the type of situation where beliefs are distorted by interests as wishful thinking. This is "the tendency to form beliefs when, and because, I prefer the state of the world in which they are true to states in which they are false" (Elster, 137). Elster is at some pains to distinguish wishful thinking from willful self-deception. The beliefs guided by preferences might be well grounded in the evidence, and in some cases they may even turn out to be true. The important point about ideology in this sense is not the propositional content of the belief, but the reasons for which it is held. Wishful thinkers are not self-deceiving, but they may well be self-defeating in adhering to distorted beliefs. Although their beliefs are shaped by their interests, it does not follow that those same beliefs really serve the interests in question. In my view it would be disingenuous to claim that we could never, under any circumstances, be faced with a dilemma of the kind I have just described, or that we are always, in every case, motivated by a disinterested desire to know the truth. At the same time, I am troubled by the view, which has become more common among scholars and culture critics in the humanities, that we have a warrant for indifference to questions of evidence. I would want to argue that the fact that an inquiry is interested is not in itself incompatible with a desire to know the truth of the matter. There is no doubt that our guiding interpretations of reality take shape against a background of preferences and desires. All the more reason, it seems to me, to take careful account of our evidence.

Evidence and the Social Experience of Research

Literary works have always provoked a high degree of curiosity about the private lives of their creators. Although this orientation builds on the appeal of gossip and anecdote, the governing aim of this type of research is simply to produce reliable narratives about authors. In this context evidence can have the fairly straightforward sense of documentary or other materials useful in the confirmation or disconfirmation of very particular claims and assertions. Samuel Schoenbaum's *William Shakespeare: A Documentary Life* is an important contemporary instance of such research that demonstrates how much useful information can be recovered from scarce and incomplete records. However, it is not at all clear even from Schoenbaum's exemplary scholarship how this very exact knowledge of Shakespeare's legal entanglements or his financial dealings would contribute to the activity of literary interpretation.

Schoenbaum's work develops out of a particularist tradition of literary scholarship. Although research of this kind continues to be undertaken, it is no longer the definitive model for scholarly activity. The aims and methods of particularist research emphasize the social experience of gathering evidence. A scholar in this context is someone who allocates a very considerable portion of professional labor to the examination of large numbers of records, documents, and other archival materials with a view to answering a very narrowly specified question. Patience, sound judgment, and detailed knowledge of the archives are the primary scholarly virtues. Factual accuracy rather than complexity of interpretation is the central methodological standard.

In order to illustrate the operations of particularist research it is useful to consider Mark Eccles' *Christopher Marlowe in London,* first published in 1934. This work is not only an example of particularist research; it also provides useful glimpses of the social background in which such research takes place. Eccles from time to time makes reference to the day-to-day activity of research—the inspired guesses about where to look, contacts made and journeys undertaken, his own reactions of surprise or frustration as he scrutinizes the records. The results of his research produce a "new chapter" in the biography of Christopher Marlowe having mainly to do with his criminal activities and those of his somewhat disreputable associates.

The gritty determination required for successful results in a particularist research program are described quite vividly by Leslie Hotson, who wrote the introduction for *Christopher Marlowe in London*:

> to root up, grub through, pry into, seek in every corner and hole, search
> diligently, grope or feel, spy out, scout about, assay and prove, trace,
> trail, or follow by the track—these alone will not produce the result
> Dr. Eccles has achieved. There must be a directing imagination to guide
> the process, and a memory stored with rare Elizabethan things.
>
> (Eccles, v–vi)

Eccles' account of Marlowe's London career reads like detective fiction. He discovered many of the details of this narrative in the Sessions Rolls at the Middlesex Guildhall, which had been organized and catalogued by J. C. Jeaffreson. In order to convey some sense of his own experience with these records, Eccles quotes Jeaffreson's "well-weighed" assessment of his own laborious examination of these records:

> The majority of the persons, thus bound over by recognizances of no
> historic moment, were mechanics who had beaten their wives or their
> neighbours' wives, labourers who had come to blows over too many
> pots of heady ale, artisans guilty of jeering at the constables, young tai-
> lors or other young craftsmen guilty of presuming to set up in business
> on their own account, instead of working as journeymen for masters
> entitled to their services, apprentices with heads broken in a recent riot,
> women at war with women of their street or yard, petty tradesmen
> accused of paltry frauds, householders charged with obstructing a
> common sewer, or persons suspected of victualling without a license.
>
> (Eccles, 102–103)

In this brief summary of the documents he has surveyed, Jeaffreson presents a fascinating sketch of everyday life in the early modern community. The socially invidious language adopted in his description of the various records, however, suggests that he was not disposed to appreciate the historical value of the materials he had at hand. The social history of everyday life had not yet become an institutionally recognized research agenda.

For Jeaffreson and similarly for Eccles most of the documents in the Sessions Rolls did not belong to the category of "evidence" because they couldn't answer any question worth asking. "Under no circumstances could the recognizances of such people and their sureties be diverting or usefully instructive" (Eccles, 103). Jeaffreson's comment rejects the bulk of the documents surveyed as historically uninteresting. They also reveal something about the various aims that govern the compiling of evidence. To begin with, documents must be entertaining or diverting as well as informative if they are to be counted as evidence. More significantly, records become interesting only insofar as they contribute to our knowledge of the lives of historically "important" individuals. Information about Christopher Marlowe or Walter Raleigh would be evidence. The rest of the material is simply a nuisance, although the tedium experienced in perusing these documents gives a certain assurance that the scholarly discoveries have been earned. For Jeaffreson and for particularist scholars more generally the sharing of evidence with like-minded persons is valued in and of itself as a social experience.

Particularist scholarship is perhaps less exact and less exacting than it claims to be. It is first of all based on rather large but completely unexamined assumptions about the reliability of the public records. Eccles does not seem to consider the possibility that the records are not only incomplete, but possibly partial in the sense of "interested." Furthermore, he is able to piece together his narrative only after he "realizes" that certain records for Christopher Morley and for Christopher Marley in fact pertain to the case of Christopher Marlowe. It may well be the case that Eccles' narrative is not only fascinating but perfectly accurate in its details. Still, his desire to make discoveries is so emphatically manifested throughout *Christopher Marlowe in London* that the possibility of wishful thinking certainly cannot be ruled out.

Particularist research wants to know exactly what Marlowe or Shakespeare did at particular moments. The focus here is on accuracy and circumstantial detail. Broader interpretation of literary works and their historical context is generally avoided. Historicist research, by contrast, is interested mainly in the big picture. The persuasive authority of historicist research is based on the high standard of general erudition demanded for scholars who adopt this orientation to their work. It is not, however, clear exactly how interpretations are actually supported by evidence. E. M. W. Tillyard, perhaps the best known of earlier historicist scholars, was given to making extremely sweeping claims about the entire population of Elizabethan England. The ideologically distorted character of his arguments has been extensively analyzed elsewhere. More recent variants of historicism have attempted to present a more complex, nuanced account of Elizabethan *mentalités*. The function of evidence in the critical practice known as new historicism is, however, fundamentally ambiguous.

Stephen Greenblatt, in "Shakespeare and the Exorcists," begins his discussion of *King Lear* by connecting that play with Samuel Harsnett's *A Declaration of Egregious Popish Impostures*. The argument here entails a typically particularist claim about the relationship between these two texts:

> Between the spring of 1585 and the summer of 1586, a group of English Catholic priests led by the Jesuit William Weston, alias Father Edmunds, conducted a series of spectacular exorcisms, principally in the house of recusant gentleman, Sir George Peckham of Denham, Buckinghamshire. The priests were outlaws—by an act of 1585 the mere presence in England of a Jesuit or seminary priest constituted high treason—and those who sheltered them were guilty of a felony, punishable by death. Yet the exorcisms, though clandestine, drew large crowds, almost certainly in the hundreds, and must have been common knowledge to hundreds more. In 1603, long after the arrest and punishment of those involved, Samuel Harsnett, then chaplain to the bishop of London, wrote a detailed account of the cases, based on sworn statements taken from four of the demoniacs and one of the priests. It has been recognized since the eighteenth century that Shakespeare was reading Harnsnett's book, *A Declaration of Egregious Popish Impostures*, as he was writing *King Lear*. (Greenblatt, *Shakespearean Negotiations*, 94)

At this point, a superscript number appears, directing the reader to a note, the usual location for recording evidentiary support for claims of this kind. The note supplies a full citation of Harsnett's book and the following supplementary information:

> Harsnett's influence is noted in Lewis Theobald's edition of Shakespeare, first published in 1733. Shakespeare is likely to have known one of the principal exorcists, Robert Dibdale, the son of a Stratford Catholic family linked to the Hathaways. (185)

As "evidence" that William Shakespeare read a particular book at a particular time this is tenuous, to say the least. In fact this is only evidence that Lewis Theobald held a certain opinion, the details of which have not been made available. The footnote doesn't explain what basis there was for Theobald's belief in Harsnett's influence or exactly why he thought Harsnett was relevant to *King Lear*. Presumably if Theobald's comments actually provided a description of the circumstantial evidence prompting his conjecture Greenblatt would have included it. However, what's curious about this footnote is not its failure to provide convincing evidence for the claim of influence. Evidence of direct influence, even if it existed, would in any case be tangential to the central arguments of Greenblatt's essay.

The real ambitions of "Shakespeare and the Exorcists" go considerably beyond source study.

> When Shakespeare borrows from Harsnett, who knows if Harsnett has not already, in a deep sense, borrowed from Shakespeare's theater what Shakespeare borrows back? Whose interests are served by the borrowing? And is there a larger cultural text produced by the exchange? Such questions do not lead, for me at least, to the *O altitudo!* of radical indeterminacy. They lead rather to an exploration of the institutional strategies in which both *King Lear* and Harsnett's *Declaration* are embedded. These strategies, I suggest, are part of an intense and sustained struggle in late sixteenth- and early seventeenth-century England to redefine the central values of society. (95)

For the purposes of Greenblatt's larger argument it doesn't really matter in the slightest whether Shakespeare read the book or whether he only heard the rumors. The point of the argument here is to examine the "larger cultural texts" and the "institutional strategies" in which the works in question are embedded. The particularist move that insists on direct borrowing is clearly intended to reinforce the persuasive authority of the larger argument. Ironically it is just as likely to have the opposite effect. Readers who are troubled by the use of tenuous or bogus evidence may well miss or reject the cogency of the larger argument.

The practice of cultural poetics—the new historicism—aims at a "thick description" of the historical context in which literary works may be most effectively read. The social background or lived environment in which early modern subjects lived has to be "thickly described" in terms of the practical, symbolic, and moral life of diverse and shifting communities, their level of technical knowledge, their politics, and the important social and religious conflicts of the period. The big picture that emerges from this research program is very different from the thin descriptions typified by abstract and finally diffuse notions like the Elizabethan world picture. New historicism foregrounds conflict, difference, and complexity. It acknowledges the crucial importance of marginal or excluded figures within the social landscape. The persuasive authority of these narratives, then, is greatly enhanced by the incorporation of a particularist element. The notorious new historicist "anecdote" is much more than colorful décor; it has an indispensable function in making historical descriptions sufficiently thick. For this reason it becomes crucial for the new historicist project to be particularly scrupulous about getting the details right.

Particularist research is committed to making very precise discoveries about singular individuals and isolated events. This requires a stringent segregation of a very select body of evidence from a much larger archive. The danger here is that the collection of evidence may become an end in itself. Furthermore, the big picture is often overlooked in a maniacal quest for detail. A strong preference for "important" people and distinguished achievement may lead to significantly distorted outcomes. On the other hand, there is something to be said for a research program that understands the importance of scale and proportion on questions of evidence. Particularist scholarship at its best provides very full evidentiary support for a modest and carefully delimited argument. Historicist research, by contrast, frequently attempts to support a very ambitious argument with very fragmentary and incomplete evidence. Here the big picture is what counts, even if this means that detail must be sacrificed. In addition, wishful thinking, this time in the form of a strong preference for certain master narratives, may substantially impair the reliability of historicist interpretations. The problem in these situations is in finding an equilibrium between too much evidence and not enough. As I hope to suggest in the next section, this is not so much a question of "looking at the evidence" as it is a matter of hypothesis formation and revision.

Authorizing Shakespeare

The use of evidence can be extremely helpful when there are strong disagreements over multiple competing accounts of a difficult question. At the present time one of the most vexatious issues in Shakespeare scholarship concerns the question of authorship. The existence of something we agree to call "Shakespeare's works" is, of course, not in dispute. What is in question is how these "works" come into being, and what valences should be assigned to the various social agents and institutional practices that contributed to their determinate formation. The standard hypothesis is simply that William Shakespeare is the author of the works in question and that their value is somehow linked to his singular creative agency. There is certainly evidence to support such a hypothesis, but the evidence is insufficient to establish exactly what it was that this Shakespeare actually wrote. However, the many difficulties that have arisen over the authorship question have given rise to at least three important alternative hypotheses: 1. Shakespeare's plays were written by some other person such as Francis Bacon or the Earl of Oxford. 2. Shakespeare wrote scripts for the theatre, but these were from time to time revised. 3. To claim that Shakespeare wrote the plays is an ideologically motivated fiction, because the institutions and practices of authorship as we know them today did not exist at that time.

The standard picture of Shakespeare as the author of the works interprets authorship according to a model of singular creative agency. That interpretation is codified by textual editors during the eighteenth century and is slowly developed through an increasingly sophisticated technical and theoretical apparatus. The moral center of this argument is an individual artist who is uniquely responsible both for the aesthetic quality of his works and for the fullness of their meaning. Although the activity of many other social agents may be acknowledged as valuable auxiliaries to the artist's achievement, these auxiliary figures pose a constant threat to the integrity of the author's work. Shakespeare's achievement is deformed and distorted by the carelessness and the self-interest of players, printers, and editors whose duty was simply to transmit the works in their original form.

The textual scholars who elaborated this account of Shakespearean authorship were very well informed about the practical and institutional context in which the works were actually produced. Indeed, their exploration of the techniques of the early modern theatre companies and print shops is a good deal better than that of most of their recent poststructuralist critics. The difficulty with the standard account is not a lack of accurate information or concrete evidence about the way the extant texts came into being. It is rather in the explanatory models that were used to interpret that information and to generate a misleading, though perhaps not altogether misguided, account of the role of individual creativity in the production of Shakespeare's plays. A strong preference for the model of singular creative agency, with its insistence on the ontological and the ethical priority of the author's strictly individualized original intentions over any concrete material embodiment of particular works, led to the formation of increasingly complex auxiliary hypotheses to account for peculiar features of the evidentiary record. The failure of this elaborate apparatus to make any significant progress toward a definitive resolution of the text of Shakespeare's works has encouraged the formation of a number of alternative proposals.

The first of these alternative accounts is the claim that Shakespeare's plays were written by a different person. Among the leading candidates for the position of the "real author" have been Francis Bacon, Christopher Marlowe, and most recently Edward de Vere, the Earl of Oxford. These stories are actually variants of the standard hypothesis which do nothing to resolve the textual problems or overcome its many other difficulties. The case depends on making some sort of decision as to whether the body of evidence that supports the contention that Shakespeare wrote the plays is better than a second body of evidence that supports the contention that the Earl of Oxford wrote them. The evidence supporting Shakespeare's claim is of the usual sort associated with claims of this kind. For example, Shakespeare is named in the accounts of the Revels Office as the "poet" of works later included in published texts. Furthermore, there is a clear and coherent chain of inferences that would account for a connection between the hypothesis that Shakespeare wrote the plays and observation reports like the appearance of Shakespeare's name on the title page of the early editions of the works. Finally, this chain of inferences does not require an elaborate set of auxiliary hypotheses. This is, of course, merely circumstantial evidence. We do not have direct observation to confirm the hypothesis; and we cannot, in the last analysis, absolutely eliminate alternative narratives.

All of these alternative narratives, however, would require extensive ad hoc rationalization both to explain away the pretty good circumstantial evidence that Shakespeare was the person who wrote the plays and to support the rather tenuous evidence that they were written by some other person. The evidence for the challenger hypothesis (for example, that the Earl of Oxford was the author of "Shakespeare's" plays) is much less satisfactory. There is absolutely no trace of direct written confirmation that Oxford wrote any plays. Much of the argument in support of this hypothesis has been aimed at discountenancing the idea that Shakespeare was the author. But the Oxford hypothesis seems weakest in its handling of the explanatory requirement in that it demands acceptance of a significant number of cumbersome ad hoc provisions before it can even get off the ground. Here, even though the evidence on both sides of the question is incomplete, there seems a very strong warrant for discarding the hypothesis that the Earl of Oxford wrote the plays in favor of the more conventional view, even though we should probably not expect alternative proposals of this kind to disappear completely. It seems unlikely that the theory of a pseudonymous author could ever have the narrative and argumentative economy of the standard hypothesis, unless a considerable body of heretofore unknown evidence were to be discovered.

A much more promising alternative to the standard hypothesis is an argument that maintains that Shakespeare is the author of the plays, but that these plays were subject to a process of continual authorial revision. This hypothesis has become more and more widely accepted in the field of textual studies. Its main virtue is that it retains the notion of singular creative agency but dispenses with the problematic aim of reconstructing a single, true text for each of Shakespeare's works. I think it is important to observe that the revision hypothesis is not based on any new evidence. It is the same old evidence that is being used here, with a new explanation for the observation reports about differences in the text that appear in the various early editions. What grounds are there, then, for preferring this new explanation? It has been argued that the older critical editorial practice, with its focus on the reconstruction of an "ideal text" based on a "lost original," was motivated by a bias in favor of a humanistic culture that privileged the printed book. In addition, these editors were hampered by a great deal of romantic ideological baggage about the ontological and ethical primacy of a sovereign, voluntaristic, and expressive subject.

But the revisionist hypothesis is also motivated by a bias in favor of the working theatre. Ideological preferences are operative here as well. The argument that one or the other of the competing hypotheses is "interested" or "motivated" does not really help to settle the issue. Although the revision hypothesis is not without its flaws, it does a better job of explaining more of the evidence we in fact have, with much less resort to auxiliary hypotheses than earlier accounts. The revision hypothesis is not a radical rejection of the standard account, but rather a reworking of its central arguments. This model of Shakespearean authorship would be even more persuasive if it were to supplement ideas of singular artistic agency with an account of collaboration and derivative creativity. In such an account authorship would be understood dialogically. Shakespeare's activity as his company's "poet" would then be situated in the context of his interactions with other literary artists, players, and audiences. The dialogic intervention of these auxiliaries would be assigned a substantially different valence than in the standard hypothesis.

The sharpest challenge to the standard account maintains that the very notion of authorship is an ideological fiction. On this view, Shakespeare may have participated in the textual production of the plays, but he was not their author because the institutions of authorship as we know them today did not exist at that time. This is a far-reaching hypothesis suggested by the narrower revision hypothesis and reinforced by other recent research on questions of copyright, licensing, and so on. The broader social context for understanding Shakespeare's activity as a writer has been very thoroughly studied in the professional literature over the past decade. It is now clear, I think, that some cherished assumptions about Shakespeare's genius that have survived from eighteenth- and nineteenth-century criticism will have to be reexamined and perhaps modified. We understand much better now that the composition of Shakespeare's plays was made possible within the specific technological and commercial infrastructure of the early London theatres. We also understand that the publication of his plays in book form was made possible by a quite different technological and commercial infrastructure in the early printing industry. Despite these advances, however, a hypothesis that requires the radical abolition of authorship does not have clear advantages over more moderate proposals to refine and modify the standard account.

First of all, a great deal depends on how carefully the hypothesis is stated. Here I think we have to look closely at the influence of Michel Foucault's widely cited essay "What Is an Author?" Foucault's essay is perhaps less original than many people have realized. The authorship question has been discussed at length in Biblical scholarship and in classical scholarship as well. Questions of oral vs. written composition, collective vs. individual authority, and deuteronomic redaction have all been discussed at length in a variety of contexts, but the results of these researches have in many ways been inconclusive. In any case Foucault's essay has been the vehicle for raising questions of authorial practice in relation to Shakespeare, and I certainly have no quarrel with the basic idea here that authorship has a specific history. However, Foucault's discussion of this problem does not aim at the careful historical elucidation of that history, nor does he suggest what ought to count as evidence in support of a particular historical narrative. What is under attack here is the very principle of self-conscious authorship itself, which Foucault maintains only comes into existence within the context of the disciplinary state apparatus.

Following Foucault, Shakespeare scholars have suggested that institution known as "Shakespeare the Man and His Works" is the creation of the editors of the First Folio, or, more recently, that Shakespeare as an author only sprang into existence with the appearance of Edmond Malone's edition of 1790. And in a recent article in the *Shakespeare Quarterly* we have a proposal to abolish the concepts of author and work, along with such traditional notions as character and even the author's words, in favor of the study of such material practices as papermaking. This article, "The Materiality of the Shakespearean Text," by Margreta de Grazia and Peter Stallybrass, presents an abundance of documentation in support of its many proposals. The problem here is certainly not with the quantity of this documentation; if anything there is far too much presumptive evidence here. The real difficulty is with the explanatory relationship between the evidence assembled and the hypothesis proposed.

It is of course entirely clear just what hypothesis the authors of this article wish to promote—that the quest for an authentic and pristine Shakespeare capable of authorizing his purported works is misguided and even disingenuous. There is an obvious irony in having named authors for an essay proposing the abolition of authorship. However, the reasons for this paradoxical state of affairs are stated clearly right at the outset. "'The thing itself,' the authentic Shakespeare, is itself a problematic category, based on a metaphysics of origin and presence that poststructuralism has taught us to suspect" (de Grazia and Stallybrass, 256). In making this statement, de Grazia and Stallybrass are invoking the authority of Jacques Derrida in exactly the same way that medieval writers might have invoked the authority of Aristotle. Since every hypothesis connected with notions of authorship is suspect on the same grounds, it eventually becomes impossible to find any proposition about authors and works that would be worth asserting. The essay concludes with the admonition that we ought to be more interested in the history of the anonymous laborers in the printing and papermaking industries than we are in "the solitary genius immanent in the text . . . an impoverished, ghostly thing compared to the complex social practices that shaped, and still shape, the absorbent surface of the Shakespearean text. Perhaps it is these practices that should be the objects not only of our labors but also of our desires" (de Grazia and Stallybrass, 283). The wish to redeem and vindicate the dignity of those anonymous laborers is certainly admirable, but that dignity doesn't depend on the abolition of the notion of authorship as singular creative agency, which is itself arguably a constituent element of these complex social practices with its own kind of dignity. I also fail to see how that dignity would be diminished even if it were the case that Shakespeare was an aggressively assertive, individualistic, or even egomaniacal author.

The larger theoretical protest against an impoverished idea of the solitary genius that forms the background to this article is not, of course, confined to Shakespeare. De Grazia and Stallybrass present two distinct arguments to support their contention that authorship is particularly wrongheaded in the case of Shakespeare. First, they emphasize the very high number and frequency of textual indeterminacies in the transmission of Shakespeare's works. The facts presented here are already well known, but de Grazia and Stallybrass are persuasive in maintaining that there is no reliable discovery procedure that could be used to reconstruct an accurate text. This evidence is, of course, fully consistent with the standard hypothesis. It works even better with a modified account of derivative creativity and serial collaboration. The participation of collaborators, revisers, and other secondary creative agents was already well understood in traditional textual scholarship. De Grazia and Stallybrass show that the specific effects of singular creative agency cannot be disentangled from other, more derivative forms of participation in artistic creation and that the social dignity of these complex, socially embedded practices must be acknowledged. But they do not show exactly what is gained in explanatory power by refusing to countenance the idea that individualized creativity has anything whatever to do with the production of textual artifacts.

The arguments of textual indeterminacy are reinforced by a discussion of the material form of the book. De Grazia and Stallybrass point out that the production of books depends on a varied and heterogeneous network of industrial practices such as papermaking, typefounding, and the production of ink: "the words of what was to become a classic text were printed in an ink that mingled not only ingredients like juniper gum, linseed oil, and lampblack but also the residual traces of the urine of the printshop workers, who each night used urine to soak the leather casing of the balls that inked the press" (De Grazia and Stallybrass, 281–282). These are very interesting details, but they are quite irrelevant to the question of authorship, however understood. It would appear, in fact, that the development of such industrial techniques must presuppose an intention to publish verbal artifacts, and this in turn suggests at least a limited conception of authorship. The examples of Publius Virgilius Maro or even Geoffrey Chaucer suggest that printers as well as the reading public could not have been ignorant of the idea of the author. De Grazia and Stallybrass evidently want to dissociate the traditional valences of this notion from Shakespeare and to emphasize the radical heterogeneity of his works. There are, however, two serious problems with the arguments for multiple agency in the production of literary works as presented in this essay. First, there is simply no gain in explanatory competence here over more traditional models. In fact, to insist on generalized concepts of discursive fields and networks of reproduction without specifying any role at all for the specialized tasks of composition and verbal articulation is simply to mystify rather than to explain the appearance of literary artifacts. Second, the argument here equivocates between explanatory and evaluative registers.

The sustained attack on authorship as an explanatory principle here is motivated by strong political and ethical beliefs. This essay represents an odd kind of wishful thinking that flows from a sincere aversion to certain pernicious effects of an exacerbated individualism and from a sincere belief that these effects would be greatly diminished if only the demons of authorship could be exorcised. In such a context of ideological protest, the dense pattern of citation and documentation—there are no fewer than 115 footnotes in an article of 33 pages—does not function well as forensic evidence. No amount of evidence, no matter how exhaustive, can provide epistemic justification for a poorly formulated, weak, or incoherent hypothesis. The arguments presented by de Grazia and Stallybrass should not be rejected simply on the grounds that they fail to conform to some sort of culturally preferred humanistic picture of a sovereign subjectivity. On the other hand, their argument ought not to be adopted simply because of a similar preference for an alternative account of subjectivity.

Well, does it matter if he did it? I think we can say the following: in the decades between 1590 and 1610, roughly speaking, William Shakespeare wrote a number of plays for performance in various theatres in London. It is not easy to say exactly what this "writing" entailed. Did Shakespeare do the writing in a room of his own, all by himself, or did he draft scenes while hanging out in a local tavern? Was he more influenced by his acquaintance with literary texts or by his interactions with other players? Whatever the details of Shakespeare's activity as a writer, there is nevertheless an important causal link between that activity and the appearance in this world of certain textual artifacts commonly known as Shakespeare's plays. These plays were popular with his contemporaries, some of whom thought they were important enough or interesting enough to warrant publication in book form. Although the concept and the practice of authorship at this time were very different from what they are today, there is no doubt that the category of the author was well known and widely understood. To suggest that ideas of authorship would have been inconceivable to writers at this time is clearly wrong.

It is not clear, however, whether William Shakespeare did or did not aspire to the status of author. Unlike a number of authors who were his contemporaries, like Ben Jonson or Michael Drayton, this William Shakespeare was not careful in preparing his works in a final form for publication or particularly scrupulous about preserving them for posterity. We don't know why he neglected this task, nor do we know what that final form would be. We just don't know. The information is lost, most likely forever, and no amount of editorial labor or ingenuity can restore or reconstruct that information. Quite a lot has survived, however, and much that is not in dispute, even though the "works" that we call "Shakespeare's" are derivative, unfinished, and incompletely determined. To account for the body of works known as Shakespeare requires a mixed and untidy hypothesis about its changing identity over time.

The plays do indeed flow from a "complex social process" that is an impure mixing of Shakespeare's activity as a writer with the labors of actors, editors, printshop compositors, and other workers who have engaged with this material over the *longue durée* of his cultural authority. It would then follow from this that we can only effectively discuss what we call Shakespeare with reference to specific social contexts of cultural production and reception. That discussion can most usefully be conducted, however, if our desires and preferences are responsible to canons of evidence and of argumentative coherence that are truly adequate in forensic inquiry.

3

Recovering Elizabethan Staging:
A Reconsideration of the Evidence

Alan C. Dessen

The discovery in 1992 of a hitherto unexamined Jacobean printed quarto with playhouse annotations yielded a rare phenomenon for theatre historians of the period—some new evidence. Throughout this century scholars have pored over and argued about a few noteworthy documents (the Swan drawing, several other drawings or illustrations, Philip Henslowe's papers, the Fortune contract, some surviving theatrical "plots," a few eyewitness accounts of performances) in an attempt to recover or reconstitute the staging practices of English Renaissance drama.[1] Such studies have greatly enhanced our knowledge about theatre buildings, theatrical personnel, and the theatre business, but a host of uncertainties persist about what actually happened upon the stages within the Globe and other contemporary playhouses.

The "new" information to be gleaned from the annotations in the Folger Shakespeare Library copy of *The Two Merry Milkmaids* does not resolve such problems and indeed contributes several new puzzles—as with the curious insertion *"Knock Act."*[2] Moreover, only those readers familiar with the evidence in the manuscripts already available with playhouse annotations will fully appreciate what this document can and cannot tell us. Nonetheless, the appearance of something "new" in an area where so much of the terrain has been repeatedly mapped and mined provides an occasion for some ruminations about what today's historian or historicist wrestling with the extant evidence can establish about what the original playgoers actually saw when they watched a given scene. The sporadic and sometimes puzzling annotations found in this quarto will elicit no "Ahas!" or "Eurekas!" from the reader (in Watergate parlance, the two annotators provide no smoking gun), but some insights do emerge from what is *not* specified and what those silences reveal about both English Renaissance playhouse practice and today's scholarly procedures and assumptions. At stake here are familiar current issues (e.g., contingency, cultural difference, indeterminacy, essentialism), but they are manifested in a comparable yet different arena where ideological battle lines are less clearly defined.

Let me start with what would appear to be a straightforward, self-evident, commonsensical proposition: that a playwright fashioning a scene might be vague or sloppy (or "permissive" in editorial parlance) about various details, but a bookkeeper preparing the same playscript for a performance would have to be much more specific about personnel and properties so as to "disambiguate" what had been left "open" in an author's manuscript. Exceptions to this "rule" have been known for some time—at least since W. W. Greg's pioneering work on playhouse documents in 1931. Nonetheless, the self-evident nature of this proposition has been irresistible, so that, despite strong objections from scholars such as William B. Long, editors still use seemingly "permissive" stage directions as evidence in their quest to distinguish between texts that are authorial and those that reflect playhouse use.

The sixteen extant manuscripts with theatrical annotations and the Folger quarto of *The Two Merry Milkmaids* provide ample evidence for such adjustments, for the bookkeepers often (but not always) clarify elements left muddy by the dramatist. In the margins of such documents are to be found (1) anticipatory warnings that a property or actor is be *"ready"*; (2) detailing of personnel when the original stage direction is vague as to number or identity; (3) the names of specific actors (a sporadic occurrence); and (4) the spelling out of properties not mentioned by the dramatist or sometimes the listing in the margin of a property that *is* cited in the playscript to ensure that it catches the eye of the bookkeeper during a performance.[3] The playhouse manuscript of Philip Massinger's *Believe as You List* provides: *"Table ready: & 6 chaires to sett out"* (654–656); *"the great booke: of Accompte ready"* (982–984); *"Gascoine: & Hubert below: ready to open the Trap doore for*

Mr Taylor" (1825–1831); "*Antiochus—ready: under the stage*" (1877–
1879); "*Harry: Willson: & Boy ready for the song at the Arras*"
(1968–1971). Occasionally such practical in-the-theatre signals survive
in printed texts: "*2 Torches ready*" (Fletcher, *Love's Cure*, VII: 205);
"*Whil'st the Act plays, the Footstep, little Table, and Arras hung up for
the Musicians*" (Massinger, *The City Madam*, 4.4.160.s.d.).

In this context, consider one of the major scenes in the center of *The
Two Merry Milkmaids*, the trial of the virtuous Dorigen, where Bookkeeper B provides some anticipatory warnings ("**Ready / Sennet / [flor-
ish** deleted] **/ table / Duke / Barr**," I2v) and then at the outset of the
scene adds some specifics not found in the printed text. Thus, with two
figures already onstage, the Quarto directs: "*Enter the Duke, Judges,*
Raymond, *with others, the forme of a Court*" (I3r); Bookkeeper B adds
in the margin: "**A Table / A Barr / A Sennet**." After a Judge says: "Bring
forth the prisoner, place her at the Barre," another Quarto stage direction reads: "*Enter* Dorigen *plac'd at the Barre*"; Bookkeeper A adds:
"**Enter Du[chess] & Guard**." At the lower left margin of I2v, moreover,
Bookkeeper A inserts "**boyes**" (i.e., *hoboys*) and below that "**Judges /
Ranoff / [s?] Carolus / and Raymond**."

In making these adjustments to the printed quarto the two annotators
have clarified some matters, as a reader today would expect from theatrical professionals preparing a text for the playhouse, but they have
also left open or vague some details that, at least to that same reader today, would seem significant in a document designed to serve as the basis
for a performance. First, the annotators *do* spell out several items not
available in the printed Quarto: from Bookkeeper B a sound effect (a
sennet at the entrance of royalty) and a table (presumably for the judges
and perhaps the duke himself); from Bookkeeper A a sound effect
(hoboys) and a guard (implicit in the Quarto's signal that Dorigen be
placed at the bar). In addition, Bookkeeper A's other annotation, which,
along with Judges and Raymond, cites Ranoff, Carolus, and perhaps a
third figure (Cornelius?), clarifies the Quarto's signal that the duke,
judges, and Raymond enter "*with others*."

Nonetheless, the resulting document is not the orderly, meticulous
"promptbook" that generations of editors have assumed to be typical of
Jacobean playhouse manuscripts. For example, the annotator does not
spell out the number of judges (subsequent dialogue has two judges
speak), distinctive costumes, the presence and number of chairs, or the

configuration of the court (e.g., where or how the table and chairs are to be placed). Also not specified is the means by which the furniture is to be introduced onto the stage: is the table to be thrust out, as with beds in some extant stage directions, or discovered by the parting of a curtain, so that the judges are seated in place at the outset of the scene, or carried out and set up upon the stage? Here then, for a major ensemble scene that requires at least two significant pieces of furniture, is evidence for some differences between authorial and playhouse presentation of the same moment, with the latter approach, as would be expected, more attentive to personnel, sound effects, and properties. Still, a coded term (*"the forme of a Court"*) is left open, at least from our point of view, to the extent that, despite the annotations, today's reader cannot clearly visualize the original staging of this scene.

In terms of reading such Jacobean evidence today what is of particular interest is a playhouse annotator's approach to such signals as the Quarto's *"with others, the forme of a Court."* A reference to *"others,"* with or without further explanation, is more helpful than it initially sounds, because four courtiers (Fernando, Cornelius, Ranoff, and Carolus) are a continuing part of the narrative in this romance (and at times the object of satire) and hence likely to be included in this public scene. In contrast, *"the forme of a Court,"* even accompanied by the subsequent call for a bar in the Quarto and a table by an annotator, seems less than fully informative to our eyes and ears. The author of the printed stage direction left a great deal to the expertise of the players; the playhouse annotators have inserted marginal signals to ensure the availability of large properties or sound effects; but they have not felt it necessary to expand or improve upon *"the forme of a Court."* And thereby hangs my tale.

This specific locution (*"the forme of a Court"*) is, to my knowledge, unique; nonetheless, it corresponds to signals found in comparable trial scenes, some of them in manuscripts with playhouse annotations. To start with two such manuscripts, for the trial of the title figure in John Fletcher and Philip Massinger's *Sir John Van Olden Barnavelt*, the order "Let him be sent for presently" is accompanied by a scribal stage direction: *"A Bar brought in"*; the bookkeeper inserts **"Barre"** and **"Table"** (1259–1260). Much more elaborately, a trial scene early in *Sir Thomas More* begins with the authorial stage direction: *"An arras is drawn, and* behind it (as in sessions) sit the Lord Mayor, Justice Suresby, and other Justices, Sheriff More and the other Sheriff sitting by; Smart is the plaintiff, Lifter the prisoner at the bar" (1.2.0.s.d.).[4]

Details in courtroom or trial scenes found in printed quartos range from the minimal (no more than "Enter . . .") to the highly elaborate. The minimal approach is easily documented: "Enter the Duke, the Magnificoes, Anthonio, Bassanio, and Gratiano" (The Merchant of Venice, Quarto, G3r).[5] Sometimes a text provides a coded term comparable to "the forme of a Court" or More's "as in sessions," as in The Winter's Tale, where at the outset of 3.2 the Folio directs: "Enter Leontes, Lords, Officers: Hermione (as to her Triall) Ladies: Cleomines, Dion" (TLN 1174–1175). Next to a general "Enter . . ." the most common procedure, as in both Barnavelt and More, is to specify a bar as the key property: twice in The City Night-cap Davenport directs "A Bar set out" (2.3.0.s.d., 3.2.0.s.d.).[6]

Some dramatists, however, call for more than a bar and a table and occasionally spell out considerably more than is to be found in the annotated version of The Two Merry Milkmaids or Barnavelt. For example, in a climactic scene in a 1590s murder tragedy the emphasis is not upon the bar or even the prisoner but upon the seating of the judges: "Enter some to prepare the judgement seat to the Lord Maior, Lo. Justice, and the foure Lords, and one Clearke, and a Shiriff, who being set, commaund Browne to be brought forth" (A Warning for Fair Women, H3v). That same emphasis upon seating can be seen in John Webster's The Devil's Law-Case, Edward Sharpham's The Fleer, and George Chapman's Chabot Admiral of France.[7] Chapman provides plentiful information for his two trial scenes: "Enter Officers before the Chancellor, Judges, the Proctor generall, whispering with the Chancellor; they take their places. To them Enter Treasurer and Secretary who take their places prepared on one side of the Court. To them The Captaine of the Guard, the Admirall following, who is plac'd at the barre" (3.2.0.s.d.); "Enter Officers before, Treasurer, Secretary, and Judges, attended by Petitioners, the Advocate also with many papers in his hand; they take their places. The Chancellor with a guard, and plac'd at the Barre" (5.2.0.s.d.).

Also informative are three scenes that involve a trial-like confrontation but not an actual courtroom. In Thomas Heywood's 1 The Iron Age the contest between Ulysses and Ajax for the armor of Achilles begins with Thersites and soldiers "bringing in a table, with chayres and stooles plac'd above it"; then the armor is "plac'd upon the table, the

Princes *seate themselues, a chayre is plac'd at either end of the Stage,
the one for* Ajax, *the other for* Ulysses" (III: 334–335). In Ben Jonson's
The New Inn to begin a Court of Love: "*Prudence* usher'd by the *Host*,
takes her seat of Judicature, *Nurse, Franke.* the two Lords *Beaufort*, and
Latimer, assist of the Bench: The *Lady* and *Lovel* are brought in, and sit
on the two sides of the stage, confronting each the other" (3.2.0.s.d.).
The most elaborate special case is the trial of Queen Katherine in *Henry
VIII*, where an unusually long stage direction drawn from details in
Raphael Holinshed concludes: "*The King takes place under the Cloth of
State. The two Cardinalls sit under him as Judges. The Queene takes
place some distance from the King. The Bishops place themselves on
each side the Court in manner of a Consistory: Below them the Scribes.
The Lords sit next the Bishops. The rest of the Attendants stand in con-
venient order about the Stage*" (TLN 1343–1349, 2.4.0.s.d.).

What is to be learned from such a survey of comparable scenes? The
unannotated Quarto of *The Two Merry Milkmaids* is more informative
about the staging of its trial scene than most printed texts; moreover, to
use a theatrical shorthand that leaves the implementation of "*the forme
of a Court*" to the players is not unusual. The playhouse annotators (as
in *Barnavelt*) then add some details (a sound effect, a second piece of
stage furniture) and some clarification (specific figures to flesh out the
Quarto's "*with others*") but not as much as today's reader might expect.
Indeed, the stage directions for comparable scenes in some printed texts
are more detailed than two of the three relevant playhouse documents
and therefore conjure up a more vivid picture of the original staging for
today's reader, especially about seating arrangements or the larger stage
configuration. In preparing the printed Quarto for playhouse use, however, the annotators of *The Two Merry Milkmaids* did not have today's
reader in mind.

To borrow from a late Elizabethan theatre critic, ay, there's the rub.
Certainly, the staging of court and trial scenes may have varied somewhat from theatre to theatre or even in the same theatre over a span of
years, but the basic configuration probably remained roughly the same:
a bar; a table; some distinctive seats and placement for the judges; and
something important that is implicit but not spelled out in the many signals: distinctive costumes for judges, sheriffs, advocates, and other court
personnel. Indeed, along with the bar such costumes would probably
have been the most significant part of the "code" to signify "a courtroom."[8] An experienced dramatist, however, especially a Shakespeare, a

Fletcher, or a Heywood attached to a theatrical company, could assume a theatrical vocabulary shared by both players who knew their craft and playgoers familiar with such scenes; such a playwright could therefore provide few or no details or could fall back upon some formula (*"the forme of a Court," "as in sessions," "as to her Triall," "in manner of a Consistory"*).

This gap between a dramatist's working assumptions and today's reader has not gone unnoticed. A particularly lucid formulation from an editor's point of view is provided by Gary Taylor. The original manuscripts (or *scripts*) of Shakespeare's plays, as Taylor notes, "were not written for that consortium of readers called 'the general public'" but "were written instead to be read by a particular group of actors, his professional colleagues and personal friends, who would in turn communicate the plays through performance to a wider public." Shakespeare could therefore "rely on this first special readership to 'edit' his manuscript, at least mentally and perhaps physically, as they read it"; and, more important to the theatre historian, "he could also rely on those readers to bring to the reading much specialist knowledge about the conditions and working practices of the contemporary theatre, and the circumstances of the specific company to which they and he belonged."

Shakespeare's ability to rely upon his colleagues, in turn, has significant implications for any attempt at "recovery" today by an editor or theatre historian, for, as Taylor goes on to observe: "The written text of any such manuscript thus depended upon an unwritten para-text which always accompanied it: an invisible life-support system of stage directions, which Shakespeare could either expect his first readers to supply, or which those first readers would expect Shakespeare himself to supply orally." The problem for the editor and especially the theatre historian, then, is that "the earliest editions of the plays all fail, more or less grossly, to supply this unwritten text." Subsequent editors, including Taylor and Stanley Wells in their Oxford edition, have sought "to rectify the deficiency, by conjecturally writing for him the stage directions which Shakespeare himself assumed or spoke but never wrote"; but, as Taylor admits, "to fill such lacunae is necessarily hazardous: necessary, if we are to relish the texts as scripts for theatrical performance, but hazardous, because the filling which modern editors concoct might not always be to Shakespeare's taste" (2–3).

For both the editor and the historian significant problems are therefore generated by the nature of the evidence. In later periods of drama other sources of useful information are available, but for English Renaissance drama eyewitness accounts of performances are few and frustratingly limited,[9] and other documents (e.g., the Swan drawing, Henslowe's inventory, the Peacham drawing of a scene from *Titus Andronicus*) are notoriously difficult to interpret. To recover what would have been obvious to the original playgoers, then, requires the teasing out of possible stage effects or shared meanings from often cryptic stage directions, the only substantive evidence available, when, in fact, the norm for most scenes in printed texts is silence or simply *"Enter . . ."* As seen above in my invocation of a group of courtroom scenes, to seek to recover the original staging or stagings is to build mosaics from widely disparate fragments, any one of which may be quirky or unrepresentative owing to authorial idiosyncrasy (as perhaps with Chapman), changes in procedure over a span of time, or varying practice in different playhouses.

As an illustration of the problems and frustrations, consider the second appearance of the ghost in the Second Quarto of *Hamlet*, where Horatio says "I'll cross it though it blast me" and the marginal stage direction reads: *"It spreads his armes"* (B3r). The Pelican editor changes this signal to *"He spreads his arms"* (1.1.127.s.d.) so that presumably the gesture is made by Horatio, not by the ghost. Q2's *It*, however, leaves open the possibility of a reaction from the ghost, perhaps in response to Horatio's "stay illusion," an option less likely to be noted or explored given the emendation.

Although the matter may not seem consequential to a reader of the scene today, a spreading of arms by the actor playing the ghost may have been a meaningful signifier in an Elizabethan theatrical vocabulary. Thus, after Horatio's injunctions for the ghost to speak, *"The cock crows"* (138.s.d.), at which point "it started, like a guilty thing / Upon a fearful summons" (148–149). At Horatio's command, Marcellus and Bernardo strike at the departing figure with their partisans, but they are unable to affect it ("'Tis here. / 'Tis here. / 'Tis gone," 140–142). In the original production the presentation of such a ghostly departure or vanishing, without access to today's variable lighting, posed various problems, with few opportunities for the kind of verisimilar staging today's interpreter takes for granted. Although apparently anomalous today, *"It spreads his armes"* may have been an onstage signifier to denote that the ghost was visible or accessible to Horatio. If the signal is read this way, at the crowing of the cock this ghost would then have repositioned its arms to denote that it had faded from sight and was therefore invulnerable to the sentinels' partisans.

Lest the reader find such a hypothetical staging fanciful, consider two instances where X sees but then ceases to see Y, who therefore *vanishes* to X but the playgoer *continues* to see Y, so that unquestionably the *vanish* effect is from the point of view of an onstage observer rather than from the point of view of the playgoer. In *1 Hieronimo*, a play roughly contemporary to *Hamlet*, the penultimate scene starts with Horatio and others at *"the funeral of Andrea"* (xii.o.s.d.); the ghost of Andrea and Revenge enter. Of the mourners onstage only Horatio can see Andrea, although he cannot hear him, so Horatio says: "See, see, he points to have us go forward on. / I prithee, rest; it shall be done, sweet Don. / Oh, now he's vanish'd" (17–19). Horatio and his group may depart here or may stay onstage, but clearly Andrea does not exit, despite "now he's vanish'd," for he has the next speech ("I am a happy ghost," 19). Clearly, from *Horatio's* point of view Andrea has vanished, but the spectator sees the ghost stay to deliver another speech and then exeunt with Revenge (23.s.d.). The effect is a *vanish* witnessed and described by Horatio but seen in very different terms by the playgoer.

Similarly, in Henry Shirley's *The Martyred Soldier* (ca. 1620), Bellizarius, about to convert to Christianity, calls upon "some Divine power" to "open my blind judgement / That I may see a way to happinesse"; the stage direction reads: *"Thunder: Enter an Angel"* (188). Initially, Bellizarius cannot see the angel; when the angel finally does speak he replies: "What heavenly voyce is this? shall my eares onely / Be blest with raptures, not mine eyes enjoy / The sight of that Celestiall presence / From whence these sweet sounds come?" The angel responds: "Yes, thou shalt see; nay, then, 'tis lost agen" (189)—somehow revealing itself, then becoming invisible once more. Here the angel is unseen, seen, and vanished not only without leaving the stage but within a single line.

No evidence survives here or in other *vanish* scenes—of which there are many—as to how an angel or ghost would suddenly become invisible. Scenes involving magic rings that make the wearer invisible (including several in *The Two Merry Milkmaids*) provide no clues. Presumably the effect in *The Martyred Soldier* was achieved by a combination of the Bellizarius actor's reaction and some expansive gesture by the angel (e.g., a spreading wide, then closing of its arms) as may perhaps have been the case in *Hamlet*, 1.1. Here, as with other supernatural vanishings or departures, we do not know enough about Elizabethan theatrical practice to dismiss *"It spreads his armes"* as an error rather than accepting it as a valid theatrical signifier worthy of investigation. The absence to my knowledge of comparable signals elsewhere in the period, however, makes such a claim problematic.

Such situations, where what was obvious then is murky today, are commonplace. In the quest for evidence the would-be theatre historian must therefore continually make allowances for Taylor's para-text or what I term the shared theatrical vocabulary. Few today would deny that invisible barriers created by an interpreter's unacknowledged assumptions and expectations block any attempt to "recover" meanings from the past, but such predisposition is particularly strong when a reader confronting the drama of another age attempts to extrapolate the staging of a given scene from words on a page even when those words come from a playscript actually used in a playhouse. As Bernard Beckerman notes, when such a reader confronts a book containing the printed words of a play he or she simultaneously puts on a pair of spectacles "compacted of preconceptions about what constitutes drama and how it produces its effects" (*Dynamics of Drama*, 3). Viewing earlier drama through such spectacles inevitably blurs or distorts the original onstage procedures and vocabulary.

The problem is brought into focus by such signifiers as *"the forme of a Court," "as in sessions," "as to her Triall,"* and *"in manner of a Consistory."* To confront a stage direction that calls for a figure to enter *in prison, in his study, in the woods,* or *in the shop* is almost inevitably to draw upon the experience gained from reading novels or watching cinema, television, and modern stage pictures linked to properties, sets, and lighting. But what if that same stage direction read or clearly implied *as in* or *as if in*? How would such an adjustment change our view of both individual signals and the larger problem?

To make my point without inundating the reader with a sea of italics, consider some pairings: (1) *"Enter Bullingbrooke with the Lords to parliament"* (Quarto *Richard II*, G4r) versus *"Enter as to the Parliament"* (Folio *Richard II*, TLN 1921); (2) *"Enter the Lords to Councell"* (Quarto *Richard III*, G1r) versus *"Enter Lords as to Councell"* (Denham, *The Sophy*, 18); (3) *"Enter Marcus from hunting"* (Quarto *Titus Andronicus*, E2r) versus *"Andrugio,* as out of the wooddes, with Bowe and Arrowes, and a Cony at his gyrdle" (Whetstone, *Promos and Cassandra*, K4r); (4) *"Enter the King sicke"* (Folio *Richard III*, TLN 1121) versus *"as he were* sick" (Davenant, *The Platonic Lovers*, II: 100); (5) "*Enter Timon in the woods*" (*Timon of Athens*, TLN 1602) versus "*as in a Wood*" (Jasper Mayne, *The Amorous War*, 18, 20); (6) "*Enter Palamon, and Arcite in prison*" (*The Two Noble Kinsmen*, D2r) versus enter "*as in prison*" (Davenport, *The City Night-cap*, 176); (7) "*Enter Faustus in his Study*" (Marlowe, *Doctor Faustus*, A-text, 30, 437) versus "*as in his Study*" (Fletcher, *The Fair Maid of the Inn*, IX: 193); (8) "*Enter* Achilles *and* Patroclus *in their Tent*" (Folio *Troilus and Cressida*, TLN 1888) versus "*as in their Tent*" (Henry Killigrew, *The Conspiracy*, H3r, I3r); (9) "*Enter before Angiers*" (*King John*, TLN 292) versus "*as before the City Corialus*" (*Coriolanus*, TLN 479–480); and, for a variation, (10), "*locks the door*" (Fletcher, *The Island Princess*: VIII, 137) versus "*seemes to locke a doore*" (Munday, *The Death of Robert Earl of Huntingdon*, 1921). Readers familiar with the drama of this period will recall many shop scenes (as in *The Shoemakers' Holiday*), garden scenes (as in *Richard II*), tavern scenes (as in *1 Henry IV*), and inside-the-house scenes but may not have encountered such signals as "*as in their shop*" (Field, *Amends for Ladies*, 2.1.0.s.d.); "*as in the Dukes garden*" (Shirley, *The Gentleman of Venice*, 2.1.0.s.d.); "*as in a Taverne*" (Glapthorne, *Wit in a Constable*, I: 231); and "*as in his house at Chelsea*" (Munday, *Sir Thomas More*, 4.4.0.s.d.).

Reading the more familiar signals (*in prison, in the shop, in his study, in the woods*) is further complicated by Richard Hosley's distinction between *fictional* and *theatrical* stage directions. For Hosley (16–17), *theatrical* signals "usually refer not to dramatic fiction but rather to theatrical structure or equipment" (e.g., *within, at another door, a scaffold thrust out*), whereas *fictional* signals "usually refer not to theatrical structure or equipment but rather to dramatic fiction" (e.g., *on shipboard, within the prison, enter the town*). The same onstage event can therefore be signaled by both *enter above* and *enter upon the walls* (of a city), with the second locution the "fictional" version of the first.

The most "theatrical" of signals can be seen in an annotator's call for a specific property such as a bar or a table. At the other extreme are those "fictional" directions in which a dramatist slips into a narrative or descriptive style seemingly more suited to a reader facing a page than an actor on the stage. Some of these "fictional" signals show the dramatist thinking out loud in the process of writing so that the details anticipate what will be evident in the forthcoming action: "*Parolles and Lafew stay behind, commenting of this wedding*" (*All's Well That Ends Well*, TLN

1089–1090); "*The King sodainely enters having determined what to doe*" (Chapman, *Tragedy of Byron*, 4.2.164.s.d.); "*Enter two serjants to arrest the scholer* George Pyeboard" (*The Puritan*, E1r). Such stage directions can be valuable insofar as they provide evidence about the dramatist's thought processes or sense of the narrative but often tell us little about what the playgoers saw.

In interpreting such evidence, however, various complications can arise when today's reader cannot be certain if a signal is "theatrical" and therefore calls for a significant property such as a tomb or a tree or "fictional" so that a sense of a tomb or forest is to be generated by means of language, hand-held properties, and appropriate actions in conjunction with the imagination of the playgoer. Such complications are further compounded by the presence of an explicit or implicit *as* or *as if*. A seemingly straightforward "fictional" signal such as "*Enter Marius solus from the Numidian mountaines, feeding on rootes*" (Lodge, *Wounds of Civil War*, 1189–1190) initially may appear to tell the story rather than provide a signal to an actor, but a starving Marius who has been alone in exile could enter "[*as if*] *from the Numidian mountaines*" so that the actor will use "*feeding on rootes*" (as in *Timon of Athens*), along with disheveled costume and hair, to signal his mental and physical state. Similarly: "*Enter Sanders yong sonne, and another boy comming from schoole*" (*A Warning for Fair Women*, F4r) may be merely a telling of the story, but, if construed as "[*as if*] *comming from schoole*," the two boys could be dressed in distinctive costumes and carrying books. Again: "*Enter old M*. Chartly *as new come out of the Country To inquire after his Sonne*" (Heywood, *The Wise Woman of Hogsdon*, V: 340) tells the mission of the old man in narrative terms but may also signal some "country" costume or other property (e.g., a staff, a basket). A "fictional" signal such as "*enter on the walls*" requires only that the figure enter *above* or *aloft*; other seemingly "fictional" signals (e.g., "*comming from schoole*") may in contrast convey some practical instructions albeit in an Elizabethan code or argot (as with "*the forme of a Court*").

For the theatre historian trying to build edifices from evidence derived from stage directions, the fictional-theatrical distinction combined with explicit or implicit *as if* signals generates a host of interpretative problems to which I cannot do justice in this essay. Let me focus upon several examples from the sampling above.

Consider first the most innocuous of terms, the preposition *to*, as used in the two pairings linked to an onstage council or parliament. Again, most of the relevant scenes merely call for a group of figures to *enter*. Some, however, follow the procedure found in *2 Henry VI*, 3.1.0.s.d., where both the Quarto (D3r) and the Folio (TLN 1292–1294) have the king and his entourage enter *"to the Parliament."* Similarly, at 3.4.0.s.d. Quarto *Richard III* (G1r) has *"Enter the Lords to Councell,"* although the Folio (TLN 1964–1966) has the same group enter *"at a Table."*

Should an entrance *"to Councell"* or *"to the Parliament"* then be read as "fictional" and hence a part of the narrative or read as "theatrical" and hence a coded instruction for a particular onstage effect? As noted in my pairing, the latter option is supported by Folio *Richard II*, where at 4.1.0.s.d. a group is directed: *"Enter as to the Parliament,"* although the *as* is not to be found in the Quarto. Compare as well Caesar's entrance *"with his Counsell of Warre"* (*Antony and Cleopatra*, TLN 3108–3109) and two Caroline signals: enter *"as at a council of war"* (Shirley, *The Cardinal*, 2.1.0.s.d.); *"Enter Lords as to Councell"* (Denham, *The Sophy*, 18).

As with courtroom scenes, other more explicit stage directions suggest how *"as to Councell"* could be staged or conceived. As already noted, the Folio calls for the council figures in *Richard III*, 3.4 to enter *"at a Table"*; similarly, in Quarto *Othello* the Venetian council scene begins: *"Enter Duke and Senators, set at a Table with lights and Attendants"* (C1r). In *King John and Matilda* (2.4.0.s.d.) Davenport provides: *"A Chaire of state discover'd, Tables and Chaires responcible, a Guard making a lane,"* so that King John, Pandulph, and the lords *"enter between them"*; in a later scene, after *"A Table and Chaires set out,"* Davenport instructs: *"Sit to Council"* (3.4.0.s.d.). Even more elaborate is *Henry VIII*, 5.3: *"A councell Table brought in with Chayres and Stooles, and placed under the State. Enter Lord Chancellour, places himselfe at the upper end of the Table, on the left hand: A Seate being left void above him, as for Canterburies Seate."* Five figures *"seat themselves in Order on each side. Cromwell at lower end, as Secretary"*; a few lines later *"Cranmer approches the Councell Table"* (TLN 3035–3041, 3055).

The elaborate description of the council scene in *Henry VIII*, 5.3 is far removed from enter *"at a table"* or *"Sit to Council"* and even farther from *"Enter the Lords to Councell,"* but all four signals can be encompassed within the simple *"enter to . . ."* formula. As with *"the forme of a Court,"* the reader is eavesdropping on a conversation carried out in an elliptical theatrical language that made excellent sense to native speakers but can be murky, even impenetrable, today.

Consider next the possibility of distinctive, even italicized onstage images that, owing to the nature of the evidence, may be obscured or eclipsed for us. To return to another pairing, in *Titus Andronicus* Marcus is directed to enter *"from hunting"* (2.4.10.s.d.), a signal that can readily be read as part of the narrative fiction rather than as a theatrical signal. But what if this stage direction is construed as *"[as if] from hunting"* and is then linked to George Whetstone's 1578 spelling out of "as out of the wooddes" in which a comparable figure had "Bowe and Arrowes, and a Cony at his gyrdle"? If *"[as if] from hunting"* can include a small animal "at his girdle," especially a bloodied animal without its limbs, consider the effect upon the "imagery" of the remainder of *Titus*, 2.4, Marcus' painful confrontation with Lavinia (*"her handes cut off, and her tongue cut out, & ravisht,"* E2r), an encounter that includes such lines as "what stern ungentle hand / Hath lopped and hewed and made thy body bare / Of her two branches . . ." (16–18).

Another pairing yields an unusually elastic set of terms, for many options are available to stage *"enter sick"* or *"as he were sick."* A playgoer then or now would recognize an entering figure as sick or dying if he or she is helped onto the stage (as with Queen Katherine in *Henry VIII*, 4.2), accompanied by a doctor (sometimes carrying a urinal), supported by a crutch, or wearing some distinctive garment: a kercher, a coif, a nightcap, or, most commonly, a gown or nightgown (as in *2 Henry IV*, 3.1.0.s.d.). In *The Telltale*, *"Isabella sick"* is juxtaposed with *"Picentio as a doctor with her water"* (1381–1382); in *Fair Em*, Trotter enters *"with a kerchife on his head and an Urinall in his hand"* (350–351). In addition, a large number of sick, dying, or counterfeiting figures are linked to beds: *"Enter Elizabeth in her bed"* (Heywood, 1 *If you know not me you know nobody*, I: 200); *"Enter Genzerick King of the Vandalls, sicke on his bed"* (H. Shirley, *The Martyred Soldier*, 1.1.0.s.d.).

What is far less visible to the reader today, however, is the widespread theatrical use of a portable chair in which the sick figure could be carried in and out expeditiously. Indeed, the evidence I have collected suggests that such a sick-chair was by far the most widely used signal for *"enter sick."* In *Othello*, after "finding" the wounded Cassio, Iago cries "O for a chair / To bear him easily hence" (5.1.82–83) and mentions the chair twice more (95, 98); when the chair arrives, he adds: "Some good man bear him carefully from hence. / I'll fetch the general's surgeon"

(99–100) and "O, bear him out o' th' air" (104); the Quarto then directs that Cassio in the next scene be brought in *"in a Chaire"* (N1r). Elsewhere in Shakespeare's plays, chairs are specified for sick or dying figures in *1 Henry VI* (2.5.0.s.d., 3.2.40.s.d.), *2 Henry VI* (2.1.66.s.d.), *King Lear* (4.7.20.s.d.), *Henry VIII* (4.2.3), and *The Two Noble Kinsmen* (5.4.85.s.d.). Examples are also plentiful in the plays of John Fletcher and Richard Brome and can be found as well in George Peele, George Chapman, Thomas Dekker, Thomas Heywood, and Philip Massinger and in many anonymous plays.[10]

In this context, consider the moment in *3 Henry VI* when Edward IV, having been surprised and captured by Warwick and Clarence, is carried onstage *"in his Gowne, sitting in a Chaire"* (Folio, TLN 2258, 4.3.27.s.d.). Given this juxtaposition of gown and chair, the initial signal for the original playgoer would have been that this figure is entering *"sick"* or *"as sick"* (all the signs are there, although they are blurred in the television production for the BBC's "The Shakespeare Plays," where director Jane Howell has Edward *bound* to the chair and hence a prisoner). In this instance, the signals are wrong or misleading, for Edward is embarrassed and vulnerable but not sick.

But keep in mind that this play starts and ends with throne scenes, with that royal seat serving as a symbol of the disorder in a kingdom in which three different figures are seen sitting upon the English throne. Indeed, in the opening scene the titular king, Henry VI, comes onstage to discover Richard of York seated upon his throne, an initial usurpation that typifies what is to follow. The presence of a king or pseudo-king brought onstage in what appears initially to be a sick-chair is therefore more than a momentary trick played upon the playgoer. Rather, that initial confusion of throne-chair and sick-chair calls attention to an important set of associations that links disease to kings and power-brokers, associations reinforced by the unkinging, rekinging, and unkinging of Henry VI in the last three acts. Memories of both the opening confusion about the throne and the momentary sick-chair image of 4.3 should then inform the final moments, where the surface order assumed by Edward ("Now am I seated as my soul delights, / Having my country's peace and brothers' loves," 5.7.35–36) is undercut by a continuing sense of the kingdom's diseases, as typified in Richard's asides (e.g., "I'll blast his harvest . . . ," 21).

What is surprising and, to my knowledge, has not been noted is how often Shakespeare introduces one or more such sick-chair moments into plays that deal with some form of diseased authority, and, moreover, how often such plays also contain scenes with thrones or other chairs of state. Eight of the ten history plays provide clear or likely evidence for such combinations (all except *1 Henry IV* and *Henry V*), along with *Othello* and *King Lear* (and perhaps *All's Well That Ends Well* and *Antony and Cleopatra*). Here, then, is what may have been a highly visible signifier in an onstage vocabulary available to Shakespeare (or to Jonson in the first trial scene in *Volpone*) but easily obscured or lost today owing to the nature of the evidence (*"enter sick," "the forme of a Court"*).

For a final example, consider the available ways to stage a "shop scene" in an Elizabethan theatre. One option was to "discover" one or more figures in such a shop: *"Enter discover'd in a Shop, a Shoo-maker, his Wife Spinning, Barnaby, two Journimen"* (W. Rowley, *A Shoemaker, a Gentleman*, 1.2.0.s.d.). Far more plentiful, however, are comparable signals that do not specify a discovery wherein "the shop" would be revealed by opening a curtain but rather direct the players to enter *"in the shop,"* a locution that *could* be read as *"enter [as if] in the shop"*: *"Enter* Signior Alunio *the Apothecarie in his shop with wares about him"* (Sharpham, *The Fleer*, 4.2.0.s.d.); *"Enter* Luce *in a Sempsters shop, at worke upon a lac'd Handkercher, and* Joseph *a Prentice"* (Heywood, *The Wise Woman of Hogsdon*, V: 284); *"Enter in the shop two of* Hobsons *folkes, and opening the shop"* (Heywood, *2 If You Know Not Me*, I: 283). In at least some scenes, moreover, the actors were not suddenly revealed "in" this place, a theatrical option that jibes with a post-Elizabethan fourth wall convention, but rather brought "the shop" with them onto the main stage, an option supported by Field's signal: *"Enter* Seldome *and* Grace *working as in their shop"* (*Amends for Ladies*, 2.1.0.s.d.). Thus, some tradesmen enter with their work rather than being discovered: *"Enter a Shoomaker sitting upon the stage at worke Jenkin to him"* (*George a Greene*, 971–972); *"Enter* Strumbo, Dorothie, Trompart *cobling shoos and singing"* (*Locrine*, 569–570). Several scenes therefore call for a setting forth of furniture on the stage: *"A Table is set out by young fellows like Merchants men, Bookes of Accounts upon it, small Deskes to write upon, they sit downe to write Tickets"* (Dekker, *If this be not a good play*, 2.2.0.s.d.).

Elizabethan players therefore had various options: (1) to draw a curtain so as to discover figures in a shop (and set up an initial tableau); (2) to have figures set forth "the shop" by means of furniture, costume, and properties (so that *"opening the shop"* may have entailed the carrying onto the stage of a stall and merchandise, perhaps even an awning); or (3) to have figures enter working or with the tools of their trade (one way of realizing *"as in the shop"*). The options are comparable to (1) a banquet revealed behind a curtain (from which figures come forth) versus (2) a table and food set up upon the stage versus (3) figures entering *"as from dinner"* (Massinger, *A New Way to Pay Old Debts*, 3.3.0.s.d.). Given the demands of a particular narrative and the investment in shop, banquet, or other place-event, the players could present considerable detail or could opt for a more economical approach *as in* or *as from*. The latter option both increases the narrative pace and, if done deftly, sets up "images" that (perhaps) link scenes together.

The only relevant scene in the Shakespeare canon is generated by Romeo's description of the apothecary's "needy shop" in which

> a tortoise hung,
An alligator stuffed, and other skins
Of ill-shaped fishes; and about his shelves
A beggarly account of empty boxes,
Green earthen pots, bladders, and musty seeds,
Remnants of packthread, and old cakes of roses
Were thinly scattered, to make up a show. (5.1.42–48)

The playgoer, however, sees no such interior, for when Romeo seeks out the apothecary ("As I remember, this should be the house"), he notes "Being holiday, the beggar's shop is shut" (55–56). In effect, whatever the actor gestures to at "this should be the house" "becomes" the shop. The apothecary then enters to Romeo's call ("Who calls so loud?" 57) and soon after provides the vial of poison requested ("Put this in any liquid thing you will . . . ," 77).

To discover a shop here would go against the dialogue and interfere with the thrust of the scene. After all, the focus is upon Romeo, not the supplier of the poison, so that an elaborate display of a shop would be counterproductive. But what if the apothecary enters "[*as if*] in his shop"? In addition to some distinctive costume, such a staging would involve some hand-held property or properties, so that the vial would be brought forth not from a pocket but from a larger supply of wares (as with figures cited above who enter bearing their "work").

Such an entrance is conjectural, although it does conform to practice elsewhere. Nonetheless, the particular asset of such an *as [if] in* approach to this moment is that the image presented would then echo comparable images presented earlier so as to set up a potentially meaningful progression. Thus, at the outset of his first scene, Friar Laurence enters *"with a basket,"* talks of filling up "this osier cage of ours / With baleful weeds and precious-juiced flowers," and, in his moralization, refers specifically to "the infant rind of this weak flower" (2.3.0.s.d., 7–8, 23). To some readers and editors 2.3 may be a "garden" scene (i.e., located in a "place" where a friar can gather weeds and flowers), but the original playgoer probably saw only an actor carrying a basket from which he produced one object, a flower.

A comparable onstage image is accessible when a desperate Juliet seeks out the friar in his cell. A reader wedded to geographical "realism" may see no connection between the "place" (garden? field?) where the friar gathers weeds-flowers and "the cell" (and such "placing" is reinforced by the locale headings in many editions), but what would the original playgoer actually have seen? Previewing the apothecary ("Put this in any liquid thing you will . . ."), the friar produces an object: "Take thou this vial, being then in bed, / And this distilling liquor drink thou off" (4.1.93–94). Here as in 5.1, the actor could pull forth the vial from a pocket, but he equally well could be carrying the same basket as in 2.3, a hand-held property that could then reappear in 5.1 as a version of *"enter [as] in the shop."* Back in 2.3 the friar had noted that within the same flower (taken from his basket) "Poison hath residence, and medicine power" and had linked these two opposites or options to "grace and rude will" within humankind (2.3.24–30). If the apothecary pulls *his* vial out of a basket, the links among the three moments need not be subtle, something to be teased out after many readings, but could instead be italicized.

To postulate such a staging, which cannot be established with any degree of certainty, is to move beyond the scripted "shop" signals cited earlier. Yet given the Elizabethan theatrical vocabulary such links and images are possible, perhaps even likely. A post-1660 sense of place-locale that distinguishes firmly among garden-field, cell, and a street in Mantua outside a shop blocks today's interpreter from even minimal awareness of a staging of the apothecary's brief appearance that would establish some meaningful connections and enhance a playgoer's sense of the choices made by the two title figures, choices visibly linked to two contrasting basket-bearing suppliers of vials. As with *"Marcus from hunting"* or *"in his Gowne, sitting in a Chaire,"* owing to the nature of the evidence something significant may be lost in translation.

Readers may quarrel with my readings of *Titus, 3 Henry VI,* and *Romeo,* which act out, among other things, my formalist reflexes and penchant for analogues and images, but in setting up such case studies my goal is to provide illustration, not explication. For today's editor, critic, historian, or theatrical professional confronting an Elizabethan play, something has been lost, something that can have significant interpretative implications. Those readers who can readily accept such a thesis but prefer bold formulations may, in turn, find something distasteful, even wimpish in the abundant sprinklings throughout this essay of the Three Ps: *perhaps, probably,* and *presumably.* But, as reflected in the participial *recovering* of my title (that for me signifies an ongoing process), firm conclusions, neat distinctions, and confident truth claims do not emerge from the extant evidence. Rather, the history of scholarship in this area is a narrative replete with Solutions and Answers that have not stood the test of time (the postulation of an "inner stage" provides one chastening example). In Brutus' terms, such a situation "craves wary walking" (2.1.15).

My purpose in this exploratory essay has therefore been to call attention to the problematic nature of the extant evidence about the staging of plays in early modern England. To build mosaics from large numbers of stage directions can be highly misleading, for such details are the exception (to butcher Hamlet's final words, the norm is silence). As Gary Taylor notes, Shakespeare and other seasoned playwrights did not have to spell out such details for their colleagues; indeed, what is surprising is how much information *has* survived. Important signifiers such as costumes are therefore not mentioned at all, other than in references to the judges, sheriffs, gaolers, foresters, doctors, clergymen, or sailors who are wearing them, probably because to the players the presence of such items was so obvious as not to need mentioning (as apparently was also the case for how an actor was to become "invisible").

What is at stake here is a form of indeterminacy related to yet different from that invoked by devotees of deconstruction. Five playgoers who saw the original performance of *Twelfth Night* might have come away with five different interpretations of the play's "meaning," but, allowing for variations in their attentiveness and placement in the theatre, they would have seen the same onstage choices and practices and would have been in tune with both the spoken and the fuller theatrical language. Today's theatre historian, however, often can only guess at what those original playgoers saw (again, I am referring to onstage actions, costumes, properties, and configurations, not to the meaning or meanings that would have been constructed from such phenomena). Choices had to be made, but the passage of time has eroded most of the evidence, probably 90 percent or more, so that what was too obvious to need recording then is murky or eclipsed today. The reliance upon inferences from printed texts of playscripts not of our age rather than upon the in-the-theatre experience of the original playgoers is at the heart of the problems confronted in this essay.

The result of such a situation *is* indeterminacy, but an indeterminacy that results not from the nature of the original phenomena but rather from the nature of the evidence about those phenomena that has survived the wide gap of time. No magical videotape of a performance at the Globe (or Rosetta Stone) is likely to surface so as to resolve such problems. To invoke again my pet analogy, in reading from a distance such theatrical signals we are eavesdropping on a conversation being conducted in a language we only partly understand.

I have no wish to end on a note of despair with a Prospero-like lament about great artifacts from the past fading into air, into thin air. Evidence *has* survived; some racks *have* been left behind. As a result, inferences *can* be drawn and connections made (and mosaics constructed, demolished, and reconstructed). To be aware of coded terms (*"the forme of a Court," "enter sick"*), *as if* constructions, and the "fictional" versus "theatrical" distinction is not to pluck out the heart of Hamlet's (or *Hamlet's*) mystery but at the least to make a start toward a fuller understanding of the larger theatrical language in which such plays were conceived. Not to make the effort is to side with Leontes, to whom Hermione can say: "You speak a language that I understand not" (3.2.79).

NOTES

1. For an excellent overview on such matters, see Andrew Gurr's *The Shakespearean Stage 1574–1642*. The most penetrating and rigorous analysis of the evidence in my view remains Bernard Beckerman's *Shakespeare at the Globe, 1599–1609*; see also Beckerman's subsequent essays for thoughtful analyses of what can and cannot be learned from documents such as Henslowe's papers and the theatrical "plots." For an investigation of theatrical practice that builds upon stage directions rather than evidence outside the playtexts, see Alan C. Dessen, *Recovering Shakespeare's Theatrical Vocabulary*.

2. This quarto was donated to the Folger in 1982, put on display in 1983, and noted as "marked for performance" but was not given close attention until July 1992, when both Leslie Thomson and William Long came across the catalogue entry. I am grateful to Professor Thomson for alerting me to this discovery and providing me with a copy of the annotations. This 1620 quarto is only the second known example of a printed text of an Elizabethan or Jacobean professional play that has been annotated for performance (the University of Chicago copy of *A Looking Glass for London and England* has been largely ignored since 1931). In her essay Thomson notes that the Folger Quarto, which is missing most of act 1 and virtually all of act 5, is annotated at two different times by two different hands (she terms them Bookkeepers A and B).

3. Such marginal notations are linked to what William B. Long terms the "glancing bookkeeper." See his informative analyses of the playhouse manuscripts for *John a Kent* and *Woodstock*, particularly 106–108 of the latter essay, devoted to the bed.

4. This scene is the only one I have found in which a curtain is drawn to reveal a court configuration already in place, although such a procedure is possible elsewhere. For a recent argument in behalf of the presence and use of a special onstage pavilion for this and other scenes in *More*, see Scott McMillin, *The Elizabethan Theatre and "The Book of Sir Thomas More,"* 96–112.

5. See also *Volpone*, 4.5.o.s.d., and *The Revenger's Tragedy*, A4r.

6. Similarly, in *The Lover's Progress* Fletcher signals "*a Bar set forth, Officers*" (V: 144); in Fletcher's *The Spanish Curate* a marginal signal adds more details: "*A Bar, Table-book, 2 Chairs and Paper, standish set out*" (II: 98).

7. Webster directs: "*Enter* Officers *preparing seats for the judges . . .*" (4.2.o.s.d.); a later signal calls not for one but for two bars: "*Enter* Crispiano

like a judge, with another judge; Contilupo *and another lawyer at one bar;* Romelio, Ariosto, *at another . . ."* (4.2.52.s.d.). Sharpham provides: *"Enter two* IUDGES *with their traine, and sit down"* (5.5.o.s.d.); when a figure replaces one of the judges, he is told: "I pra'y assume his place" (17).

8. For a discussion of the relationship between costume and "place," see chapter 5 of Dessen, *Elizabethan Stage Conventions.*

9. For some shrewd comments on the limitations of the evidence provided by such playgoers' reactions, see Gurr, *Playgoing in Shakespeare's Time,* 105–114. For two such eyewitness accounts that have emerged in the last ten years, see the essays by Berry and Braunmuller.

10. For a fuller discussion of the sick-chair and a sampling of the evidence, see Dessen, *Recovering Shakespeare's Theatrical Vocabulary,* chapter 6.

4

Performance-Game and Representation in *Richard III*

Robert Weimann

Talk about "performance" in connection with Shake-speare more often than not tends to convey an interest either in the performance *of* his plays in the theatre or in the issue of performance *in* the dramatic text itself. Although this state of affairs continues to reflect, even while it modifies, the unhelpful dichotomy between stage-centered and text-centered approaches, the underlying difference in the reading of performance is symptomatic of a duality—as yet scarcely noticed—in the concept itself. There are two connotations of performance that ultimately derive from the transactive function of performative action itself. In order fully to appreciate this bifold connection of performance, it is not enough to dispense with the text/performance dichotomy; performative action itself needs to be relocated at that crucial point where dramatic language and cultural institution, representation and existence, can be seen to interact.

To illustrate this approach (one that cuts through traditional boundaries between dramatic criticism, theatre history, and cultural theory), let me start from a concept of performance that, in its transactive function, is no innocent vehicle of any linear or unitary mode of mediation between dramatic script and theatrical institution. In fact, performance in theatre can be said to be a dichotomous and highly changeful activity.

Its epistemological ambivalence can best be summarized in Julian Hilton's phrase: "performance is simultaneously representation and being" (152). Performance is representation insofar as it seeks in fiction to represent what image, speech, and thought a given text conveys about the world of the play and its meaning. But performance also and at the same time is "being"—that is, existence—in that performative practice (as distinct from its representational effect) constitutes an irreducible investment, on the part of actual (not fictional) agents, of their mental and visceral energy, their time, skill, competence, and, even, their sociocultural status and interest. Even as the performer proceeds to embody his/her part, the achieved impersonation does not cancel out the process of em-bodi-ment. On the contrary, the art of performance seems to thrive on the actor's stage presence, at least as far as that presence draws on the inalienable strength and agility of the agent, with all traces of his/her body, gender, age, and other forms of existence that go with and counterpoint the histrionic representation of fictitious roles.

Representation and Playing: Elizabethan Performance Revisited

To make this theoretical and cultural distinction seems especially important in an approach to performance *in* and *of* Shakespeare's plays. For reasons that closely connect with "bifold authority" in the uses of theatrical space,[1] actors in Shakespeare's theatre can both conceal or foreground performative agency; in doing so, they serve either a thoroughly textualized, representational "purpose of playing" (*Hamlet*, 3.2.20),[2] or a histrionic type of game and showmanship conveying, in Joseph Hall's words, their "own self-resembled show."[3] Although, as I shall emphasize, transitions between and amalgamations of these positions abound, the distinction seems useful and consequential in that it recognizes and responds to a basic differential in the uses of theatrical space: the articulation of performative agency dwindles in the *locus* (the represented site of verisimilitude allowing for an emphatic assimilation of roles) but seems to thrive on the *platea* (the space for a more "self-resembled" type of audience-addressed play in performance). But, again, the difference between them is never absolute; rather, as Shakespeare proceeds, it tends to be overlaid by increasingly complex and experimental constellations of text, space, and embodiment.

For our present purpose, these brief and entirely schematic considerations must suffice when, in the Elizabethan theatre, the element of duality in performance is seen to implicate an entirely unfixed series of links and gaps between textually determined representation and performative play-action. Here the relationship of "representation" (as an act of counterfeiting an "absent," fictitious state of affairs) and play-action (with its relatively unmediated existential underside) is not at all an invariable one. There is plenty of room for continuity, in the sense that the actor subsumes his own voice, gait, and looks under the needs of representation as authorized and inscribed in the text. But there is also evidence of discontinuity, as when textually oriented representation (although important throughout) fails to account for certain aspects of performative practice. Over and beyond the authority of the written text as the realization of represented meaning, there is a playful function of performative practice itself. Wherever in the early modern theatre the meaningful "purpose of playing" could be reconciled to the residual oral culture of playful game and sport, the actor continued to present himself as an at least partially self-directed agency of play and laughter. In these circumstances, the performer was not altogether "lost" in what he performed.

In the Elizabethan theatre, relations between text and performance were in a state of flux and realignment. No doubt it is tempting to assume, as John Russell Brown does, that this "actor-centred theatre would provide an encounter with Shakespeare's plays at which everything was at risk, and from their prepared positions the actors, with the audience could probe, penetrate and ride high upon the plays in their moment-by-moment life" (112). Such highly flexible relations between the presenter and the presented went hand in hand with a linguistic and, in the widest sense, semiotic fluidity in the relations of signifier and signified. Hence there could be continuity as well as a friction between written text and performed play: the dramatic written text, in the process of its performance, could mimetically be reproduced and complemented but also, to a certain extent, reinvented and re-signed.

The range of semiotic and semantic variability was especially broad in view of the actual conditions of production. As long as actors shared their performance space with spectators, the autonomy of textualized meaning could not be complete. Before the advent of the proscenium stage (where performers did obtain a separate space for their roles, one that was consistently symbolic in its apartness from the social occasion) actors might playfully say "more than is set down for them." To judge by Hamlet's stricture, such self-resembled agency of clownish playing must have been notorious at the turn of the century; its continuity was blamed because "in the mean time some necessary question" pre-scribed in the text of "the play" tended to be neglected. But for the Prince of Denmark to attack "them that will themselves laugh" (3.2.38–43) was to acknowledge the ongoing strength of the Tarlton tradition in performance, and to do so even after Will Kemp, "Jestmonger and Viceregent generall to the ghost of Dick Tarlton,"[4] had left the Lord Chamberlain's Men.

Despite increasing odds, the authority of self-directed game and jest-ing appeared impervious to a purely literary humanistic type of criticism—so much so that, more than a generation later, it must have been possible for an inventive performer to "fribble through." The phrase is from Richard Brome's play *The Antipodes* (1636), where Lord Letoy says of his own company of players:

> Well sir, my actors
> Are in all readiness, and, I think, all perfect
> But one, that never will be perfect in a thing
> He studies: yet he makes such shifts extempore,
> (Knowing the purpose what he is to speak to)
> That he moves mirth in me 'bove all the rest.
> For I am none of those poetic furies,
> That threats an actor's life, in a whole play,
> That adds a syllable or take away.
> If he can fribble through and move delight
> In others, I am pleas'd. (quoted in Wiles, 34)

The authority of the actor continued to be such that, in a certain context, he was free to adapt the text to his own self-directed sense of "mirth" and "purpose." Even after Ben Jonson went out of his way in print to as-sert the authorship of his "works," the political economy of theatrical production continued to allow actors (literally as well as metaphorically) to appropriate the text of the play to their own needs: the play in any case was theirs, since most Elizabethan dramatists, after having sold their script to the actors, had abdicated any personal claim upon it.

As Peter Thomson has recently reminded us, the relationship be-tween performers and dramatists was one "between actor-employers and playwright employees" (93). This state of affairs allowed an unusual

scope to the work of the inventive actor, especially when time for rehearsals was exorbitantly limited. Neil Carson, in his study of Henslowe's diary,[5] arrives at an estimate that would make modern actors
shudder: on the average no more than two weeks were available for
preparing a new play; within this brief period rehearsals proper would
be preceded by the transcription of the author's manuscript as well as the
cutting and pasting (and, of course, the memorizing) as well as the cos-
tuming of parts. As Thomson suggests (88 ff.), this hasty passage from
page to stage would not appear implausible "in the theatre untram-
melled by the demands of directors and designers"; the absence of the
latter would go hand in hand not only with the reduced amount of integration and disciplining among actors but, positively speaking, with a
readiness to leave certain (unrehearsed) scenes "to the improvisatory
inspiration of the flavoured actors."

The "Execrable" Play of "Contrariety"

No doubt these theoretical and historical considerations must remain
quite schematic as long as the generic and figural context is left in the
dark in which the gap between textualized representation and performative energy had to be accommodated. This context cannot exclusively be
associated with any one traditional convention of speech or acting
(among other things, it includes clowning as well as disguise).[6] For our
purpose, the postallegorical adaptation of the figure called Vice is of particular interest. If anywhere in the Tudor theatre there flourished a
configuration of performative strategies that was radically removed
from the neoclassical poetic of representation, it was to be found in this
singing, dancing, punning frivolous descendant of allegorical evil.

Humanist precept had strongly prescribed "delightful teaching"
along unambiguous lines of demarcation between the image of sinfulness and the mirror of virtue, aiming in general at "pictures, what should
be, and not stories what have bin" (Feuillerat, III: 29). But the figure of
Vice not only tended to defy the tidiness of this distinction but, even
worse, exemplified a "great faulte" in the theatrical uses of laughter: the
Vice stood for a grotesque mélange of boisterous comedy and heinous
sinfulness, the irreverent strategy, "forbidden plainly by *Aristotle* . . .
that they stirre laughter in sinfull things, which are rather execrable
then ridiculous" (Feuillerat, III: 41). But such "loude laughter" about the
"execrable" was symptomatic of the dissociation between represented
role and performing actor; it tended to privilege, on the part of the per-

formers, a comic response to what was hostile to the received order of things. Here was a gulf between the homiletic aims of allegorical representation (in its own way holding up a mirror to "pictures, what should be") and that frivolous site of performance where fondness and deformity, the laughable and the horrible, could scandalously be conflated. On the earlier Elizabethan stage, this state of affairs allowed (or so a humanist like Philip Sidney believed) "no right Comedie in that Comicall part of our Tragidie" in which the performer, unheedful of learned precept, constituted "a kinde of contrarietie" (Feuillerat, III: 40).

Sidney's phrase here is deeply revealing: "laughter in sinful things" is indeed "execrable" when the word is read as denoting an inversion of the sacred (as derived from *ex-sacrare*: "to reverse what is set apart as holy"). The act of reversal may of course be adumbrated in any textualized form of mimesis; even so, in the theatre the actual tool of reversal presupposes a performative agency which, notoriously, was provided by the actor who, in playing the Vice, can project "a kinde of contrarietie." Sidney, as we shall see, might have remembered the phrase from George Wapull's *The Tide Tarrieth No Man*, where the Vice Courage is designated as a force "contrarious" as well as "contrary" (see esp. ll. 93–110).

In Shakespeare's reception of the Vice there was, especially in a tragic context, scarcely any space left for the extemporal wit of "rhyming mother-wits" (as Christopher Marlowe styled them in the prologue to *Tamburlaine*, part I). But even when the distance between the image of representation and the site of performance could be physically or orally negotiated, the element of "contrariety" continued to be prominent: inscribed in the text itself, this "contrariety" was of general importance to Shakespeare's adaptation of the Vice; in fact, it appeared to constitute, or at least thrived in, the very gap between textual representation and those "fond and frivolous jestures" that Richard Jones had "purposely omitted" from his text of *Tamburlaine* (Cunningham, 111). Although "greatly gaped at" in performance (as the printer admits), these "graced deformities" must indeed have been execrable in relation to the "worthiness of the matter it selfe" in representation. But if, in Marlowe's *Tamburlaine*, this particular piece of "contrariety" was canceled out through Jones's censorship, in Shakespeare it received a different treatment in the first place. Not content with juxtaposing these "graced deformities" and "such matter of worth," Shakespeare assimilated the element of execration at a deeper level, absorbing the deformation itself within what Jones had called "so honourable and stately a history"

(Cunningham, x). Shakespeare used deformity in a physical, judicial, even socio-pathological sense so as to reconstitute the theatrical representation of "such matter of worth" as graced the history of royalty on the unworthy scaffolds in the liberties of London.

In *Richard III*, the absence in a Renaissance figure of nobility of "this fair proportion" was particularly striking when an ungentle hunchback conveyed a "misshapen" (1.2.250) character's sense of isolation. Such images of apartness can be traced in several other adaptations of the Vice, but especially in those where the image of their isolation was suspended in, or complemented by, *platea*-like uses of a privileged type of performance space. It is in the space of "aside," with its surplus of awareness and audience rapport, that the frivolity of the Vice (just like the fondness of the Clown) continued to thrive: here was the institutionalized site on which the arts of performance could bring forth (and infiltrate into the text) "jestures . . . far unmeet for the matter" of serious representation.

In this context of "contrariety," the descendants of the figure called Vice in Tudor drama continue to assert the efficacy of a playful type of game and feigning, even as they do so through their inscription in Shakespeare's dramatic representation. Hence Aaron in *Titus Andronicus* tends to speak "aside" (3.1.187–190, 201–204; 4.2.6, 25): the position of difference, spatially borne out by a site nonrepresentable, or at least invisible in the text, is symbolically followed up and endorsed by his "slavish," "servile" memories, his blackness coupled with a fierce desire for self-liberation: "Away with slavish weeds and servile thoughts! / I will be bright and shine in pearl and gold" (2.1.19–20). In Iago, the sense of dispossession symbolically affirms (and to a degree motivates) highly effective uses of the traditional site for evil manipulation. His sardonic signature tune, "Put money in thy purse" (1.3.341, 342–343, 345, et passim) recalls the chorus-like refrain of the old Vice but symbolically associates the absence of material means, an awareness of the hardness of things, the need for making both ends meet.

In an altogether different vein, Edmund is a "whoreson" (*Lear*, 1.1.23) who, as illegitimate son of the Earl of Gloucester, feels "branded" in his relation to the legitimate:

> Why brand they us
> With 'base,' with 'baseness, bastardy—base, base'—

. . . .

> Fine word, 'legitimate.'
> Well my legitimate, if this letter speed
> And my intention thrive, Edmond the base
> Shall to th'legitimate. I grow, I prosper.
> Now gods, stand up for bastards! (1.2.9–10; 18–22)

The recurring attributes of dispossession, bastardy, and apartness (anticipated in Faulconbridge, the bastard in *King John*) may suggest how the unsanctioned world of the underprivileged and indecorous, always already "unmeet for the matter," can actually be made integral to it. The question was how to traverse the distance, proscribed by neoclassical authority, between "matter" and "impertinency"; how to have "Matter and impertinency mixed" (4.5.178), so as to overcome any preordained opposition between "reason" and "madness," seriousness and frivolity, decorum and "deformity"—between the closure of representation and the aperture of performance. It is largely in rebellion against this binary scheme of things that Shakespeare's evocations of Vice mobilize the play at large: they embrace the contrarious thrust of a "bifold authority," through which the kinetic energies of performance—the scheming, cunning élan of theatricality, the unbound spirit of moral indifference and ideological negation—can unfold their ambidextrous design from within the text of representation itself.

As the descendants of the Vice enter (even, partially, raid) the world of history and representation, their isolation is suspended in symbolic figures of emplotment: thus, the apartness in downstage performance and the dispossessed, "branded," and deformed attributes in the representation of character are made to authorize and fortify one another. The image of social or moral isolation reflects (and is sustained by) a nonsymbolic space on the platform stage. Speaking from the same downstage, *platea*-like position, the Vice's descendants adopted a similarly frivolous air of showmanship, the conspiratorial show of alliance with a "gaping" audience; sustaining the distance, whenever called-for, from the self-enclosed illusion of dialogue by a specifically liberating use of language, a capacity for word-play and anachronism, for proverbial expression and the language of *sermo humilis*.

Here then was a whole context in which the performative dimension of the Vice survived the decline of allegory in the Morality play. This space—mutually supportive in its linguistic, spatial, and social conventions—was conducive to continuity, so that a late Vice like Courage can persist in being "contrarious" to empathy in representation and "contrary" to consistency in characterization.[7] In this context (if anywhere), the self-conscious voice of the itinerant performer continued to be heard, even in the newly set up amphitheatres, authorizing the sheer pleasures of entertainment together with the craft, the craftiness of the game, and of course the drudgery of staging, memorizing, and performing a play.

In the old Vice, invariably played by the principal actor (Bevington, 80), this voice was institutionalized in a *travail théâtral* that was incompatible with the constraints of either too much doubling or too consistent a form of characterization. The leading player/character was in charge of overseeing and directing the play, providing links and explanations wherever necessary, filling in the necessary intervals between change of dresses and appearances. Thus, ambidextrously serving both impersonation in a fiction and existentially needful requirements for entertainment *in persona*, the Vice would use his overwhelming stage-presence for improvised juggling, dancing, and playing, as Nichol Newfangle does in Ulpian Fulwell's *Like Will to Like*, "as oft as he thinketh good" (Dodsley, III: 344). But the most efficient and conclusive linkage between these two "contrarious" functions was for the actor of the Vice to turn his stage directorial function itself into some kind of entertainment: to dis-play his own job in staging the play, to offer his acts of go-between and manipulation as some kind of game, which the audience is invited regularly to see through and thus, in a manner, join.

Hence in the liminal quality of his showmanship, the strange, Janus-faced actor/character was deeply rooted in an important socio-theatrical function, in a cultural practice that must have served as his most viable and enduring matrix. Here was a highly transgressive master of ceremonies, an agent of theatricality, easily crossing the boundary between plot and complot, emplotment and manipulation. Carrying all before him, a person of some authority among his peers, this figure, offstage and onstage, must have stood for the most active and articulate agency of staging and performance. Constantly drawing and crossing the line between representation and showmanship, this entertainer must have stood for the arts of performance as a great game, a mixture (even in the symbolism of his role) of appropriation and dispossession, of evil greed and good fellowship turning sour. Small wonder that the pattern of bi-fold order in this potent agent of liminality lived on, to be remembered and uniquely inscribed in Shakespeare's plays—especially so in the early history of *Richard III*.

Vice of Kings: Betwixt Game and Representation

Richard Gloucester's wooing of Lady Anne may first of all suggest how "Th' abuse of distance" (*Henry V*, Chorus, 2.31) is turned into a game of performance out of which the popular Renaissance stage can "force" a representation of, literally, unbelievable density. The scene (*Richard III*, 1.2) has carefully marked frontiers: its threshold is crossed twice; for there is a sort of prologue as well as an epilogue to this scene, both spoken by Gloucester alone on the stage. His language (blank verse in direct address) is forthright but "conspirational" in the sense that, in sinister comedy, he draws the audience into his "secret close intent," debating with them the odds and "gains":

> For then I'll marry Warwick's youngest daughter.
> What though I killed her husband and her father?
> The readiest way to make the wench amends
> Is to become her husband and her father,
> The which will I. (1.1.153–157)

This is a *platea* occasion, with its correlative in Gloucester's uses of language. Note how the scheming Duke forgets the decorum and illusion and falls in with the common idiom of the day: the daughter of the Earl of Warwick, wife to the late Prince of Wales, is referred to as a "wench." The vulgar language of petty tradesmen is cited for proverbial wisdom ("But yet I run before my horse to market," 160), and to reassess his own politic schemes, the Duke must "count my gains" (162). Anachronism offers another sort of transgression, as when "George be packed with post-haste up to heaven" (146). Whatever breach of decorum (and laughter with terror) we experience, this use of language draws on a horizon of ordinary understanding which helps encode the signs and images, even the syntax, in a grim kind of *sermo humilis*.

For such discursive practice there is of course no authority either in the chronicles or in Thomas More's portrait of the ferocious witty tyrant. But in Shakespeare, the ordinary idiom of tradesmen is followed by the poignant wit and stichomythic rhetoric of courtship and persuasion: Gloucester makes good his "secret close intent" and displays "the readiest way" to win the wench (1.2.33–212). After Lady Anne's fierce hatred has melted in the heat of his violent play of wooing, Gloucester, again alone on stage, congratulates himself, not so much upon the outcome of a represented action as upon the achieved level of its performance:

> Was ever woman in this humour wooed?
> Was ever woman in this humour won?
> I'll have her, but I will not keep her long.
> What, I that killed her husband and his father,
> To take her in her heart's extremest hate,
> With curses in her mouth, tears in her eyes,
> The bleeding witness of my hatred by,
> Having God, her conscience, and these bars against me,
> And I no friends to back my suit withal
> But the plain devil and dissembling looks—
> And yet to win her, all the world to nothing? Ha! (215–225)

Appealing to an authority that is in the performance rather than the role, the actor/character stands back as it were and looks at his own part in the preceding scene. Instead of replaying the aggressive strategy of his impudent courtship, he proceeds to relish the virtuoso quality of his "dissembling looks." The opening question is "frivolous" enough; its repetition urges the audience (and grants them time) to respond. The outgoing bravura is that of a self-congratulating entertainer who rejoices over an uncommon feat, success against formidable odds. What the performer (rather than the performed) reviews is the high degree of his professional competence. The sheer pleasure at the outcome of the game finds its climax in the sardonic "Ha!"—the Vice's oft recurring expletive of satisfaction: it is the moment of supreme triumph, when the full extent of "contrariety" through execration emerges. The exultation is unmistakable; the triumph of achieved equivocation is celebrated and, as such, shared out with the audience who, right up to the actor's exit, are involved on a level where the arts of representation and the playing of the game, never quite the same, come to complement and supplement each other.

In this epilogue-like perspective (that can mark the end of the play just as, here, the end of the scene) two locations of authority engage one another: the authority of what is represented is made to collapse in, or at least come to terms with, the authority of what is performing. The fictitious representation of Gloucester's role as suitor is undermined and overshadowed by the histrionic competence required to counterfeit it.

At this juncture, there is neither complete rupture nor perfect continuity between what was represented in a fiction and what (and who) was doing the performing. Instead, there is a kind of balance in "contrariety," a strange, almost weird kind of poise, (dis)continuity between the symbolism of representation and the craft of performance.

If, then, the actor/character of Gloucester is both the performing agent and the performed object of a textualized representation, the ambidextrous engagement between the two dimensions has the use and "abuse of distance" at its center. At its liminal site, two levels of authority can be seen to negotiate: in its outcome, the signs of Gloucester's isolation as a character ("And I no friends to back my suit withal") are intercepted and appropriated by the virtuoso quality of the performance itself. The measure of Gloucester's success in courtship is that he has nothing but "the plain devil and dissembling looks" at his disposal. This could with equal poignancy be said in reference to the common player who confronts "so great an object" (*Henry V*, prologue, 11) of performance as (in the guise of the evil Duke) having to court the widow of the Prince of Wales.

Thus, the game in playing the scene is to emphasize both the area of continuity and the sheer distance between "that brave prince," "A sweeter and a lovelier gentleman," "this sweet prince," "no doubt right royal" (226–234) and the "dissembling" performer who, a disadvantaged outsider, seems dispossessed of the luminous pleasures of the court whose emblematic seat of splendor he is about to appropriate. Gloucester scarcely conceals his surprise that Anne will "yet debase her eyes on me" (251). The Folio reading ("abuse") is even more emphatic about the lowering of status. In either case Richard, in his own bustling ambition and mobility, finds the language ("But first I'll turn yon fellow in his grave," 265) and elicits sufficient solidarity for the audience in horror and laughter to go along with the disadvantaged upstart ("misshapen thus?" 255). Hence, when Gloucester appears to rouse his "dissembling looks" from a lower ground, the real actor—poor devil—who performs this role must confront the difficulty (well described in the language of the prologue to *Henry V*) that "a crooked figure"—a veritable o, a social nil—must induce the audience to "make imaginary puissance" (15, 25) in coming to terms with ferocious springs of power.

This reading of the wooing scene cannot of course do justice to the entire, complex role of Richard Gloucester, who is the most Marlovian of Shakespeare's heroes, a "Machiavellian" intellect of ruthless self-aggrandizement, minister as well as scourge of a corrupt and murderous world. At a later stage, and especially after having gained the throne, he—entirely surrendering the *platea* position of showmanship—is turned into an object of retributive justice. But since the agents and prophets of this justice are either faceless and theatrically ineffective (like young Richmond) or compromised by their own ugly hunger for revenge (like Margaret), the status of the hero's shifting space in the play remains unchallenged, even when responding to no single, univocal code or telos. Since the configuration of the Vice cannot be "moralized" as purely the opposite of virtue, the appeal of the play as drama actually thrives on an "execrable" design of unlawful empowerment and fortitude in the teeth of defeat.

In this respect, Shakespeare's reception of the figure called Vice projects a specifically theatrical site of "contrariness" through the challenge, in the image and language of performative energy, of "the worthiness of the matter" of historiography in representation. The idea is not at all to denounce "so honourable and stately a history," but to assimilate it to a stage representation through a performative strategy of appropriation that is decidedly different from, even "contrarious" to, the discourses of historiography and contemporary politics: the representation of greatness is redefined in that its image is made to process, through performative action, its frivolity and recklessness.

Since the discursive and performative space for this difference in the image of the great is unsanctioned in the dominant order of things, Gloucester's "dissembling looks" conceal an unsuspectedly large area of social confusion and topsy-turvydom. Hence early in the play, upward mobility as blandly practiced through courtship and murder can easily be retracted; the thing itself can be disowned when, handy-dandy, Richard appears to complain to Elizabeth, "Since every jack became a gentleman, / There's many a gentle person made a jack" (1.3.72–73). Here, characteristically, complaint and offense go together in a contrarious juxtaposition. But this piece of contrariety is doubly dubious in a twofold sense, when the line can be read as celebrating two meanings of one conceit: suggesting upward exchange of roles in the world of both society and the theatre, the dark dialectic of appropriation and self-projection is at work in a performance practice where every ordinary actor in this history does, and therefore undoes, "a gentle person."

Although the emphasis on this self-reflexive aspect of textually inscribed performance practice must not be pushed too far, the mimesis of game and sport was inseparable from the play of turning the status of things upside down. Note the facility with which Richard can assume the plain forthright voice of indignation: "Cannot a plain man live and think no harm?" (1.3.51). Along these lines, he is honest Gloucester, contemptuous of false, "apish courtesy" (1.3.49). It is within this role-playing (which recalls the "honesty" of Iago) that critics have perceived "a comedian so cheeky, frank, and enthusiastic in his wickedness that most of his betters seem unpardonably dishonest and dreary" (Ornstein, 63). Such outspoken "frankness" in his showmanship is part and parcel of a larger duplicity of meaning. On a rather obvious level, Gloucester of course is free to play with an absolute host of moral and political choices because, unlike Margaret, Elizabeth, and Edward, he does not recognize any authority except his own appetite and self-interest: "I have no brother"; "I am myself alone" (3 Henry VI, 5.6.81, 84); he is not bound by norms of affection or kinship. But more subtly and hardly less consequentially, the game he performs is that of a player in front of a looking-glass, an actor who counterfeits the counterfeiting, who "descants" on the shadow of his own "deformity." The image of the "glass" serves almost as a leitmotif upon his first appearance (1.1.15; 1.2.242, 249); but in marked contrast to the element of closure in Marlowe's "tragicke glass" (prologue to Tamburlaine, 7), Gloucester's mirror serves to emphasize not representation but its limits—insofar as these are foregrounded by a player who, first and foremost, performs the act of playing: "Shine out, fair sun, till I have bought a glass / That I may see my shadow as I pass" (1.2.249–250). The rhymed couplet aims at the mimesis of mimesis; the "glass" in question is an insubstantial pageant; instead of Tamburlaine's stately "presence" in representation, this "shadow" reveals the performer in self-reflexive effigy.

Once the purpose of playing in a history play is "princes to act, / And monarchs to behold the swelling scene" (Henry V, prologue, 3–4), the actors playing those princes can find the measure of their performance (and their excellence) in the profession itself. Theirs is a kind of authority that, "But in a fiction, in a dream of passion," can set an example by which the Prince of Denmark seeks to assess his own inactive performance ("What would he do / Had he motive and the cue for passion / That I have?" 2.2.554, 562–563). Similarly, the perfect touchstone for the politics of "dissembling looks" in the world of Richard III is the performance that seeks to excel, at least to imitate, not so much the represented "picture in this tragicke glass," but the "shadow" in the mirror of "the deep tragedian."

> Tut, I can counterfeit the deep tragedian,
> Tremble and start at wagging of a straw,
> Speak, and look back, and pry on every side,
> Intending deep suspicion; ghastly looks
> Are at my service, like enforcèd smiles,
> And both are ready in their offices
> At any time to grace my stratagems. (3.5.5–11)

These, of course, are Buckingham's words as he, entering "in rotten armour, marvellous ill-favoured," is baited by Gloucester to perform his part well in the bloody farce, staged to collude in the murder of Lord Hastings before the eyes of the Lord Mayor and those that might "misconster" (59) the deed. Again, what authority there is resides on the level of the performance—a touchstone especially supreme in face of the absence, or even the destruction, of moral authority in the represented world of the play. As far as Gloucester avails himself of norms, including those of royalty and public service, they are at once used as masks of falsehood behind which there is nothing but empty space for a brazen-faced pursuit of power legitimated by power alone.[8]

At this point, the Vice-world of unlimited performance fully unfolds its destructive potential—again, in Richard Jones' language, "far unmeet for" an official reading of "the matter" of political history. Gloucester, precisely because power is his sole aim and point of departure, utterly discredits the authority of power pure and simple. What seems remarkable is how, in the reckless game-world of performance, the readiness to waive the political norms and choices of Tudor ideology combines with a startling aloofness from the Protestant mode of legitimation. As Thomas Sorge suggests, the play explores the clash between secular power and Protestant conscience (215, 221–225), a contest between two vast locations of authority: the Tudor ideology of order, office, and obedience is shown as in a troublesome relation with such justification by faith as inspired a self-authorized Protestant frame of mind. Richard, in his ambidextrous posturing, can be shown to straddle the conflict, exempting himself from both demands. To reject both locations of authority is to establish a noncommittal site, unbound by their norms, where the play of power and the game of conscience can engage one another in uncommon playfulness.

Thus Gloucester, in order to achieve powerful room at the top, is free to "clothe" his murderous ambition by appeal to divine authority:

> But then I sigh, and with a piece of scripture,
> Tell them that God bids us do good for evil;
> And thus I clothe my naked villainy
> With odd old ends, stol'n forth of Holy Writ,
> And seem a saint when most I play the devil. (1.3.332–336)

Scripture provides a mock authority, a mode of authorization that is viciously abused when the traditional as well as the Protestant meaning is (de)moralized into its devilish opposite. It is another case where virtue and vice are turned upside down, and where Richard's specific role, the sinister design behind his farcical use of contrariety, appears rooted in the topsy-turvy world of a bottomless mimesis. Again, his "execrable" stance vis-à-vis the ultimate, sacred source of authority is inseparable from his unbounded capacity, not just for performing, but for relishing a self-directed game of equivocation. Note the professed competence for counterfeiting, the scarcely concealed gusto in playing the role of the devil in the disguise of "a saint." Here is an amoral performative agency, dis-playing unprecedented audacity in turning upside down the hallowed order of sin and saintliness. More than elsewhere in the play, the Vice self-consciously foregrounds the shameless art of his signification, disrupting the order of his continuity, stability itself, between the textual signs of orthodoxy and their actually performed reading and meaning. Here, it may well be said that performance crowns all: the "frivolous Iesture" of pious deception amounts to more than a misreading, a merely verbal upsetting of a sacred signified. What Gloucester delivers is both a representation of hypocrisy and a stage direction. It is impossible to think that, in spelling out his proposed abuse of biblical piety, the performer would not, in Sidney's words, "stirre laughter in sinful things," mimicking his own outrageous reading and interpretation of "Holy Writ."

Biblical language, in the form of a reference to "the great judgement day," is again appropriated in the following scene, and again it is used to rouse laughter and terror in a stunning game of contrariety. When the two Murderers contemplate Clarence, their victim, the question of their "warrant" leads to a grim and outrageously comic paraphrase of the uses of authority between secular and spiritual locations of validity.

> *Second Murderer.* What, shall I stab him as he sleeps?
> *First Murderer.* No. He'll say 'twas done cowardly, when he wakes.
> *Second Murderer.* Why, he shall never wake until the great judgement day.
> *First Murderer.* Why, then he'll say we stabbed him sleeping.
> *Second Murderer.* The urging of that word 'judgement' hath bred a kind of remorse in me.
> *First Murderer.* What, art thou afraid?
> *Second Murderer.* Not to kill him, having a warrant, but to be damned for killing him, from the which no warrant can defend me.
>
> (1.4.97–109)

By moralizing two meanings into the language of the Last Judgment—a topos central to the Vice's performance in *Mankind* and *The Tide Tarrieth No Man*—this exchange adumbrates the gravediggers' scene in *Hamlet*. Note the comically achieved sense of incongruity when secular power with its "brief little authority" can legitimate a crime without being able to control the ultimate instance of its retribution. Although the Second Murderer can easily, and at considerable length (131–141), borrow from the Book of Common Prayer (in particular, the commination service, where the workings of Conscience are spelled out), his own resort to it is in the manner of "courage contrarious." Conscience is treated as the most volatile site of authority; if it does not reside "in the Duke of Gloucester's purse" (125), it is "a dangerous thing." Small wonder when "every man that means to live well endeavors to trust to himself, and live without it [conscience]" (139, 140).

The murderers' scene, of course, serves as a grotesque variation on Gloucester's fate when, having ascended the throne (4.3) and sloughed off the accoutrements of the Vice, he is fully drawn into the ungrotesque world of history as pure representation. In his heaviest moment, his dreams on the eve of battle, "conscience" is on his lips no less than four times. But even here its semantic underside is deeply divided, marked by the absence of any univocal center of meaning: "My conscience hath a thousand several tongues" (5.5.147). For King Richard, confronting the ghastly images of his vicious doings (as premonitions of his own undoing), conscience is an organ of contrariety itself.

If, finally, Richard's inward language is greatly disturbed, the signs of his outward physiognomy point in a similar direction. His hunchback signifies the prominence of deformed corporeality; his deformity can, of course, be read as the symbol of personal deprivation: one who is "cheated of feature by dissembling Nature" (1.1.19). Since "nature" itself cannot help but counterfeit its own products, there is for him neither a divinely sanctioned order nor any genuinely plausible scheme of nature. Small wonder when Gloucester, in the dissembling concert of all "the idle pleasures of these days," has "no delight to pass away the time, / Unless to spy my shadow in the sun / And descant on mine own deformity" (25–27). To "descant," as the Arden editor notes, is to "enlarge upon a theme" or, by "figurative extension" from this meaning, "to sing a melody against a fixed harmony" (Hammond, 127). Gloucester, in fact, does both: on the stark performative of his corporeality he enlarges upon the theme (and shape) of his own "deformity"; he figuratively descants, that is, extends (and jars) its meaning by turning his voice against any one fixed representation of it, against any fixed mode of signifying the hump on his own performing shoulder. The hunchback functions like those prophetic but "imperfect speakers" in *Macbeth* (1.3.68), an equivocal representation that cunningly disrupts continuities between signs and meanings. Hence Richard's words as his brother Clarence departs for the Tower: "Well, your imprisonment shall not be long. / I will deliver you or lie for you. / Meantime, have patience" (1.1.115–117). Words like "deliver" and "lie for you" are twisted into a sinister ambivalence where hope and support (in Clarence's understanding) are, handy-dandy, exchanged for threats and deceits. It is another perfect game of equivocation. The dark irony in his forecast ("your imprisonment shall not be long") constitutes a nonrepresentable play with bifold meaning where the promise of imminent release and liberty turns into a prophecy of doom.

The point is not, simply, that Richard's language draws on the absence of stable relations between signifier and signified, but that, in exploiting the instability of these relations, he involves the audience in some degree of complicity with his own contrariety. Going beyond his role within the representation of a plot, he draws the onlookers into a complot, while Clarence is quite unaware of the menacing undertone. It is the spectators who are privileged to have more knowledge about the play world than its own representations are made to contain. Gloucester before his decline (which ironically connects with his *rise* to royalty) is the medium of this awareness, the darkish light of recognition that helps penetrate the surface of the "worthinesse of the matter it selfe." As spectators listen to this "moralizing" of two meanings in one word, as they follow his frivolous gestures, read in the twinkling of his eye, they literally profit from what he (in both senses of the word) betrays. It is his duplicity, his ambidextrous double-dealing with both game and representation, that *nolens volens* invites complicity. But then, as if to affirm contrariety on every level, Richard, in sharing out his superior awareness, can snare the audience's sympathy—only to betray their trust. Having ascended to the throne and consummated his ambition, he forgets about the vicious alacrity of a mounting spirit. What remains, after his apartness is ended and the play with "conscience" is over, is a "tragicke glass," the worthy narrative of a ferocious feudal magnate, shouting and dying, unhorsed and immovable, in front of a *locus*, his own "stately tent of War," in the self-enclosed armor of his murderous caste.

NOTES

1. See "Bifold Authority," in which I have further developed this spatial differentiation.

2. Unless otherwise noted, all quotations are taken from Wells and Taylor's Oxford edition of *William Shakespeare: The Complete Works.*

3. The context of the phrase deserves to be recalled (*Virgidemiarum* [1597]. 1.1.33–44; cf. Hall, IX: 58):

> midst the silent rout
> Comes leaping in a self-misformed lout,
> And laughs, and grins, and frames his mimic face,
> And justles straight into the prince's place:
> Then doth the theater echo all aloud
> With gladsome noise of that applauding crowd.
> A goodly hotch-potch! with vite russetings
> Are matched with monarchs and with mighty kings.
> A goodly grace to sober Tragic Muse,
> With each base clown his clumsy fist doth bruise,
> And show his teeth in a double rotten row,
> For laughter at his self-resembled show.

4. Thomas Nashe's phrase, in *Almond for a Parrot* (1590). On the Tarlton tradition in performance, see Wiles, esp. 11–23.

5. See Carson for significant illustrations of "the speed with which these plays were mounted" (74).

6. On the performer in disguise, see my "Textual Authority and Performative Agency."

7. See, in this connection, my revisionist reading of the figure called Vice in Tudor drama in "'Moralize Two Meanings' in One Play."

8. See Iser's reading of the play, according to which the "order of rule" (Herrschaftsordnung) and the "Interests of power" (Machtinteressen) divide and, between them, open up the modern, autonomous "realm of politics" (61–84).

5

The Shopping Complex: Materiality and the Renaissance Theatre

Kathleen E. McLuskie

In 1991 the Young Vic company, an Arts Council subsidized theatre in London, presented a production of *Timon of Athens*. Performed in modern dress, the production was dominated by images of consumer style. In his affluent phase Timon evoked the hero of Thomas Wolfe's novel *The Bonfire of the Vanities* (intertextuality is unavoidable here), equipped with a mobile phone, surrounded by elegant business furniture, meeting the former clients from whom he seeks support in a squash club. The subject matter of the play presented itself as a scathing critique of the 1980s Thatcherite boom, but the elegance of the production's physical style offered a celebration of the pleasures of consumption, summarized in the program credits which listed some of the most desirable names of 1980s consumerism—Nicole Farhi, Colibri, Moet and Chandon, Canon, the Dorchester Hotel, Coutts & Co., Ladbrooke Racing, etc.

One of the play's most telling moments was the central banquet. The setting was a reception at which elegant, dinner-jacketed, affable men (no women were present) tastefully admired the masque of Amazons (dressed by MBA costumes of Osnoburgh Street) as their modern counterparts might have relished similar corporate hospitality at a private view at the Royal Academy or a first night cast party at the Young Vic itself. The Amazons were dressed as eighteenth-century ladies and danced a formal minuet to the subdued applause of their audience. However, once the formal part was over, the ladies ripped off their paneled skirts to reveal the fishnet stockings and body suits of the up-market whore. The men took off their jackets and ties and the taking-out dance of the masque became an orgy. The moment created a powerful image of the connection between the prostitution and patronage of the arts which had been a subject of recent journalistic discussion. It drew on the liberal critique of the glorification of the market and in particular the discussions within feminism and artistic circles about the commodification of both women and art.

Later in the play, Timon becomes a figure excluded from society who repudiates all social relations as driven by greed; here too an easy modern parallel suggested itself. Timon became an emblem of the homeless dispossessed, the victim of the rationalizations of "market forces" which had closed down the mental hospitals and reduced the eligibility for public housing. He looked like the denizens of "cardboard city," the location not far from the Young Vic Theatre in which the homeless of London had set up camp under the concrete pillars which supported the walkways of the South Bank arts complex. The image was reinforced in the production program by a photograph of a homeless man sleeping in the snow and a cartoon which showed city gents, losers in recent financial crashes, joining the tramps and winos round a wasteground fire. However, the proliferation of these images showed that their pleasing ironies had become a little stale even as they were being forged. Trevor Nunn's use of the "cardboard city" image was foreshadowed and echoed in a number of plays that season.[1] And the cardboard city had itself become a tourist venue.

Soon after that production the Conservative party won its third general election. The housing policies which had contributed to the plight of the homeless had also made a number of former council tenants into owner occupiers. The economic boom which had produced the vulgarities satirized in the Young Vic Timon had enriched enough people to make them nervous about supporting a political opposition committed to wealth redistribution through taxation. The market represented in plays had provided a set of intellectually and aesthetically satisfying images which offered the additional pleasure of seeming socially relevant if not subversive. The market for plays, on the other hand, declined under pressure from funding cuts in the Arts Council budget. David Thacker, the director of the Young Vic company, left it to join Trevor

Nunn at the Royal Shakespeare Company, whose international reputation provided it with enough cultural capital to ensure continued corporate sponsorship.

The Young Vic production of *Timon*, like all theatre events, had a social meaning generated by a complex interaction of theatrical creativity, material circumstances, and social critique. Interviewed for the program notes, Trevor Nunn described how

> during a meeting to discuss the financial problems of the Young Vic, David Thacker asked me if I would do a Shakespeare production for him. When I thought of the tradition of relevant classics at The Young Vic, and of the budgetary constraints too, it seemed to me that a twentieth century or contemporary presentation of *Timon* was not only right in the circumstances, but answered in some way the demand that the play be an unsettling piece of direct address—raw and provocative.

Nunn's easy elision between the actual financial problems of the Young Vic and the theme of *Timon* derives from the assumption, commonplace among theatre practitioners, that Shakespeare "is extraordinarily relevant to how we live now." However, that relevance has to be mediated through modern dress production—"the tradition of relevant classics"—whose aesthetic pleasures derive from the abilities of directors and performers to translate the texts into recognizable images and relevant concerns. This in turn depends on the paradoxes of the material circumstances of modern theatre: Shakespeare is expensive to produce but even when the plays enact a social critique, the name of the bard can be satisfyingly linked with Royal Insurance, or Hewlett Packard or, as Alan Sinfield has recently pointed out, the arms manufacturing branch of the British state (*Faultlines*, 1–10).

The connection between Shakespeare as a modern cultural icon and the ideology of a reactionary establishment has become a commonplace of political criticism (see Dollimore and Sinfield, Holderness, and Sinfield, "Royal Shakespeare" and *Faultlines*). However, this attention to the material and ideological positioning of a cultural icon is in tension with the sense of the potential in Shakespeare and Renaissance drama for social critique, which is seen as part of its theatrical creativity and its political power. The English playwright Howard Barker, for example, has often used the early modern period as a setting for his own work, which includes an adaptation of Thomas Middleton's *Women Beware Women*. In his "Conversation with a Dead Poet" he summed up the connection between contemporary Britain and the English Renaissance: "England in this era is a money and squalor society also. The connections were obvious" (26). However, the very obviousness of these connections gets in the way of precise historical and critical analysis. It reifies "the market" into a metahistorical image as applicable to the 1980s as the 1580s, a procedure which may be theatrically creative but is analytically confused. It allows a rhetorical elision between the emergent early modern market and the highly developed, all pervasive, and infinitely adaptable market of late-twentieth-century capitalism.

The connection between early modern and the postmodern market is made easier by the way in which dramatic texts provide powerful poetic and theatrical images which generalize "the market" both as a set of social values and as a set of economic relations. No less a figure than Karl Marx, as Richard Wilson shows (11), could read the image of Timon's revulsion from gold "as the hub of the cash nexus where the 'visible god' of money circulated values" through Shakespearean England. For many critics since Marx, the resonant symbolism of the pound of flesh in *The Merchant of Venice* and the emblematic connection between prostitution and commerce in *Measure for Measure* offer paradigms of the increased commercial activity noted both by historians of the market and, most tellingly, by contemporaries.

The commonplace connections between the market and sharp practice, particularly sexual sharp practice, were dramatically elaborated in speeches and scenes which, like Nunn's production of *Timon*, both celebrate the vitality and satirize the moral dangers of the market. In Thomas Dekker and John Webster's *Westward Ho*, Mistress Honeysuckle is urged to use shopping as an excuse to get out of the house to meet her lover, saying that she will visit "the pawne to buy Lawne; to Saint Martin's for Lace; to the Garden; to the Glass-house; to your Gossips; to the Powlters; else take out an old ruffe, and go to your Sempsters" (Dekker, *Dramatic Works*; 2.1.214–217). The speech has a wonderful particularity: it creates a dramatic sense of London life, but it also seems to offer corroboration of the historical account of the growth of the consumer market, the production and consumption of "brass cooking pots, iron frying pans, earthenware dishes, knitted stockings, even a lace frill for a cap or apron" (Thirsk, 175). However, the metaphoric force of the theatrical image allowed it to do more than simply reflect the material reality of shopping in early modern London.

Mistress Honeysuckle in *Westward Ho* later justifies her own gadding to find pleasures thus:

> Why should I long to eate of baker's bread onely, when theres so much
> Sifting, and bolting and grynding in every corner of the Citty; men and
> women are borne, and come running into the world faster than Coaches
> doe into Cheap-side uppon Symon and Iudes day: and are eaten by
> Death faster, then Mutton and porridge in terme time. (2.1.324–328)

This densely packed image refers to the ineffectiveness of market regulation of bread sales, sexualizes the production and circulation of that staple commodity, and holds the whole image together in a grotesque allegory of London as a meal for Death.

The effectiveness of these rhetorical strategies lay in the way that the generalized image of the market could be animated by an authenticating particularity to create both local effects of realism and more extended scenarios for complete plays. In the purpose-built theatres, partly because they followed the familiar patterns of public building, it was easy to recreate shopping scenes, in many cases literally, as the doors and discovery space of the tiring house walls are turned into shop fronts in which the action unfolds. Arden's murder is comically thwarted when Black Will and Shakebag have their heads broken by a careless apprentice shutting up his shop; Jane Shore in Thomas Heywood's *1 Edward IV* is the first of many heroines to be seduced in a shop;[2] and Touchstone's shop is both the actual and the ironized location of the action in *Eastward Ho*, itself a play which parodies the warmer-hearted world of shopping in *The Shoemaker's Holiday* or Heywood's *2 If You Know Not Me You Know Nobody*.

These different representations of shopping are both an artistically opportunist exploitation of theatrical resources and a way of negotiating the conflicting traditions of celebration and satire with the phenomenon of the market. In Heywood's *1 Edward IV*, for example, Spicing and Chub, the leaders of a group of comic rebels, describe the exciting prospect of London's shops to their companions:

> You know *Cheapside*: there are the mercers' shops
> Where we will measure veluet by the pikes,
> And silkes and satins by the street's whole bredth:
> We'le take the tankards from the conduit-cocks
> To fill with ipocras and drinke carouse,

Where chains of gold and plate shall be as plenty
As wooden dishes in the wild of *Kent*.

No sooner in *London* will wee be,
But the bakers for you, the brewers for mee.
Birchin lane shall suite vs,
The costermongers fruite vs,
The poulters send vs in fowl,
And butchers meate without controul:
And euer when we suppe or dine,
The vintners freely bring vs in wine.
In anybody aske who shall pay,
Cut off his head and send him away. (Heywood, I: 10–11)

The scene's dramatic function is to undermine the rebels' seriousness
and to indicate their irresponsible ignorance of the true nature of trading. It provides a dramatically useful contrast with the sturdy appren-
tices who will rout them in the energetic battle scenes which ensue. It
is similar to Shakespeare's representation of Jack Cade and his rebels,
though Cade's assertion, "There shall be in England seven halfpenny
loaves sold for a penny, the three hoop'd pot shall have ten hoops, and I
will make it felony to drink small beer" (2 *Henry VI*, 4.2.65–68), in
spite of its faulty arithmetic, involves rather more sophistication as an
economic concept. It indicates the contingency of fixed measurement
and its inadequacy, like so much Elizabethan market regulation, to act as
a brake on high inflation. However, Cade's account has none of the celebratory particularity of Spicing's image of Cheapside; the sense that
London and its shops have everything to offer even if rebels and "those
desperate, idle, swaggering mates, / That haunt the suburbes in the time
of peace" (Heywood, I: 18) have no legitimate access to it.

That celebration of London's shops is even more evident in Heywood's
attempt to bring together all the different sectors of the retail trade in
part 2 of *If You Know Not Me You Know Nobody*. The play combines the
great Merchant Gresham and the building of the Royal Exchange; the
story of Hobson the jolly small shopkeeper and the whole is given a political coherence by the final presence of the Queen and the victory of
the Armada. Using the characteristic theatrical style of the public amphitheatres the action gives a physical reality to the images of economic
growth. The foundations of the Royal Exchange are physically laid onstage with a golden coin placed on the foundation stones for the cheerful

workers to share. When John Tawneycoat the pedlar comes to Hobson's shop to reequip his pack for the rural fairs, he asks for horning busks and silken bridelaces, washed gloves, and carnation girdles and asserts that the market for London fashions has been fully extended into country fairs.[3]

These comic and celebratory images of early modern shopping stand in a complex relationship both to the historical evidence about the development of a consumer economy and to the ideology of market relations. The scenes at the Royal Exchange gloss over the fact that, like many a modern shopping mall, Gresham's grandiose venture was a failure and he had drastically to reduce the rents to fill up the shops for the royal opening (Dorothy Davis, 104–105). That market is presented as shopping at its most seductive where "good citizens and their fair wives" will rub shoulders with courtiers and there will always be the buzz of sexual potential even when the eyes are chaste and the ladies "blush to turn their vizards off" (quoted in Bruster, 5). In the more down-market shopping venue, the conflicting economic interests of rural pedlars and city suppliers are similarly glossed over in the male camaraderie of sexual jokes. Hobson and the pedlar engage in a punning contest about poking sticks and the length of a Puritan's poker as the country girls' desire for modern fashions is sexualized into the standard jokes about the fashion for wearing yellow, the cuckold's color. The rehearsal of this familiar routine of standard jokes about draperies provides a theatrical pleasure which keeps at bay the sense of the conflict between market competitors and between men and women in the market. This conflict was the material of satire rather than comedy, but in either genre it involved the manipulation of theatrical tropes: in one case to produce a narrative of tragic betrayal in which women are the object of sale; in the other a set of bawdy jokes.

In its comic treatment of shopping, Heywood's play seems to gloss over real economic conflict, yet the almost casual juxtapositions of other parts of the narrative reveal the central ideological contradiction: the desire to celebrate economic growth while retaining the idealized social relations of a fantasized preeconomic era. When the great merchants argue over their legal rights to a piece of land, Hobson wishes for continuity with a prelapsarian era when "All *Adams* earth, And *Adams* earth is free for *Adams* sons, / And tis a shame men should contend for it" (Heywood, I: 267). The possibility of transcending the market economy is provided by the ideal of alms-giving and the use of economic surplus for charity rather than for conspicuous consumption (Stevenson). This notion is given a dramatic reality in the moving scene where Hobson rescues the poor laborer carrying his emblematic spade, seeing "as in a looking-glass, / I see the toil and travell of the country, / And quiet gaine of cities blessednesse" (Heywood, I: 305).

The economic thought of a culture locked into the contrasts between profit and charity was unable to deal with economic-historical evidence that the growth of the retail trade went some way to absorbing the surplus labor created by population growth and changes in the organization of rural labor (Thirsk, 174–175). The play dramatized instead the contradictions between the celebration of economic growth and the need to reaffirm the social commitment to a coherent and egalitarian social order. It explicitly resists the inevitability of the relationship between predator and prey insisted upon by city comedy satirists: it offers instead a dramatic version of both the preaching and the practice of those energetic middling sort of men who engaged day to day in the organization of cities and market regulation and the distribution of food (Rappaport; Archer).

The emphasis on images of a coherent community provided the theatrical pleasures of pathos and bawdy which diverted attention from the mundane business of the exchange of goods and services. For in the midst of the celebration of shopping and trade, the characters display a comic unconcern for the market. Both Gresham and Hobson—and, in his own way, Gresham's deviant nephew Jack—evince the dramatic qualities of good humor and comic theatrical power. Gresham comically accepts the enormous losses incurred in the failure of the sugar monopoly with the King of Barbary in which his only profit is a pair of slippers. Hobson's concern for fair dealing makes him refuse due payment of ten pounds for goods because of a confusion over the name of the pedlar who has received them. For the theatrical values of the play create a comic community not only between the characters in the action but with the audience, who are invited to share in the fun.

The dramatic treatment of the market in early modern drama elides the representation of economic relations with an account of a moral economy reinforced by the pleasures of performance. Sentimentally or satirically, the plays lay forth the contradictory impulses which create their narratives, offering an account of the connection between ideologies of the market and an emerging market economy which satisfyingly

invites a materialist reading. Using the drama as paradigm for this reading of early modern culture is further encouraged by the fact that both
moralists and apologists for the theatre in early modern times did the
same thing. In his recent work on *Drama and the Market in the Age of
Shakespeare*, for example, Douglas Bruster quotes Stephen Gosson's famous description of the theatres as "the very markets of bawdry, where
choice without shame hath been as free as it is for your money at the
Royal Exchange, to take a short stock, or a long band, or a French ruff"
(6). Gosson's analogy was, of course, commonplace: Thomas Dekker
refers, in *The Guls Horne-booke* to the "Poets Royal-Exchange" (sig.
C2; 27) and Thomas Middleton wittily compared the "fashion of play-
making" with sartorial change in the preface to the Comic Play-Readers
of *The Roaring Girl* (3), theatre with prostitution in the epilogue to *The
Family of Love* (sig. A2).

These commonplaces, of course, tell us nothing precise about the
actual economics of theatre, and recent accounts of the theatre and the
market have acknowledged this by sidestepping the problems. Bruster
explicitly abandons economics for a "poetics of the market" and, more
explicitly, Richard Halperin indicates that calling his book *The Poetics of
Primitive Accumulation* is "not to oblige myself to refer repeatedly to a
specifically economic narrative but to mobilise the genealogical force of
this narrative and to articulate it with other areas of the social formation" (13). The process of articulation in such critical procedures
nevertheless requires a broadly stable foundation upon which to support and contain all the elements. This foundation seems to be available
in the records of payment, the buying and selling involved in mounting
theatrical productions. Such evidence of commercial activity can then
be generalized into paradigms of market relations. The "circulatory
rhythms of production and consumption," which Stephen Greenblatt
influentially idealizes in *Shakespearean Negotiations* as the motor of
early modern culture, can be used to link the enigmatic jottings of
Philip Henslowe's account book, the ambitious investments of the great
merchant companies, and the metaphorical exchanges of sexual and political ideologies.

These satisfyingly coherent connections, however, need to be put under some critical pressure before they can be accepted as equally satisfactory evidence of the historical circumstances of early modern theatrical
production. Too often such analogies are effected by reading the most
commonplace actions as symbolic of larger social relations. Greenblatt,

for example, reads Henslowe's accounts of the purchase of costumes as indicating that the theatres (undifferentiated by references to particular companies) "were willing to pay high prices for objects with high symbolic valence," picking out "a pope's mitre; three imperiall crowns &c" from a list of more commonplace items (*Shakespearean Negotiations*, 9). The choice of these objects justifies the critical procedure, for it highlights the way that, once played on the stage, the most commonplace items become symbolic objects, signifiers of status and gender and class. However, in analyzing the nature of the theatrical market we have to be careful not always to read the symbolic at the expense of the material. Greenblatt goes on to repeat the assertion that the plays were costumed with gentlemen's castoffs, a symbolic transgression often commented on in antitheatrical polemic but rather undermined both by the evidence of payment for costumes (the gray gown for Grissil, the £10 for Alice Arden's dress [Carson]) and by the anger and resentment produced by the one occasion when sets and costumes, for a university performance of John Suckling's *Aglaura*, were reused by the King's Men for a performance of the play at Blackfriars (Bentley, I: 57–59). The point here is not to stultify creative readings of these texts with a leaden positivism but rather to indicate the metaphoric rather than the materialist force of notions such as the "institutionalised, profitable market" (Bruster, 8) when they are used to link the moral economy of the drama (the market *in* plays) to the commercial economy of early modern theatre (the market *for* plays). The idea that the theatre was a representative market institution, a model of capitalist commerce, smooths over the instability, the stopping and starting and the bewildering set of temporary and ad hoc alliances among actors, playwrights, and entrepreneurs which constituted the production of early modern drama. It does so partly because the notion of an "institutionalized" market with its echoes of Louis Althusser's Ideological State Apparatuses allows the question of the relationship between the marketability of the plays and the circulation of their ideologies to be evoked without analysis.

And yet, for the materialist, some connection must be found between the commercial relations of the theatre and its circulation of ideologies in dramatic form. This connection can be found by addressing the specificity of particular companies and times. It depends, in particular, upon distinguishing between the situation of Shakespeare and that of his dramatic contemporaries. As a shareholder in the King's Men,

Shakespeare was part of one of the most stable and privileged of the
theatrical companies. The King's Men was, according to Bentley, "the
only London company which has a continuous existence throughout our
period, and of course it was already one of the oldest London troupes at
the time of Shakespeare's death" (I.57–59). The continuing commercial
viability of the King's Men was, as Andrew Gurr has shown (*Playgoing*,
165), not unconnected to their opportunism in securing a Bankside base
by moving the Globe in 1599 and in consolidating their operations at the
Blackfriars theatre after 1608. Even those commercial moves, however,
shrewd as they may seem to be in retrospect, were not enough to secure
the kind of accumulation of profit which might have provided the stability associated with an "institutionalized profitable market." The continued existence of the company required the constant and repeated support of their patrons against petitions from the Blackfriars residents,
difficulties with censorship, and simple financial support during the long
plague closures of 1625 and 1637 (Bentley, I: 42–45). The other playing
companies' fortunes fluctuated much more markedly. Their operations
were in the market in that they bought plays and costumes and materials for production, paid rents, and charged for attendance at performances. However, their vexed relations both with the men who financed
them (Francis Langley, Philip Henslowe, and Christopher Beeston) and
in some cases with the descendants of their own shareholders suggest
that, far from being institutionalized, the market relations of the early
modern theatre were in the process of formation, a process which continued even after the theatres had closed.[4]

These rather more volatile relations of the theatrical market are no
more accurately represented in the plays than is the market for other
commodities. The practitioners of theatre had a different agenda and
were able to draw on a much more highly developed discourse of the
market to ensure it. Their treatment of the theatrical market in the inductions, prologues, and plays within plays served rather to debate, as-
sert, and provide pleasure from the status of playing and the myth of its
professionalization (Mann). Around the turn of the century a cluster of
plays, including *Poetaster*, *Jack Drum's Entertainment*, and *The Knight
of the Burning Pestle*, created images of the theatres in which they performed and in a sense created the audience whom they wished to attract.
As in the representation of the market for goods, they offer an image of
the theatrical market as an arena of constant conflict between rival play-

wrights, rival players, and players and their audience. The conflict, however, revolved around a limited and coherent set of objectives: the need to establish a cultural position, the hustling for patronage, and above all the importance of staying in London and staving off the dread fate of touring "with . . . pumps full of gravell . . . after a blind jade and a hamper and stalk upon boards and barrel heads to an old cracked trumpet."[5] The way in which these images recur and the comic devices they employ for theatrical pleasures show, once again, that they are a set of tropes working through the myth of the penniless writer saved from poverty, artistically demeaned by association with players and misunderstood by a philistine audience (G. K. Hunter). They produced a version of the drama and its market which could in its turn be consumed by and thus construct its audience as consumers of dramatic productions. Prologues, inductions, and extra dramatic moments in these plays and, indeed, the many versions of the debate over popular and elite culture in the theatre served to establish the superiority of the London-based players over the touring companies and one London-based company over its competitor. They did so by flattering the cultural status of the audience who found themselves in such an up-market theatrical venue.

The combination of localized theatrical pleasure and the construction of an audience whose status, however temporarily, was attached to that pleasure may have been one of the most important features of the market for drama in our period. By offering an image of the theatre as purchasable and engaged in a debate with itself over the cultural status of that purchase, these scenes constructed their audience as the consumers of a particularly valued commodity. The dramatization of market relations, including those in the theatre, translated the economic relations of theatre into cultural relations in which the theatres can trade. And the currency of this trading is the tropes of representation in which these theatres deal: Pistol's knowledge of the plays of the last age, the sense in *Eastward Ho* that Quicksilver's quotations from *Hamlet* are as much a sign of his style as the tennis racket he hides under his cloak, the number of inductions and prologues which address the audience in terms of the newness or the special nature of the plays they are about to see—all show the representation of the dramatic market for plays becoming an extension of the celebration of shopping itself.

The induction to Francis Beaumont's *Knight of the Burning Pestle* is only the most obvious representation of the competition for cultural status centered on the styles and themes of drama. The Grocer who intrudes upon the action is offered as a travesty of the ignorant playgoer. He insists that the old shows are the best shows and that the boy players should revert to presenting "the life and death of Sir *Thomas Gresham* . . . and the building of the Royall Exchange" (I: 11). The boy player can then get a laugh with suggestions for a play about Fat Drake and the repairing of the Fleet privies. But the references to actual plays in the public theatre repertory perhaps disguise the fact that the Grocer's ancestor is Bottom the weaver; an exponent of the "huffing part," the simpler and always past theatre which is invoked in order to validate the theatrical experience on offer in the main action. It would be dangerous, therefore, to accept the dramatic conflict between Beaumont's Grocer and the boy players, or between Jonson's stage keeper and scrivener in the induction to *Bartholomew Fair,* as evidence of a real divide, either between popular and elite culture or between residual and dominant modes of representation.

In creating the illusion of that divide, Beaumont and his boy players were themselves engaged in a struggle to create a new audience and secure a market niche for a new product. However, the attempt to accumulate cultural capital with the induction to *The Knight of the Burning Pestle* was a flop. The address to the reader of the printed edition attempted to recuperate the situation by suggesting that this was because the audience missed the "privy mark of irony" which its performance involved. However, that may itself have been a sales pitch aimed at the discriminating purchaser of the printed version since the equally ironic style of, for example, *Eastward Ho* had been a runaway success at Blackfriars some four years earlier.

It is worth noting that the plays which were mocked as old-fashioned in the induction to *The Knight of the Burning Pestle — The Travels of Three English Brothers, The Four Prentices of London,* and *The Building of the Royal Exchange*—are not in fact the plays of a previous generation but part of the active repertory of Worcester's Men, newcomers on the London theatre scene after 1602, and therefore direct competitors of the Children of the Revels. By 1604 it was they and not the Children of the Revels who had gained the patronage of the new queen. Far from being consigned to a dustbin of popular taste, the story of "the building of the Royall Exchange" was revived at the Cockpit in 1623 by the company who succeeded Queen Anne's Men and again in 1636 by Queen Henrietta's Men, a company organized by Beeston, who carried with him the Queen's Men's repertory as he reorganized subsequent troupes. It is perhaps only a final irony that *The Knight of the Burning Pestle* was revived at court by the same company.

The economic organization of Queen Henrietta's Men and its place in the market (Bentley, I.219–222) were quite different from that of the Children of the Revels, who had originally performed the *Knight of the Burning Pestle*, and different again from Worcester's Men, whose productions they had mocked. However, the market for drama had rendered both their playtexts and the ideas which informed them into commodities which could be recycled with their theatrical pleasures intact. In 1632, Queen Henrietta's Men performed Thomas Nabbes's *Covent Garden*, which reused the trope of a contrast between fashionable and unfashionable companies, between London players and country players, between chivalric tales and sophisticated realism, to advertise the Cockpit theatre:

> But tell me *Ralph*, are those Players the ragged fellows that were at our house last Christmas that borrowed the red blanket off my bed to make their Major [Mayor] a gowne; and had the great Pot lid for Guy of Warwicks Buckler?
>
> No, *Dobson*; they are men of credit, whose actions are beheld by every one, and allow'd for the most part with commendations. They make no yearely Progresse with the Anatomy of a Sumperterhorse, laden with the sweepings of Long-Lane in a dead Vacation, and purchas'd at the exchange of their owne whole Wardrobes. They buy not their Ordinary for the Copie of a *Prologue*; nor insinuate themselves into the acquaintance of an admiring Ningle, who for his free comming in, is at the expence of a Taverne Supper, and rinses their bawling throats with Canarye. (Nabbes, III: 9)

Covent Garden was set in the new urban development to the west of the city, and it celebrated London as a center of conspicuous consumption with the theatre at its heart. Dobson and Ralph discuss the Cockpit theatre (the place in which the audience were seated), and the exchange flatters the audience with the same opposition between a reified popular culture and the current fashion as had been used two decades earlier in *Poetaster*, *The Knight of the Burning Pestle*, and the induction to *Bartholomew Fair*.

This evidence of revivals (Knutson), the coexistence in time of plays with apparently contrasting views of market relations, and perhaps above all the instability of the market for drama all indicate some of the difficulties of setting up too easy a thematic connection between the market *in* plays and the market *for* plays, particularly when those connections rely on the discourses of the market generated by the plays themselves. Compared with the economic relations of the theatre, its cultural relations were much more coherently developed and as such were in a position to act as the currency of a cultural market. However, this cultural market must not be seen as entirely autonomous from the economic market. This circulation of cultural currency was ultimately dependent not simply on "social energy" but on the precise and changing economic relations in which the playtexts were owned, the particular combinations of energetic not to say opportunist entrepreneurs such as Beeston, the pressure of plague and patronage on undercapitalized companies, and the tensions created by the instability of the institutions of contract law which allowed texts to become commodities reproduced and reproducible in a variety of theatrical contexts including our own.

It is this *reproducibility* of the early modern playtext which seems to me to be the most important result of the operations of the early modern theatrical market. Precisely because the commodified text dealt with recurring tropes and images, it was the more easily separable from particular theatrical and social contexts, more open for its meanings to be reconstructed with the cultural toolkit of a different audience. It allowed the plays to be "not of an age" and, if not for all time, for the times when their varied and contradictory representations of imperialism or the role of women or the market itself could be reanimated by contemporary preoccupations, to generate theatrical if not political excitement.

NOTES

1. One of the most extended uses of the image was in the National Theatre production of Tony Harrison's *The Trackers of Oxyrhynnous*, in which he adapted a Greek satyr play to explore the decline of popular culture into the commercialized squalor of modern consumerism.

2. Compare Dekker, *The Shoemaker's Holiday*, 3.4; and Heywood, *The Wise Woman of Hogsden*, 1.2.

3. McKendrick, Brewer, and Plumb locate the penetration of rural markets by London fashions in the eighteenth century. The general problem of

the periodization of the development of a consumer economy is discussed by de Vries.

4. Relations between the players and the men who financed them are illustrated in the "Articles of Grievance" brought against Henslowe; the protracted lawsuit brought by Susan Baskerville against members of the former Queen's Men; and the so-called Sharers Papers indicating the grievances of King's Men players against the controlling group in charge of the company. For this material, see Chambers, II: 237–238; Bentley, IV: 158–160, and II: 43–47.

5. Ben Jonson, *Poetaster* 3.1.51–53: in my discussion of the debate over the theatrical market in "The Poets Royal Exchange," I accepted too readily the theatrical version of the urban players' view of touring. Revisionist theatre historians, informed by the enormous wealth of data supplied by the Records of Early English Drama project, now suggest that touring, even for London-based companies, was a significant part of their activities until well into the seventeenth century (Greenfield).

6

Coriolanus as Tory Propaganda

John Ripley

Late-nineteenth- and early-twentieth-century commentators seldom credited Restoration adaptors of Shakespearean tragedy with either aesthetic sensibility or literary craftsmanship. H. N. Hudson, Thomas Lownesbury, G. C. D. Odell, and Hazelton Spencer brought themselves to catalogue the redactors' omission and transposition of scenes, additions, and alterations to language primarily, one suspects, for the pleasure of anathematizing the adaptors' hubris. When moved, albeit infrequently, to account for the improvers' alleged "mangling" or "bungling," they invoked French neoclassical dramaturgy, although obliged simultaneously to acknowledge ceaseless violations of virtually every axiom of its aesthetics. Many of the adaptations are as innocent of unity of place or time as Shakespeare's original; scenes of onstage violence are endemic; and the principles of poetic justice are routinely flouted.

At the heart of Victorian and Edwardian objections to the Restoration adaptors' sacrilege was a determination to place Shakespeare's plays beyond history and ideology,[1] rather than view them as a site of social struggle. Nahum Tate's highly politicized adaptation of *Coriolanus*, titled *The Ingratitude of a Common-wealth* and first staged in the winter of 1681–1682,[2] was a frequent target of their condescension and scorn.

When examined with a less universalist bias, Tate's redaction suggests that he recognized with greater acuity than his later detractors both *Coriolanus'* historical and ideological situatedness as a Jacobean document and its potential as a cultural commodity for adaptation to other, and equally distinctive, historical and ideological sites. To examine Tate's text as a pre-Malonean artifact is at once to discover a good deal about the time-specific political and aesthetic reflex points in Shakespeare's original and to vindicate Tate to some degree as both critic and theatre artist.[3]

For purposes of this essay, I propose to examine one alteration by one Restoration adaptor. I do not suggest that all contemporary redactions are amenable to the method I employ, nor shall I attempt to generalize my conclusions. I hope only to demonstrate that Tate's *Ingratitude of a Common-wealth*, far from being a work of gratuitous philistinism, is an instructive example of the transformation of a highly fluid Jacobean dramatic text into a stable instrument of Restoration propaganda.

To clear the ground for a fresh look at Tate as a serious artist, the traditional charge that he was at best an incompetent neoclassicist and at worst a literary vandal may be dismissed at the outset. Despite the disdain of traditional scholarship, the fact remains that he was a poet laureate, a friend and protégé of John Dryden, and an individual who enjoyed, if scant reputation for genius, at least some social and artistic prominence in the life of his time.[4] If he had chosen to write strict neoclassical revisions of Shakespeare, one must assume that he was capable of doing so. The fact that he did not suggests that he had some other aesthetic end in view. The notion that he was a literary vandal also deserves a decent burial. Tate, in common with his contemporaries, repeatedly expresses his regard for Shakespeare's plays as creations of enduring merit rather than as a literary junkyard from which scrap might be plundered for recycling. The prefaces to these adaptations generously acknowledge the adaptor's debt to Shakespeare and often credit the strength of the original with whatever value the revision may have. As Tate put it in his dedicatory epistle to *The Ingratitude*, "*Much of what is offered here, is Fruit that grew in the Richness of [Shakespeare's] Soil; and what ever the Superstructure prove, it was my good fortune to build upon a Rock*" (sig A 2). Unless Tate is judged guilty of sheer hypocrisy, for which there is no warrant, his observation carries two implications: (l) that for him *Coriolanus* had not merely value as a source work, but integral, foundational worth; and (2) that its continued relevance demanded renovation and reconstruction, to be undertaken with some trepidation ("whatever the superstructure prove").

The foundational value lay, as we shall see, in the relevance of Shakespeare's narrative to the Restoration political crisis, while renovation was dictated by the indeterminacy of *Coriolanus'* ideology and the uncongenial aesthetic style which sustained it. While the basic narrative is clear enough—Rome is at war; the commons is discontented; Martius seeks political power, is denied it by the populace, and deserts to the enemy—and the action doubtless reflects with some accuracy social stresses in Jacobean London (Leinwand), the play's fictional incidents discover no unequivocal ideological imperatives. While *Coriolanus* relentlessly probes the acquisition, use, abuse, and loss of power at both the institutional and individual level, it offers the reader or theatregoer no secure ethical or psychological vantage point from which to view the action. Few literary works so cynically press the recognition that "our virtues / Lie in th'interpretation of the time" (4.7.49–50).[5] Thanks to the dramatist's fluid and relativistic portrayal of the contest for power between patricians and plebeians, William Hazlitt was able to condemn Shakespeare's "leaning to the arbitrary side of the question" (IV: 214), Bertolt Brecht, to see the play as "the tragedy of a people that has a hero against it" (258), and Samuel Taylor Coleridge, to praise the dramatist's "wonderful philosophic impartiality" (I: 79).

Coriolanus' unstable signification may be identified with a deliberate literary technique termed by Annabel Patterson "functional ambiguity," a strategy adopted by Elizabethan-Jacobean writers "in which the indeterminacy inveterate to language was fully and knowingly exploited by authors and readers alike" (18) to elude government censorship. Patterson's thesis is extended by Paul Yachnin to hypothesize the existence of a "powerless theater" during the period 1590–1625 when

> the players promulgated the idea of the disinterestedness of art, extended the techniques of "functional ambiguity" practiced by early Elizabethan playwrights, and advertised that plays were separate from the operations of power. . . . The dramatic companies won from the government precisely what the government was most willing to give: a privileged, profitable, and powerless marginality. (50)

Coriolanus' political ambivalence is supported by, and a product of, an aesthetic style more cognitive than affective in its appeal, which privileges indeterminacy, incongruity, and unresolved tension. Its structure evinces no one center of interest, but multiple foci—the Roman-Volscian military campaign, the civil-political struggle, the mother-son relationship; its characters are enigmatic and distorted; sense of place and sensuous ambience are largely absent; contradiction and paradox are endemic (McKenzie); and the conclusion brings no transcendence or release.

The theatre for which Tate sought to redesign *Coriolanus* was not the "powerless" institution of the late Elizabethan-Jacobean era as posited by Yachnin, but effectively a tool of the state. The day-to-day survival of players and playwrights depended on political patronage, and they were expected to pay their dues as often as called upon.[6] Tate's adaptation of *Coriolanus*, unlike its original, decisively identifies itself in the *Epistle Dedicatory* with a political position: "*The Moral therefore of these Scenes being to Recommend Submission and Adherence to Establisht Lawful Power, which in a word, is Loyalty.*" The *Ingratitude of a Common-wealth* is one of a number of dramatic contributions to an anti-Whig propaganda campaign waged by the Tories between 1680 and 1683.[7] Three years before Tate's play appeared, the Popish Plot had intensified anti-Catholic sentiment and strengthened the power of the Whigs. In May 1680 an Exclusion Bill was introduced in the House of Commons, denying the Roman Catholic Duke of York the right of succession to the throne, a strategy which proved so divisive that Charles II dissolved Parliament in March of 1681 and over the next few months missed no opportunity to discomfit the Whigs. At this point the theatres rallied to the Tory cause with a series of productions attacking those who would threaten the peace, overthrow authority, and return the country to the miseries of civil war. Tate's *Ingratitude* was one of the first propaganda rounds fired. The aesthetic form in which Tate recast Shakespeare's creation was precisely contrived to modulate its disorientation and alienation into fully declared meaning, to stabilize its moral and tragic focus, to enforce credibility through sensibility, and to consummate the exercise in a burst of quasi-religious transcendence.

Any consanguinity between Rome's political crisis and Jacobean exigencies was left by Shakespeare for his public to intuit; Tate's audiences were given more limited hermeneutic rein. "*Upon a close view of this Story,*" Tate informs his readers, "*there appear'd in some Passages, no small resemblance with the busie* Faction *of our own time. What offence to any good Subject in Stygmatizing on the Stage, those* Troublers *of the State, that out of private Interest or Mallice, Seduce the Multitude to* Ingratitude, *against Persons that are not only plac't in Rightful Power above them; but also the Heroes and Defenders of their Country.*" For Tate the resemblance between consular Rome and Restoration England apparently lay in similarities between Coriolanus and James, Duke of York, and the political turbulence of both periods in which the citizenry and their leaders played a key role.

Like Martius, James had a distinguished military record, but was politically naive and incompetent and wanting in tact and moderation. Both men were banished by the country they served. In the public turmoil that attended the Bill of Exclusion (to say nothing of the Popish Plot and the threat of a French invasion), Tate found the Whigs, in much the same fashion as the tribunes, to be exploiting the tensions of the times and the gullibility of the citizenry. Tate seems to have had no intent to allegorize the Jacobean narrative, but chose less ambitiously merely "*to set the Parallel nearer to Sight.*" In Shakespeare's telling account of an aristocrat driven into exile by an ungrateful rabble, spurred on by irresponsible leadership, he found a subject which could be reworked to carry a contemporary visual and verbal warning: Whig opposition to established authority was dangerous; indeed, the fomenting of popular discontent of the sort advocated by the Earl of Shaftesbury could well return the country to the horrors of the Civil War era. The racked young Martius, the dying Virgilia, the mad Volumnia at play's end speak eloquently and emblematically to the perils of factionalism.

The impartiality (or ambivalence) of *Coriolanus'* politics, later remarked by Coleridge, had scant attraction for a propagandist. Tate's first task, then, was to tilt the play's precariously balanced sympathies significantly to the right, which meant that Martius had to be written up and the plebeians and tribunes written down. While Tate allows Martius a want of political sensitivity, he takes particular pains to purge the character of outright antidemocratic sentiment. His outburst beginning "Shall!" in which he demands why the senators have "Given Hydra here to choose an officer" (3.1.90–112) and the tirade shortly afterward in which he scorns a governmental system in which "gentry, title, wisdom / Cannot conclude but by the yea and no / Of general ignorance" (3.1.126–155) are excised. His plea for the repeal of the tribunate (3.1.166–170) is abbreviated and his arrogant assertion "I do despise them! / For they do prank them in authority, / Against all noble sufferance" (3.1.22–24) disappears. His observation when required to beg plebeian voices—"It is a part / That I shall blush in acting, and might well / Be taken from the people" (2.2.144–146)—is rephrased to run rather more tactfully: "It is a Part, that I shall Blush in Acting; / Methinks the People well might spare this Method; / Better Constrain'd to do it" (19). The tribunes' assertion that their power will sleep if he is elected (2.1.222–223) and Sicinius' contention that Martius has "Envied against the people, seeking means / To pluck away their power" (3.3.93–99) are also blue-penciled.

However carefully Tate might ameliorate Martius' antipopulist views, it was impossible to purge his radical elitism entirely without doing serious injustice to the historical character or destroying the energy and tension at the heart of Shakespeare's play. In a strategy adopted many times since, Tate set himself to denigrate the character and behavior of the plebeians so that Martius' disdain for them seems less a political act than a civilized response to barbarity.

Tate's retouching required a delicate hand: his political parable must not denigrate the English underclass as a whole since Charles relied on broadly based popular support. In the end, however, not even the most naive theatregoers could descry any decent citizen of their acquaintance in Tate's caricature of an ignorant and violent rabble; nor could the same theatregoers miss the consanguinity of Tate's plebeians with the frenzied mobs, inflamed by Popish Plot hysteria and Whig manipulation, who roamed the streets staging pope-burnings and other incitements to civil disorder (Whiting). Comic and brutish, they are deliberately shorn of any redeeming features Shakespeare allows them. The excision of Menenius' "For they have pardons, being ask'd, as free / As words to little purpose" (3.2.88–89) may be taken as representative.

The mob's callous stupidity is epitomized by the First Citizen, a role now fattened by the reallocation of other citizens' speeches and some new material. Mindlessly overconfident, he sets the tone for the rabble's ominous, yet bitterly comic, abuse of power with his line, "Let 'um feel our Swords, that take away the Use of our Knives; not that I mean any Harm Neighbours" (2). Their willingness to vote in compliance with the last suggestion they hear is highlighted in an addition preceding the Voices episode; and in an expanded passage following the Voices scene the 1 Cit. demonstrates a lamentable inability to weigh accurately the most obvious evidence of his eyes and ears.

Stupidity is compounded by cowardice. Not content with retaining Shakespeare's indication that the plebeians "steal away" when invited to attack the Volscians in order to obtain grain (1.1.248), Tate reduces them

to terrified hysterics when Cominius returns from his embassy to the
Volscian camp. Similar instances of rabble-baiting abound. On Martius'
departure into banishment, he consigns them, in a rewritten execration,
to human society's barbaric outer reaches:

> Poyson each other
> Devour each other: Commerce cease amongst you;
> Rob one another: nothing you can Steal,
> But Thieves do lose it. (35)

Toward such louts, Martius' behavior is deemed not merely appropriate
but obligatory.

Hard as Tate is on the "blind Compliance" of the people, it is their
"popular Misleaders," the tribunes, epitomized offstage by Shaftesbury,
his minions, and organizations such as the Green Ribbon Club (Ronalds,
81), for whom he saves his heaviest salvoes. Shakespeare treats Brutus
and Sicinius with unusual harshness, but allows them at least some degree of political sagacity and psychological insight. Tate lets no mitigat-
ing feature remain. Sicinius' shrewd advice to Coriolanus, "If you will
pass / To where you are bound, you must inquire your way, / Which you
are out of, with a gentler spirit" (3.1.53–55), is a typical excision. Martius' denunciation of them, cast in contemporary political vernacular lest
the point be missed, fairly reeks of Tory wrath at the popular threat to
aristocratic exclusivity:

> *You, Faction-Mongers,*
> *That wear your formal Beards, and Plotting Heads,*
> *By the Valour of the Men you Persecute;*
> *Canting Caballers, that in Smoaky Cells,*
> *Amongst Crop-ear'd Mechanicks, wast the Night*
> *In Villanous Harrangues against the* State.
> *There may* Your Worship's *Pride be seen t'embrace*
> *A smutty Tinker, and in extasy*
> *Of Treason, shake a Cobler be th'wax't Thumb.* (27)

In the end, the tribunes receive their comeuppance at the hands of the
rabble they sought to exploit. At their last appearance, the 1 Cit. is
shouting, "Some comfort yet, that we have these Vipers to *Carbinado*;
Come Neighbours, we'll see them smoak before us. Away, away with
'em." And, without Shakespeare's humane intervention by Menenius,

the company exits, *"Haling and Dragging off the Tribunes"* (46) to an unwholesome destiny.

Although in Tate's parti-pris Tory universe the subverters of public order receive their just deserts, the evil that they do lives after them. The expulsion of Martius, and the civil and domestic disorder that ensues, brings disaster upon the innocent as well as the guilty. The climax of Tate's political homily, far from being gratuitous sensationalism or defective poetic justice as his critics have contended, provides the catharsis vital to stabilizing the moral and tragic focus.

In the play's final moments, as vividly and horrifically as possible, Tate limns the outcome of civil strife. Factionalism, he implies, is an inevitable prologue to disaster in the national family, emblematically portrayed at curtain-fall by the dead Martius with his lifeless wife and child on either arm.[8] Tate's projected audience-response must have been not unlike the viewer's reaction to baroque religious art envisioned by Cardinal Paleotti: "If we see the martyrdom of a saint rendered in lively colours . . . we must be of marble or wood . . . if our piety is not stimulated afresh" (Hauser, I: 77). Political piety, expressed in "Submission and Adherence to Establisht Lawful Power," could hardly fail to respond to Tate's passionate theatricality. A greater contrast with the emotionally ambivalent finale to Shakespeare's play, in which the hero dies unenlightened in mid-bellow, can hardly be imagined.

The didactic function of Tate's project found expression in an uncomplex and profoundly unified structure. Tate's decision to set *"nearer to sight"* the parallel between Shakespeare's Rome and Restoration England, which amounted to a redrafting of Shakespeare's perspective, demanded that the audience's attention be confined to a single theme—the dangers of factionalism. The multiple foci in Shakespeare's *Coriolanus*—the ongoing Roman-Volscian military struggle, the patrician-plebeian conflict, and the mother-son attachment—rendered it as ineffective a vehicle for political indoctrination as Parmigianino's *Madonna of the Long Neck*, with its anatomical distortion and perverse perspective, would have been as an object of pious contemplation.

Tate's revision was thorough and radical.[9] In order to highlight the patrician-plebeian struggle, he downplayed considerably the Roman-Volscian conflict. His act 1 comprises four scenes, as compared with the original ten: Shakespeare's 1.1 in which Menenius and Martius meet with the plebeians, 1.3, the episode between Volumnia and Virgilia in

Martius' house, and two brief battlefield sequences (part of 1.4 and a consolidation of 1.8 and 1.9). Only enough action remains to establish Martius' military stature and to introduce Aufidius. The effect is to remove the equivalent of foreground clutter and to place the plebeian-patrician struggle at center stage with minimal distraction or delay.

From 2.1 Tate removed all the preliminaries to Martius' triumphal return, including Menenius' contretemps with the tribunes and his encounter with Volumnia and Virgilia, 166 lines in all. No scene is cut in its entirety, since this act is the play's political core, but the internal revision is substantial. The sequence in which the cushion-layers assess Martius' character (2.2.1–36) is eliminated, as is the tense exchange between the tribunes and Menenius prior to Cominius' eulogy (2.2.37–66). The plebeians' good-natured banter at 2.3.18–35 disappears in favor of a sequence after the Voices episode in which they are shown as slow-witted and lacking in judgment. A number of Martius' more defiantly ungracious exchanges are cut (2.3.94–102, 105–111), and the tribunes' inflammatory appraisal of the Voices ritual is rendered more pointed and succinct.

In act 3 the introductory update on Aufidius' status (3.1.1–20) is deleted to maintain the focus on the growing patrician-plebeian tension. The confrontation itself is considerably abbreviated and recast, partly to accelerate the narrative, but mainly to mitigate Martius' antipopulism and to magnify the tribunes' knavery. The episode in which Martius is persuaded to reconcile himself with the plebeians (3.2) becomes less an exercise in maternal blackmail than the impassioned plea of a Roman matron for compromise in the face of potential national disaster. Martius accedes, not out of conditioned reflex, but out of patriotic sensibility. His concession, however, proves to be of no avail, and 3.3 sees him banished with greater expedition than Shakespeare allows.

Martius' farewell sequence (4.1), which Tate appends to act 3, is heavily rewritten to highlight the strength of the familial bond in anticipation of the Intercession scene and the act 5 denouement. Tate's Volumnia is mellower, his Virgilia more vocal than Shakespeare's originals. And as a final touch, Young Martius is summoned to add pathos to the leavetaking. The subsequent slanging match between Volumnia and the tribunes (4.2) and the encounter between Adrian and Nicanor (4.3) vanish.

Martius' arrival in Corioli and his abbreviated reflections on the world's slippery turns (4.4) launch Tate's act 4. The role of Aufidius' servants in 4.5 is curtailed to expedite Martius' pact with Aufidius, now

shorn of its nuptial imagery. In an attempt to clarify Aufidius' hitherto
obscure motivation for Martius' assassination, Tate replaces the episode
between Aufidius and the Lieutenant (4.7) with a new unit introducing
the villain Nigridius, the play's *diabolus ex machina*, who for his own
purposes whips Aufidius' jealousy to fever pitch and looses the forces
which precipitate the ugly finale. Shakespeare's 4.6 and 5.1, the sequences in which the Roman citizens learn of Martius' approach, are abbreviated, combined, and transposed to follow the Nigridius episode. Act
4 concludes with the Intercession scene (5.3), in the course of which
Menenius makes a curtailed appeal as prologue to the women's embassy.
The matrons' suit is not Shakespeare's psychological subjugation of a
man-child by a manipulative parent, but a reasoned and humane appeal
by an individual family on behalf of the national family to one who is at
once protector and aggressor; and, as on an earlier occasion, Martius is
persuaded against his better judgment to place patriotic duty above personal pique. The moral mechanism is perfectly clear; Shakespeare's am-
biguities are fully resolved. Martius' cynical inversion of a cliché of classical Renaissance art: "Behold, the heavens do ope, / The gods look down
and this unnatural scene / They laugh at" (5.3.183–185) is now rehabil-
itated and celebrated as a moment of mystical transcendence:

> O Mother-Goddess, dread *Volumnia*, turn:
> What have you done? Behold the Heav'ns divide,
> And *Gods* look down on this amazing Scene!
> O Mother Goddess, Heav'n-born Advocate. (51)

Menenius' sour chat with Sicinius on his return to Rome (5.4) is cut, together with the news that Volumnia's suit has succeeded. The enigmatic
episode (5.4) in which Volumnia and Virgilia cross the stage in silence
disappears in favor of an explicit civic welcome, dominated by a loqua-
cious Valeria and fully acknowledged by its recipients.[10]

Most of act 5 is Tate's own. Volumnia, Virgilia, and Young Martius
return to Corioli to warn Martius of impending danger; Aufidius confesses to Nigridius a long-standing passion for Virgilia and on the arrival
of the Martian family has them confined. He then proceeds to accuse
Martius before the Volscian council. In a much-revised 5.6, Martius and
Aufidius quarrel before the Volscian lords, and at a predetermined moment the Volscian general "*Stamps with his Foot, the Conspirators
Enter, and help him to Wound* Martius, *who kills some, and hurts*
Aufidius" (59). The lords conveniently rush off to deal with civil unrest

elsewhere, leaving the two ailing combatants to expire at leisure, amid the accelerating violence of the play's final moments.

A telling apotheosis of the Martian family at play's end, and the ultimate success of Tate's political homily, relies heavily upon the audience's affective response to the principal characters. And Tate's dissatisfaction with Shakespeare's portraiture was as acute as his discontent with his multilinear structure. Character commentary from a variety of sources, ambivalent and contradictory speeches and actions by the play's protagonists, ambiguous silences and lacunae, not to mention the almost total absence of revelatory soliloquies, represented the very antithesis of transparent communication. And Martius came in for a lion's share of attention.

Shakespeare's churlish, alienated, and elusive hero, although an improvement on Plutarch's lout, was not a type to pluck the heartstrings. Not only must his political position be harmonized with the play's propaganda objective, as noted earlier, but his portrait must be redrawn more sympathetically if his death is to assume the status of martyrdom and trigger the appropriate emotional response. Martius' act of national betrayal, as might be expected, was therefore downplayed to the point of invisibility; and his attack on Rome was rationalized as a legitimate reprisal against an ungrateful city for the excesses of mob-rule. By astute textual cutting, highlighting, and strategic insertions, the renovated avenger, in contrast to Shakespeare's alienated, almost mystic, machine, stands forth as an unequivocally pious and noble warrior, dutiful son, and loving husband and father. In the play's final moments, his grief-stricken and helpless endurance of his family's pain was finely calculated to win the audience's compassion and initiate them into both the horror and the exaltation of the martyred family.

Psychological complexities no longer have a place. All references to Martius' aloneness are excised; suggestions that he is a victim of reflex behavior (1.1.41–42 or 3.1.256–257) disappear. Intimations that he is susceptible either by nature or by childhood conditioning to manipulation by the tribunes, Volumnia, or anyone else are rigorously pruned. The tribunes and plebeians are permitted to rail at him from time to time, but their charges are meant to be discounted. Anything like unworthy comments or actions by himself or censure by his equals are suppressed. The shifting, often contradictory, assessments of his character from a variety of observation points (for example, the cushion-layers, Menenius, Volumnia, Aufidius, Cominius) are cut, pruned, or somehow harmonized to create a unified impression.

In a series of insertions he is shown as pious as he is brave. At the conclusion of act 1, following his battlefield triumphs, he cries: "Now let us Sacrifice to th'*Gods*, and Pray / For many Rival Days, to This on *Rome*; / Then Yield our Pious Rites, to our Slain Friends" (14–15). Piety is complemented by warm domestic feeling. In the scene of his departure at the gates of Rome, for example, the doting parent, overcome with emotion at Young Martius' request to accompany his father into exile, is obliged to have the boy removed since "he raises in my Breast / A Tenderness that's most Unseasonable" (37). Examples could be multiplied. At play's end the figure who greets death in sentiments reminiscent of artistic treatments of the flight of the redeemed soul—"So, grasping in each Arm my Treasure, I / Pleas'd with the Prize, to Deaths calm Region Fly" (64)—attains the status of secular martyr. To his enemies, only opprobrium remains.

Tate's pursuit of a unified vision demanded not only the domestication and demystification of Martius, but the reduction of the play's subordinate characters to a strictly functional role. Volumnia, with her unhealthy hold on her son excised, emerges as an idealized mother figure selflessly committed to family and country. All idiosyncrasy is suppressed. No mention is made of wound-counting; she does not evince any uncertainty over Martius' new name (2.1.174); nor is she overtly ambitious for the consulship for him (2.1.196–200). On Coriolanus' banishment, Tate's anxious matron discovers a "Womans Tenderness," a "Mothers Fondness," and a fund of "panting Fears" (36) unknown to her Junoesque original. The difference between the Volumnias of Shakespeare and Tate is tellingly epitomized in her final lines in the Intercession scene in which the understated, suggestive force of the Jacobean matriarch's "I am hush'd until our city be afire, / And then I'll speak a little" (5.3.181–182) yields to flamboyant explicitness: "We'll speak no more, till *Rome* be all on Fire. / Then joyning Curses with the Crowd, expire" (51). In similar fashion, the wordless, wonderfully inscrutable stage-cross with which Shakespeare's Volumnia quits the play is superseded by a display of partisan-wielding madness. The averted eyes of the Jacobean matriarch have now been repainted to stare back unambiguously at the spectator with maternal love, patriotic ardor, and finally terrifying irrationality when the forces of disorder have done their work.

Tate's decision to domesticate Martius meant that Virgilia would consequently assume a higher profile. Not at all taken by Shakespeare's whim to render Martius' spouse virtually mute, Tate metamorphoses her into a veritable chatterbox and a markedly more assertive soul than her Shakespearean counterpart. The Intercession scene, thanks to the appropriation of a fair number of Volumnia's lines, finds her impassioned and persuasive. Her determination to return to Corioli to rescue her husband completes the portrait of a woman of spirit, fortitude, and decisiveness. All in all, she is a fitting wife for a Roman general and an effective counterbalance to Volumnia. Her suicide, to avoid rape by Aufidius, and the noble character of her final moments identify her with a long line of female martyrs enshrined in baroque art.[11]

Young Martius, given several more appearances than Shakespeare provides, invariably accompanies his mother, as in so many seventeenth-century paintings where, as affective devices, children cling to, peep round, fly above, or are carried by their elders. Here the harrowing sadism of the boy's murder is crudely exploited to prompt revulsion at political upheaval and the barbarity it implies. The sensational pathos of his exchange with his dying father tints the moral in precisely the "lively colours" advocated by Cardinal Paleotti:

> *Boy.* I fain wou'd clasp you too; but when I try
>   To lift my Arms up to your Neck,
>   There's something holds 'em.
> *Cor.* Thy Torturers my Boy have crippled 'em,
>   And gash't thy pretty Cheeks.
> *Boy.* I know you Lov'd 'em;
>   But truly 'twas no fault of mine; they did it
>   Because I would not cry. . . .
> *Cor.* O Nature! A true Breed!
> *Boy.* 'Tis grown all Dark o'th sudden, and we sink
>   I know not whether; good Sir hold me fast. (63–64)

Menenius, like Volumnia, loses much of his unique individuality. Out of a desire to avoid any diversion of interest from the nuclear Martian family, Tate purges the multifaceted patrician of all hint of the frail and endearing humanity with which Shakespeare graces him. When Tate had finished, Menenius was little more than a judicious statesman and a model Tory. In the end, he, too, perishes, receiving his quietus in an offstage attempt to rescue Young Martius from the clutches of Nigridius.

Tate's Aufidius, unlike Shakespeare's Volscian, who exists in the most complex relationship to Martius as deadly foe and alter ego, is little more than a plot device: a mean-minded foil to Martius' highminded nobility, a convenient enemy to whom he can desert, and the instrument of his destruction. To render the audience's antipathy doubly certain, he is made the would-be ravisher of Virgilia as well. The portraits of Aufidius and Nigridius call to mind the sadistic torturer/executioners in baroque pietistic art, who by their craven viciousness heighten sympathy for the long-suffering martyr.

Hardly less attractive to the propagandist than *Coriolanus'* even-handed politics and capricious characterization was its want of *"imaginative* effect or atmosphere . . . the use of the supernatural . . . a treatment of nature which makes her appear . . . as a vaster fellow-actor and fellow-sufferer,"* noted by A. C. Bradley more than two centuries later (458). In an effort to lend his adaptation affective resonance, Tate invokes an armory of florid, if somewhat hackneyed imagery—fire, stars, Roman gods and goddesses, winds, storms, darkness and light, sunset, dying roses, owls, ravens, and vultures—and for good measure contrives several passages of sustained atmospherics, typified by Martius' premonition of catastrophe as he passes through Rome's gates for the last time:

> I know not what presage has struck my Breast;
> But Oh! Methinks I see Destruction teem,
> And waiting for my Absence, to Discharge
> The battering Storm on this perfidious Citty:
> So when the murmering Wind, from out his Nest,
> *Jove's* Royal Bird to the open Region calls;
> Aloft he Mounts, and then the Tempest Falls. (37)

Ultimately, however, the creation of persuasive ambience was for Tate less a function of verbal imagery than of *mise-en-scène.* In contrast to the fluid, revolving action on the Jacobean Globe platform, thrust into its audience and permitting a multiplicity of observation points from each of its three sides, the Theatre Royal, Drury Lane, which housed Tate's adaptation, was a structure designed to contain, control, and frame the dramatic event in the interests of a calculated aesthetic and emotional response. The major novelty of the Restoration stage was its painted shutters and wing flats, placed behind a proscenium arch, and offering, aided by artists' obsessive attention to sightlines, a unified pictorial effect from any point in the house. Scenic elements were not intended to be in any way realistic, but rather a background to the dramatic action, which proceeded for the most part on a seventeen-foot-deep apron to which the actors gained access directly from the upstage area or through proscenium doors (Leacroft, 95). The play was thus placed within a niche from which it spilled at intervals onto the apron and so interfaced in a controlled manner with the world of the spectator. The visual realization of a particular dramatic moment, pictorially composed and framed by the proscenium arch, was quite as important to the cathartic climax as the text itself.

If Tate's directions represent theatrical fact rather than a playwright's wishful thinking, the presentation of his political morality must have been fairly lavish. The 1681–1682 season was a financially difficult one for the King's Company (Lennep, 299), but Thomas Killigrew, the theatre's proprietor, may have regarded Tate's production as a last-ditch investment. The theatricality of the stage directions tends to support the claim of the text to represent the play "as performed," and the fact that the court considered the entertainment fit for the Moroccan ambassador (see note 2) suggests that some money had been spent on it.

Tate's adaptation reduces the twenty-nine scenes of modern Shakespeare editions to fourteen;[12] and the baroque concern for physical environment is immediately apparent. Rome has scant visual presence in either Shakespeare's stage directions or dialogue, and sometimes it is difficult to know whether the Volscian action is set in Antium or Corioli. One feels as if the playwright had taken to heart aesthetically Sicinius' rhetorical question, "What is the city but the people?" (3.1.197). Tate, through the provision of two major backshutters, one designated "The City Rome" (act 1) and the other "The City of Corioles" (act 4), decisively resolves geographical confusion. Everywhere mass, movement, color, and light are pressed into service to leave no doubt as to locale. The sense of Rome is further established by processional effects. When Martius returns from the wars, Shakespeare anticipates only modest visual display. The Folio direction at 2.1.160 reads, "*Enter Cominius the Generall, and Titus Latius: betweene them Coriolanus, crown'd with an Oaken Garland, with Captaines and Souldiers, and a Herauld.*" The people, one notes, are deliberately excluded, and their participation is later narrated by Brutus (2.1.203–219). What matters to Shakespeare at this point is the distanced, formal encounter between mother and son.

Tate, however, substitutes a Roman triumphal procession, presumably against the "City Rome" shutter, in which Coriolanus enters *"in Triumph, met by the* Nobility and Commons *of* Rome" (15). Precisely what spectacle was offered at the Theatre Royal is not indicated in the text, but it must have been considerable to judge from Volumnia's observation: "Not Thee this Pomp, but Thou Adorn'st thy Tryumph" (15). Here Tate takes the opportunity simultaneously to celebrate the grandeur of republican Rome just before factionalism mars it, to elevate the hero by colorful display, and, as the procession crosses the apron from one door to the other, to draw the audience into the action as bystanders who share the same fictive space. The propaganda value of Tate's triumphal procession is patent.

Another sort of visual technique animates the scene in which Martius is proposed for consul (2.2). Shakespeare provides for two Officers *"to lay Cushions, as it were, in the Capitoll,"* that is, on the unlocalized apron. Their conversation is followed by *"A Sennet. Enter the Patricians, and the Tribunes of the People, Lictors before them: Coriolanus, Menenius, Cominius the Consul: Sicinius and Brutus take their places by themselves: Coriolanus stands."* Shakespeare's conservative, dynamic processional entry is restaged by Tate as a spectacular and static discovery. The direction runs "Scene *Opening, shews the* Senate *sitting in the Capitol*; Coriolanus *in a White Robe, as Candidate for the* Consulship" (17). Shakespeare's contrived posing and the byplay with sitting and standing, which allow Martius to signal his political intractability, are excised in favor of an exercise in history painting: within a postproscenium setting, the general, dressed in white, stands in the foreground against a formal, spectacular human and architectural backdrop to receive due recognition from representatives of a thriving and grateful state. This scene visually reinforces the impression of Roman grandeur created by the triumphal procession, the sense of a society engaged in the orderly institutional exercise of power. The Voices (2.3) scene which succeeds it is staged on the apron, backed by a "Street" shutter which closes on the Senate setting. The political heart of the play, from the Voices scene to Martius' departure into banishment, seems to have been played as a continuous unit on the forestage before the same "Street" shutter. Shakespeare's direction *"Enter seven or eight Citizens"* is replaced by *"Enter the* Citizens *in vast Numbers."* The throng of supers, their dynamic entry, and their proximity to the audience as they give and withdraw their voices, demand the death of Martius, and ultimately hound him into exile underlined with devastating clarity the risks inherent in popular suffrage. By collapsing real and fictive space, Tate makes affective capital of an ugly political coup, rendered all the more disturbing by the distanced grandeur of the Senate episode which preceded it. Confronted on the one hand by the citizens' bovine stupidity and violence, and on the other by Volumnia's patriotic eloquence and Young Martius' pathetic attachment to his exiled father, theatregoers were affectively maneuvered into knee-jerk support for the Tory position.

Tate's Corioli is as visually specific as is his Rome. The battlefield sequence in act 1 is staged *"before the Walls of* Corioles"; and on his arrival in Corioli, Martius delivers his "A goodly city" apostrophe in front of "The City of Corioles" shutter. References to Antium are deleted here and elsewhere. At the conclusion of his abbreviated soliloquy, the shutter is withdrawn to reveal *"The Inside of the Palace; Musick Plays; Servants pass hastily over the stage."* Shakespeare's encounter between Martius and Aufidius takes place in front of Aufidius' house, suggested by no more than the tiring-house facade; Tate moves the action to an elegant interior, taking advantage of color and light to lend significance to the interview.

The Intercession scene, in its turn, was contrived with a richness of atmosphere reminiscent of Rembrandt or Rubens. Shakespeare sets the episode on a bare stage, furnished merely with some sort of seat. Only Aufidius and Martius are present at the scene's opening. Later the matrons enter in clothing indicative of hard times and accompanied only by whatever attendants are proper to such a down-at-heel troupe. The scene is more intellectual than emotional, focusing upon the bodies of the principals as they stand, kneel, and hold hands. The rhetoric, with its paradoxical and tortured argumentation, beneath which a dominant mother engages in a life-and-death struggle with her emotionally dependent son, is paramount. In the end, the scene leaves unanswered as many questions as it resolves.

No scene in Tate's adaptation better illustrates his exaltation of clarity over ambiguity and feeling over intellect. Like the earlier Senate sequence, it is staged as a discovery, with all the visual thrill revelation affords. The direction reads "Scene *Opening, shews* Coriolanus *seated in* State, *in a rich* Pavilion, *his Guards and souldiers with lighted Torches, as ready to set Fire on* Rome; *Petitioners as from the* Citty *offer him Papers, which he scornfully throws by: At length* Menenius *comes forward, and speaks to him:* Aufidius *with* Nigridius, *making Remarks on 'em"* (46). The action is arrested at a crucial moment, allowing the audience to feast their eyes on the rich pavilion and its colorful masses of guards and soldiers over which chiaroscuro effects produced by the torches play. Here is a grand frame for a grand action—in Tate's reading, not the subjugation of an overgrown boy by a hectoring matriarch, but the conquest of a warrior's passion by the rational and patriotic appeals of a Roman wife and mother. Through mimed action, the audience is prepared for Coriolanus' obduracy, and the probable futility of the suit Volumnia and Virgilia will press. After the summary dispatch of Menenius, Martius orders, "Now plant our Fires against the Gates of *Rome*"; and as the soldiers "*Advance with their Lights, Enter from the other side*, Volumnia, Virgilia, *and* Young Martius, *with the rest of the* Roman Ladies *all in Mourning*" (47). The line of matrons, tastefully attired in black gowns of contemporary cut,[13] must have created a stunning effect as they passed slowly over the apron, their funereal frailty juxtaposed against the colorful, torch-lit military figures opposite. It is within this spectacular visual context that the women make their case, gaining affect all the while from the painterly ambience. Tate's atmospherics might not have supplied what Bradley missed in Shakespeare's script, but the imagination could not fail to be seized, or the emotions stirred. So impressive was Tate's staging of this scene that the procession of mourning matrons remained a fixture of *Coriolanus* revivals until after World War I.

Following the episodes in which Volumnia and her party return to Rome and Nigridius and Aufidius plot, both played on the apron, the shutters were drawn off to reveal "*A Palace*," perhaps the interior of Aufidius' palace employed earlier. Upstage the Volscian lords are discovered "*as set in Councel*," presumably picturesquely grouped at a table. Aufidius and Coriolanus enter from opposite proscenium doors not long after. Their fight takes place downstage of the stunned assemblage of Volscian senators, who rush forward as Martius falls, only to exit a moment later. The rest of the scene makes its impact not by visual splendor but by intense and controlled exploration of human pain, each segment of which is marked by precise blocking. Martius falls somewhere near the curtain line, facing outward toward the audience. Aufidius and Nigridius die upstage of him, probably near the conspirators killed earlier by Martius. Virgilia, brought in by way of a proscenium door, is placed on one of Martius' outspread arms and proceeds to her death-speech. Volumnia then enters and apparently puts Young Martius on her son's other arm, thus indicating a new unit of action. Volumnia's mad soliloquy follows, concluded by her murder of Nigridius. Her exit marks the beginning of the death throes of Young Martius, terminated by his vain attempt to embrace his father. On his son's death, Coriolanus confronts his own dissolution, leaving the audience to contemplate an empty up-stage council table, downstage of it the bodies of the scene's villains, and nearest the audience the tableau of the martyred family. Tate's final episode, growing in disciplined intensity throughout, is not mere sensa-tionalism for its own sake, but a theatrical exemplar of Judith Hook's perception that in baroque art "ultimate reality in the shape of some all-embracing unity was perceptible only in moments of intense passionate experience" (12). Tate's final scene must be regarded, I think, as an at-tempt at secular transcendence:[14] even as the contemplation of the suf-ferings of religious figures in art led to spiritual insight, so, he might have argued, could the contemplation of political martyrdom in the the-atre foster wiser statecraft.

Tate's alteration, far from being Thomas R. Lounsbury's "ridiculous travesty of the terrible" (195), is a thoughtful attempt by a Restoration literary figure to make a serious political point; and the fact that he chose *Coriolanus* rather than another drama as a vehicle evinces an awareness of the play's political potential all too rare in its theatrical and critical history. Apart from the redaction of Tate, only John Dennis (1720) and Bertolt Brecht (1952–1955) overtly confronted in the theatre the play's political vitality, while scholarship since the eighteenth cen-tury has engaged in what amounts to a critical conspiracy to displace the play's political concerns with character analysis.[15] From G. G. Gervinus' 1849 dictum that although "political relations are inherent in the sub-ject," the "sort of characters which have to decide in these situations . . . is everywhere the actual centre towards which the poet worked, and his leading thought here . . . is of a moral psychological nature" (747–748) to Stanley Cavell's 1983 conclusion that "the psychoanalytic perspective has produced more interesting readings than the political" (2), the deval-uation of *Coriolanus'* political interest has been more or less perennial.

If Tate's adaptation teaches us anything, it is that *Coriolanus* has substantial political content, and the extensiveness of his revision at-tests to its pervasiveness. Simultaneously, too, the alteration highlights the intricate balance of the play's political sympathies, evidenced by the lengths to which Tate was obliged to go to bias the piece in favor of "the right-hand file." Tate's thoroughgoing and ultimately unsatisfac-tory renovation makes it clear that *Coriolanus* does not readily lend itself to service as an ideological vehicle, as Dennis and Brecht were to learn in their turn. Its interest lies ultimately in its observation of political dynamics as an ongoing process; viewed thus, the play's tensions admit of no resolution. Martius is removed from the action, but the political and military struggle continues. To attempt to stabilize the drama's fluidity, or manufacture transcendence and release at curtain-fall, is as futile as to seek to put a collar on human interchange. To observe the play's power struggle is to participate in an ongoing revelation, not to reach a conclusion.

Tate's redaction, even as it obliterates the play's Manneristic identity, calls attention stroke by stroke to its aesthetic distinctiveness. As the structure is simplified and regularized, the richness and complexity of the original more insistently reveal themselves. At the moment of their disappearance, the interdependence of the disparate foci, their capacity to resonate against and reinforce each other, becomes transparent, revealing how much of the Roman-Volscian narrative and the mother-son relationship must be sacrificed to make *Coriolanus'* political attributes prevail.

While it may be argued that the play's characters are intensely private, ambiguous, and finally unsympathetic, Tate's experiment convincingly demonstrates that this is where their fascination resides. To pluck the heart out of their mystery is to destroy them. Like the portraits of Bronzino, their interest lies in their enigmatic motives, their ambivalent relationships, their self-conscious poses, designed as much to obscure as to reveal. Out of the actors' and audience's fresh readings of their secrets from ever-changing personal and cultural perspectives the play is forever reborn.

From Tate's attempt, as from Dennis' and Brecht's subsequent efforts, it becomes apparent how indissolubly Shakespeare has melded the dancer and the dance. To bias *Coriolanus'* overdetermined political vision, to fix its tantalizingly fluid aesthetic, is to diminish it, to deprive it of the mechanism for self-renewal. One wonders if this perception motivated Brecht's last entry in his working diary, "Couldn't one do [*Coriolanus*] just as it is, only with skilful direction?" (quoted in Heinemann, 219).

Tate's Victorian and Edwardian detractors were partly right; the play does have an artistic integrity, which so far has defied the best efforts of improvers. They were wrong, however, to assume that the recreation of Shakespeare in the cultural image of one's age merits condemnation rather than consideration. On the contrary, redactions like Tate's are indicators of the unique Elizabethan/Jacobean situatedness of the original text, sensitive guides to cultural values at particular historic moments, and, perhaps, unwitting pointers to a play's more durable (dare one say intrinsic?) features.

NOTES

1. "Withered be the hand, palzied be the arm, that ever dares to touch one of Shakespeare's plays," declared Hudson (II: 277–278).

2. The only surviving performance date is for January 14, 1681/82. *The Calendar of State Papers Domestic* notes: "This evening the Morocco ambassador with all his attendants will be treated at the King's playhouse with a play that has relation to that country, viz., Caius Martius with dancing and volting." See Lennep, 304.

3. Margreta de Grazia observes that editors of Shakespeare prior to Edmond Malone authorized their practice by their own literary credentials. Malone, she argues, "abstracted Shakespeare from the process by which he had been made correct and comprehensible by Taste and Judgement and by which in turn Taste and Judgement had been enriched and fortified by Shakespeare. The new [Malonean] criterion of authenticity converted the Shakespearean texts into a new kind of object: one lodged in the past rather than integral to current cultural concerns" (71). De Grazia's remark has, I think, as much relevance to Shakespeare's adaptors as to his editors.

4. Dryden invited Tate to write *The Second Part of Absalom and Achitophel* and contributed a preface to Tate's translation of Ovid's *Epistles* and a prologue for Tate's drama *The Loyal General*. See Christopher Spencer, 24.

5. All line references are to *The Riverside Shakespeare*, ed. G. Blakemore Evans.

6. See Jones, Nicoll, Whiting, and Wikander.

7. Helpful studies of Tate's adaptation include Allen, Ayres, Gallion, and McGugan.

8. The slaughter of innocents as the outcome of factionalism is a feature of a number of Shakespearean adaptations of this period, and the analogy between family and state is frequently pressed by divine right theorists from James I to Robert Filmer. See Wikander.

9. Of Shakespeare's 3,409 lines, Tate has retained 1,274; he is directly indebted to Shakespeare for 60 percent of the 2,124 lines in his adaptation. See McGugan, xxviii.

10. Tate's revision expands substantially the role of Valeria and trans-

forms her into a Restoration coquette. Her comic presence, disconcertingly out of keeping with the style and tone of the redaction, no doubt represents a concession to the contemporary audience-demand for increased participation of actresses in Shakespeare performances. See Lucyle Hook.

11. Walter Benjamin, in his analysis of Germany's baroque martyr-drama, with which Tate's *Ingratitude* has certain affinities, notes that the hero is frequently "a radical stoic, for whom the occasion to prove himself is a struggle . . . ending in torture and death. A peculiarity is the introduction of a woman as the victim in many of these dramas" (73–74).

12. Scene changes are not always marked. On two occasions I have provided for scene changes when they were obviously called for but not indicated: the entrance of Brutus and Menenius (43) after the exit of Aufidius and Nigridius (obviously a Corioli scene) and again in act 5, when after the exit of Volumnia and Virgilia, determined to depart for Corioli, Aufidius and Nigridius must enter on a Corioli setting.

13. Actresses regularly wore up-to-date fashions in historical plays. As late as 1792 (*Star*, April 2), Sarah Siddons was censured for wearing contemporary costume as Volumnia. In 1796, if the *Morning Chronicle* (October 4) is to be believed, Volumnia apparently sported gloves!

14. For an example of secular transcendence in visual art, Tate need have looked no farther than Peter Paul Rubens' *Apotheosis of James I* on the ceiling of the Banqueting House at Whitehall.

15. Only in the first half of the nineteenth century, presumably in the aftermath of the French Revolution, was the political character of the play stressed, particularly in the criticism of William Hazlitt, Nathan Drake, Friedrich von Schlegel, Hermann Ulrici, and Charles Knight.

7

The Rhetoric of Evidence: The Narration and Display of Viola and Olivia in the Nineteenth Century

Laurie E. Osborne

In examining the theatrical past, theatre historians like Marvin Rosenberg focus on kinetic performances as they have actually occurred, and performance critics like Michael Goldman focus on the potential for performing the dramatic text independent of any actual historical performance. The distinction is between an excavation or recovery effort on the one hand and an imaginative projection based in the conditions of theatrical production (including the playtext) on the other. The first can invoke the absent performance only by subjecting it to a narrative structure necessarily distanced from its material occurrence; the second generally avoids the particularities of individual theatrical productions in order to narrate the possibilities for enactment. To put it concretely, the theatre historian tells us what Maria Tree did onstage in her crossdressed role as Viola, but only by substituting narration for action; the performance critic may use Tree's experiences in the 1820 production, but her aim will be to describe the potential for performance within the text and the prevailing theatrical and acting conventions. In either case, performance criticism or theatre history, the actual performances are irrecoverable.

More recently critics have begun to combine these efforts in a blend of theatre history and performance criticism which I will call performance scholarship. In performance scholarship, the commitment to archival historical detail coincides with the critical aim of understanding the potentialities of theatrical enactment. Despite the obvious benefits of this union, what continues to be missing from these endeavors is, not surprisingly, performance itself. Instead of performance as such, performance scholars provide us with critical reconstructions of performances, based upon evidence that is textual in nature—archival material, published texts, diaries, reviews, prompter's notes, etc. Visual material might seem to be an exception to this claim, but as I shall try to illustrate visual material also becomes inescapably textual in nature when used as evidence. Moreover, if the evidence with which we produce our narrative reconstructions is perforce textual, so (obviously) are these reconstructions themselves. In this sense, performance scholarship is produced and reproduces itself by means of persuasive textual strategies—argumentative structures, narrative emplotments, and the like; performance scholarship, in other words, may be understood as functioning rhetorically. It is with these rhetorical functions that I am concerned here—the persuasive effects at work, intentionally or not, in the evidence that helps to generate and is regenerated by performance scholarship.

More specifically, I propose to examine some of the evidence we might use to recover the aural and visual effects of the performances of *Twelfth Night* in the early nineteenth century. In the first instance, I am concerned with Leigh Hunt's review of Maria Tree's Viola in an operatic version of the play and with William Oxberry's biography of the actress. In the second, I focus on two illustrations of Olivia's unveiling in 1.5, the first from the *Inchbald's British Theatre* edition of the play (1808), the second from the short-lived pre-Raphaelite journal the *Germ* (1850). In both instances, I am dealing with material that might be taken to represent performance with particular immediacy—more so than such other types of evidence as playbills, receipt books, and theatre statistics. However, this immediacy may be questioned: in the first instance by attending particularly to aspects of the evidence which resist the analysis of vocal effects; in the second, by exposing the distance between the illustrations and the performances they purport to evoke. In both cases, the gap between the absent performance and its reconstruction is filled by powerful rhetorical effects that I wish to describe and analyze.

As performance scholars, we face the problem Hayden White located in the production of history: "the facts do not speak for themselves, but the historian speaks for them, speaks on their behalf, and fashions the fragments of the past into a whole whose integrity is—in its *representation*—a purely discursive one" (*Tropics*, 125). White argues that historians produce narratives which depend on the emplotment of "facts," creating discourses which many historians resist analyzing in terms of their literariness. Although, as performance scholars, we acknowledge our motives of emplotment when we seek to recover or construct the performance of the dramatic text, the force of narrative in our work tends to become invisible, particularly when the rhetorical effects of our evidence condition its use within our work.

Though White frequently discusses evidence as though it were neutral material rendered rhetorical in the historian's construction, he notes that "the historically real, the past real, is that to which I can only be referred by way of an artifact which is textual in nature" (*Content*, 209). By positing a radical separation between an inaccessible past and the written artifact which supposedly refers to it, White opens up a space to meditate on the linguistic analyses required for the production of history. He treats especially intellectual history, which, exploring the dichotomy between classical and documentary texts and in contrast to the more straightforward reconstructions of political and economic history, is "shot through with ideological elements" (*Content*, 187).

Theatre history and performance criticism fall somewhere between these two modes; they deal with classical texts, like Shakespeare's, and with documentary evidence ranging from reviews to playbills. Many scholars of performance now address the emplotment of evidence in reconstructions of theatrical history. For example, when Joseph Donohue takes up evidence as it functions in the historiography of the theatre, he too insists that "no amount of actual information, however seemingly comprehensive, can mask the inadequacy of argument and rhetorical purpose" (191). For both White's history and Donohue's theatre historiography, evidence as a category exists only within the structures imposed upon it by history, or more precisely by the rhetorical purposes of the historian's/critic's writing. It is to these structures, I argue here, that we should be paying special attention.

Nonetheless, however rhetorically motivated may be the materials we use as evidence, that material must preexist our structures for them to establish or corroborate anything. Thomas Postlewait deals with this problem by arguing that evidence should be evaluated in the context of generic conventions. Hence, in dealing with theatrical autobiography, we need to keep in mind the limited validity of anecdotal histories and the frequently self-serving motives of the authors ("Autobiography," 248–252). Postlewait's suggestion represents one normalizing mechanism for evaluating evidence—namely, determining its appropriate context. I would go still further and argue that both intentional and unintentional rhetorical structures within textual evidence inevitably influence the rhetorical forms of the arguments which use that evidence. Moreover, the influence which I posit is neither exclusively supportive nor historically neutral. Often, the overt rhetorical purposes at work in the evidence are at odds with those of the argument. Just as often, discursive practices which register the evidence's inability to recreate performance create still different rhetorical effects. From textual evidence, we produce critical texts which propose to convey scholarly "truth." But performances, like histories, are sloppy, self-contradictory, and in many ways incoherent. The totalizing stories we tell about performance are far different from the diverse materials we survey in constructing those stories, but the rhetorical structures of those materials, often marked by the persistent failure to capture performance in text, have noticeable effects in the production of performance scholarship. From these crossed purposes arise conflicts and unexpected complicities between critical approaches to performance on the one hand and the materials they employ as evidence on the other.

The early-nineteenth-century evidence of Maria Tree's musical performance as Viola is a useful starting place. Viola's vocal abilities exist as one of the shadow versions of *Twelfth Night* suggested in the Folio, where Viola tells the sea captain she will entertain Orsino, "For I can sing, / And speak to him in many sorts of music / That will allow me very worth his service" (1.2.57–59). Hence Tree's singing makes concrete one potential performance registered in the first available performance text. But her particular talent and early-nineteenth-century concerns about gender norms are the more significant factors in contemporaneous accounts. Tree's greatest strength was apparently her singing; her praised appearances as Viola occur during Henry Bishop's operatic reworking of the play in 1820. After a very successful revival of *Comedy of Errors*, *Twelfth Night* was the second Shakespearean play to be rewritten as light opera, followed by *Two Gentlemen of Verona*, in which Tree played another crossdressed page, Julia.[1] With the addition of songs stolen from other plays and the sonnets, these operatic productions flourished in the early nineteenth century and helped to showcase Tree's particular vocal talents. Hunt's review of the production mentions Tree's singing prominently, and Oxberry quotes just such a review, which asserts that "her tones go right to the heart" (204). Both critics explicitly mark the significance of this feature in this 1820 production of *Twelfth Night*. Yet the evidence in these documents inevitably exceeds the revelation of one particular feature of performance. Despite the attention which both Hunt and Oxberry tender to her singing skills, their analyses of the production and the actress' place in it return constantly to her appearance in a revealing crossdressed costume, to her modesty and vulnerability. And these meditations on the actress in male attire persistently divert Hunt and Oxberry from their presumed purpose of analyzing or narrating Tree's vocal performance.

For example, Hunt is drawn into an admiring discussion of Tree's singing in the production because he "never saw or heard her to more advantage in solos" (227). However, he does not give any hint of what her songs are like other than "deep and tender," nor does his analysis of her vocal powers extend beyond a brief mention of "the strength and fullness in the lower notes which, being unusual in a female, appeared to fall in with the character she had assumed as a male" (228). To be sure, these comments address the aural effects of Viola in production, yet the sounds associated with Tree's performance are ultimately not what most draws Hunt's attention.

After mentioning her singing and briefly alluding to the interest arising from her recent illness, Hunt's review takes an unexpected turn. He launches into an extremely lengthy description of her leg:

> (as such subjects are eminently critical), we must be allowed to say that her leg is the very prettiest leg we ever saw on the stage. It is not at all like the leg which is vulgarly praised even in a man, and which is doubly misplaced under a lady—a bit of balustrade turned upside down; a large calf, and an ankle only small in proportion. It is a right feminine leg, delicate in foot, trim in ankle, and with a calf at once soft and well-cut, distinguished and unobtrusive. We are not so intolerant— we should rather say ungrateful and inhuman—on the subject of legs, as many of our sex, who, without the light of a good ankle, can see nothing else good in a figure. We have a tender respect for them all, provided they are gentle. But it is impossible not to be struck, as an

Irishman would say, with a leg like this. It is fit for a statue; still fitter where it was. . . . We are sorry we cannot speak so well for the rest of the performance. (228)

Hunt then juxtaposes Tree's legs with other actors' performances. The irony of treating Tree's leg as an intrinsic part of performance is particularly obvious, given that Hunt himself complained several years earlier that "the disguise of women in male attire, though it continues, and will continue, welcome in the spectators from causes unconnected with dramatic decorum, always strikes one as a gross violation of probability, especially if represented as accompanied with delicacy of mind" (42). Nonetheless, the discussion of Tree's leg takes over Hunt's evaluation of her singing of the role; in effect his interest in her body displaces her singing as the focus of his commentary on her performance. This shift in his rhetorical strategy passes unremarked within a review which predominantly treats the details of the actors' portrayals. Although the careful wittiness of Hunt's description seems to indicate his rhetorical control, the abrupt switches in subject and diction within the review mark contradictions in the rhetoric of his text which influence those who use it or reviews like it.

Notable examples of such influence appear in *Oxberry's Dramatic Biography*, which attempts a more thorough discussion of Tree's singing skills but ultimately recapitulates conflicting, yet revealing rhetorical elements of his evidence. In examining the observations he offers of her singing, we soon discover that the specific songs or tunes and even the quality of her voice preoccupy her biographer only in the context of the scandalous details of her near-suicide and ultimate departure from the stage to marry. Throughout his dramatic biography, Oxberry offers, contradicts, and qualifies his own evidence, as he includes and rewrites a series of narratives concerning Tree's life. In effect, Oxberry takes up positive reviews like Hunt's in order to write Tree's biography, while his own skeptical opposition to his chosen accounts produces a negative evaluation of Tree. These interpolated texts include their own self-conscious rhetorical and narrative flourishes, wherein description of her acting recoils into analysis of her modesty much as it does in Hunt's review. The influence of these rhetorical strategies—particularly descriptive narration and displacements from performance to the actress' modesty—is evident in Oxberry's own uses of these rhetorical strategies even as he attempts to reverse every piece of evidence he offers about

Tree. Even though the overt rhetorical strategy of his biography is to contradict his evidence, the materials which he includes have distinctive (though unintentional) effects on both the structure and rhetorical strategies of his biography.

Oxberry first signals his contrarian approach to evidence by quoting the remarks from the *Examiner* at length because "our own impressions of our heroine, as we have hinted, are not so favorable as those of most of the critics of the day" (204).[2] By including an excerpt from the *Examiner's* laudatory comments, Oxberry acknowledges that the "remarks are generally talented, and, we believe unbiased"; he therefore at least initially proposes to offer an objective account of her stage performances. The writers "are almost convinced, that the great poet himself, could he have witnessed Miss Tree's performance of his Viola, his Julia, his Ophelia, or his Imogen, would have experienced the perfect content of seeing his own idea faithfully reflected by his acting" (205). They quote *Twelfth Night* in claiming that her tones " 'give echo to the very seat where Love is throned' " (204). At the same time, the praise in the passage Oxberry quotes is extravagant and accompanied by a continual return to the question of Tree's modesty in male disguise, which embeds her theatrical performance in discourses of gender propriety.

For example, the *Examiner's* account of Tree's stage career as "a first rate singer" mentions only briefly her talents for singing and acting. Most of the evidence quoted here concentrates on her admirable modesty, claiming that "nothing, perhaps, can be a stronger proof of native modesty than the manner in which she played in male attire" (205). The lengthy discussion of her enviable modesty in revealing attire ends in remarks which echo Hunt's preoccupations: "Then her figure was beautifully formed; and her 'masculine usurped attire,' which was always the most tasteful and becoming imaginable, displayed it to peculiar advantage" (206). By quoting from *Twelfth Night's* Viola in conjunction with the direct reference to the character, this reviewer is able to identify Tree very strongly with Viola's modesty, as it was perceived in this period.

Oxberry, however, denies both Tree's singing skill and her modesty, but not before making it very clear that he cannot present any piece of evidence without qualifying it or disagreeing with it. For example, he includes a "strongly but unjustly deprecated" essay written in *From the News of Literature and Fashion* which recounts in the form of a conversation Tree's attempt to kill herself after her fiancé, Mr. Bradshaw, sought to end their engagement. This narrative of her experience, which records both her rescue from self-destruction by her servant and her ultimate reconciliation with Mr. Bradshaw, claims as the cause of her difficulties the potential mother-in-law's opposition to including an actress in the family. After reporting this anecdote, Oxberry acknowledges that "it will be obvious to our readers that correctness of the details of a circumstance like the foregoing, was near impossible" (209) and amends the motives of Mr. Bradshaw to include "vexation, given by Captain Forbes' applications on account of Covent-Garden theatre as well as maternal control" (209). Oxberry ostensibly brings in such evidence to supply the objectivity he lacks, but he is not content to let a single piece of evidence he offers stand as the truth of Tree's situation. Even so, the evidence he brings in consistently affects his own argument, most notably in the production of narrative which he adopts as a rhetorical strategy.

He most pointedly establishes his own narration by constantly referring to Tree as "our heroine." He also offers his own version of the story of a young actress immediately following the tale of Tree's marital adventures. Oxberry's alternative version is framed specifically as narrative:

> Really the situation of a young actress, in the present day, is little better than a slave. Just review the life of one. From twelve years of age until eighteen, kept eight hours a-day singing and playing the piano; dieted and kept to particular hours, from eighteen to twenty-five; hurried from theatre to theatre, and from town to town. . . . All this while carefully excluded from any intercourse with one of the other sex, who might render her happy. Her every movement watched by her anxious relatives, lest, by taking a husband of her own choice, she should defeat their hopes of subsistence on her exertions. At twenty-five, they begin to look out for her; and the very person who is supposed to perform the principal character in this drama of matrimony, is little consulted about it. At length, the musical victim is sold off to some rich booby, who she heartlessly weds—she is raised into a circle of society to which she is unused, and for which she is unfit; for her studious and industrious existence has allowed her little chance of mixing in company. What are the results? Taken from a station where, as an exhibitor, she was delightful, to one in which she is a novice, and consequently awkward, and where she has no means of display—she disgusts the very being she should

charm—he curses his folly—she, her parents' cupidity—and the great
dramatic alliance becomes the fruitful source of lasting misery. We do
not apply these observations to Miss Tree, though we think her one of
the victims of some system of this kind. (209–210)

If Oxberry truly does not intend this story to reflect on Tree—as it certainly seems to do—then what is this narrative doing here? He recapitulates the impulse to narrate implicit in his most recent piece of evidence, countering the story in *Literature and Fashion* with a veiled one
of his own of Tree's life as a young actress. Just as importantly, he concludes this episode by anticipating that his own narrative will encounter
opposition: "we make the remark generally, respecting the young syrens
of the present day, and dare their friends to a refutation of the truth of
our allegations" (210). Thus he not only adopts the structure of marital
narrative implicit in his evidence but also anticipates a continuation of
the kind of dialogue which serves as one rhetorical form in the *Literature and Fashion* excerpt he includes.

Oxberry's extremely contentious use of evidence and his anticipation
of subsequent refashioning of his own statements mark all evidence as
inherently subject to revision and qualification by those who use it as
their own. His argument deliberately opposes the evidence he offers at
the same time that the multiple rhetorical purposes in his evidence are
recapitulated within his biography. The common thread here is the
troubling prospect of actresses marrying and bringing their skill for display into the domestic sphere. The conflict between performance and
maidenly modesty/appropriate social display becomes an explicit issue
in the young actress' inability to display herself appropriately and grace-
fully in the domestic sphere. Although Oxberry deliberately avoids the
more scandalous possibilities of the young actress who actually mixes
with male company, his comments persistently imply that performance
and self-display are qualifications which women must have in both theatrical and domestic situations.

Most interestingly, however, this story serves as Oxberry's transi-
tion into his own rather harsh critique of both Tree's singing and her
modesty/appearance: "Now, then, to our own statement of what our
heroine was in our estimation" (210). The multiple possessives of this
single line paragraph signal a decisive move to Oxberry's own opinions,
coyly veiled until this point behind his use of evidence. However, by this
point, the evidence so clearly links the performative and the social that

Oxberry's abrupt juxtaposition of Tree's singing and her modesty may seem less arbitrary than it is.

His dispraise of her singing begins with the claim that "Miss Tree had not, naturally, good voice: her voice like Pearman's, was the result of art" (210). Along with contradicting the supposedly impartial evidence he offers of her performance, Oxberry instantly allies Tree with the narrative of the young working actresses he has just produced and whose relevance to Tree he had disclaimed. He has difficulty distinguishing what was wrong with her voice and once again imagines opposition to his opinions. At one point, he asserts even that "without calling in aid of a musical type, it is difficult to explain ourselves on these subjects" (211). These difficulties in verifying events and producing vocal quality lead into a devastating summary: "Our objections to her as a general singer are these:—She could be loud, but not energetic—she could be plaintive, but she never rose to the beautiful in melancholy—she could be lively, but never fervid—she could execute every sort of thing in a second-rate style, she could not excel in any" (211–212). At this point, Oxberry's oppositional style is never more evident.

While maintaining a skepticism which pervades this memoir, Oxberry offers his perspicacity in trying to evaluate her voice "objectively" as the contrast to the overblown praise he has quoted. However, both within his quoted remarks about Tree's voice and within his own assessment, her performance resists discursive capture while her modesty and person do not. The conflicting rhetorical features I noted in Hunt's review—the displacement of concerns about performance onto concerns about female propriety and appearance—recur in the *Examiner* commentary which Oxberry uses and in turn become part of Oxberry's own rhetorical strategies.

In fact, he moves directly from her "musical pretensions" to an outright assault on her modesty: "hers was the affectation of nonaffectation—the assumption of timidity—the show of modesty . . . amid all this farrago of modesty and delicacy, how came Miss Tree to dress Ariel the way she did? . . . She likewise willingly assumed Patrick, in *The Poor Soldier*. So much for the cant of delicacy!" (212).[3] Ultimately, Oxberry asserts that Tree's relative lack of talent made it impossible for her to compete with the "lively ladies of the stage, [and so] she hit upon the expedient of 'doing a little timidity,' and the scheme told" (213). Her performance blends into her appearance, scantly clad as Ariel or in male attire as Patrick; maidenly modesty becomes a tactic, in effect the successful performance of an actress whom he chronically characterizes as second rate in her acting ability. The dangers of her ability to pretend skill in singing and in modesty pervade Oxberry's biography, effectively replacing the biographer's inability to reproduce performance with the actress' unexpected ability to feign appropriate female modesty. The available discourses of dangerous female behaviors of the nineteenth century take the place of the unavailable singing voice which Oxberry seeks to criticize and control.

On the basis of such contradictions and displacements, I would claim that the comfortable discourses of nineteenth-century female propriety became a refuge for both Hunt and Oxberry as they encountered the apparent inadequacy of text to match performance. Their rhetorical moves into prose poems of praise for Tree's limbs, general narrations of the young actress' life, and abruptly juxtaposed criticisms of her singing and her modesty all strongly link the difficulties in representing performance to the problems of staging gender roles, especially in the case of the actress.

These textual influences extend even to the use of evidence which is not so resolutely textual, so involved in narrative, and consequently so likely to shift into discourses of gender in response to female performance, which indeed would seem at first glance to escape the dangers of textuality altogether and recuperate some of the spectacle of theatrical performance itself. I am thinking of the representations of the visual arts, in particular two versions of the frequently represented unveiling of Olivia in act 1, scene 5 of *Twelfth Night*.[4]

Such illustrations sometimes represent extradramatic scenes (Ophelia's drowning, Lady Macbeth's death, the opening storm of *The Tempest*). This is not the case, of course, with the unveiling of Olivia, which occurs in the playtext. At the same time, we must be careful about inferring actual performance conditions or practices from such illustrations. As Stephen Orgel has argued in "The Authentic Shakespeare," the construction of visual images related to stage productions could serve a variety of purposes from self-aggrandizement to an imaginative refashioning of actual staging. Even deliberate efforts to capture stage images halt the kinetic enactment of the play in mid-gesture, arresting performance both in the physical image and in the artist's construction of a static moment. On the whole, although clues to performance can be recovered from the visual arts, the material demands of their construction and the necessary intervention of the artist's sensibility and skill distance the image from performance as well as freezing it into a stasis unnatural to performance.

To these substantial qualifications of the relationship between such engravings and the stage, I would add and expand upon a third: such images rarely, if ever, appear without some kind of textual positioning. The two examples I have in mind are contextualized in very different ways, but in both cases the writing of the image becomes a crucial aspect of its function as evidence, so that in the process the image accrues rhetorical features which affect the arguments to be made about it or by means of it.

The first engraving appears as the title-page illustration for volume 4 of *Inchbald British Theatre*'s version of *Twelfth Night*.[5] This engraving (figure 1), painted by Howard, engraved by Noble, and published by Longman & Co. in 1808, appears opposite the title page which claims to offer the comedy, "as performed at the Theatres Royal, Drury Lane and Covent Garden, printed under the authorities of the managers from the promptbook, with remarks by Mrs. Inchbald." Beyond the assertions of theatrical origin for the edition and, by implication, for the engraving, the scene itself is entitled "TWELFTH NIGHT" at the top and includes Olivia's name, her line ("Look, sir, such a one I wear"), and "Act I, Scene V" to indicate placement in the comedy. Thus the engraving embeds its image—almost like a quotation—between the title of the play and the lines and their reference.

The line itself is interesting, not least because neither figure in the engraving has her mouth open to speak it. We are thus dependent on the text to identify the speaker. Olivia is positioned on the left, implicitly allied with her speech heading below; Viola/Cesario is apparently the listener, positioned by the gendered address "Sir" and his own masculine usurped attire. Further, this speech suggests Olivia as the agent in control of the encounter as she demands that Viola look while she holds her veil up from her face to enable the glance she solicits. The lighting of her figure and the frame of her arm and veil insure that the viewer's gaze, as well as Cesario's, will be drawn to Olivia's face. Thus a reader must construe text and image together and, even if unfamiliar with the play, will "read" Olivia as the speaker although the image itself suggests only silence.

However, the engraving also records a gesture which escapes the text's interpolation, in part because Cesario is not given any text here. Viola holds her hand outstretched toward Olivia, but why? Aside from

Figure 1. Olivia:
"Look, sir, such a one
I wear." Act I, Scene V.
Courtesy of the Folger
Shakespeare Library.

offering a gestural reinforcement of the engraving's concentrated interest in Olivia's self-revelation, this display of Viola's outstretched hand
opens up a number of possible interpretations, but confirms none. The
most pressing issues are whether Viola's gesture, like Olivia's, derives
from a staged image and, whatever the origin of her gesture, what motivates Viola to reach for Olivia at this moment. These questions are unanswerable precisely because the engraving exceeds the text with which
it interacts.

Thus despite its visual component, the engraving's evidentiary function is textual. The lines which invariably accompany the visual representation do not and cannot fully account for the image. In part because
of its excess, the image itself provokes and requires narration, an aspect
of its evidential use which I have just enacted. In fact I have been drawn
into narrating this image in order to point out Viola's gesture. My as-

sumption that her hand is outstretched toward Olivia narrates the static gesture, placing it within an action and calling for the motive of that action.[6] The engraving is not only surrounded by text, but also can only function as evidence once rewritten in textual, even narrative terms which direct the viewer's eyes.

The words which grace the bottom of the engraving raise still more subtle issues. This line directs our attention to the ambiguous evidence offered by the text itself as it proposes to offer the promptbook in published form. The caption rewrites the performance edition's text for that line—"Look you, sir, such a one wear I"—which, in its turn, rewrites the Folio text: "Look you, sir, such a one I was this present" (1.5.237–238). This multiplicity leaves completely unresolved the question which line was used in performance. Although we might assume that the Folio text is not a viable alternative, the line beneath the engraving also differs from the *Inchbald* text and therefore serves to raise the issue of what kind of evidence of performance either text or image can offer. Performance editions—that is, published texts like Inchbald's which claim performance as their source of editing—may offer cast lists from different years and versions of the text which do not match the promptbook markings of their presumed editor or include introductions as well as engravings, which refer to lines that are omitted from the text presented.[7] Neither text nor image can offer direct, straightforward alignment between evidence and theatrical event. Even the marked promptbook set out as the model for performance cannot fully control the enactment, which is always subject to the material intervention of sickness, recalcitrant props, hostile audiences, faulty memories, and even weak singing.[8]

With this resistance of performance and the question of Viola's response in mind, I turn to my second engraving, "Viola and Olivia" (figure 2). This image reworks the "staging" of Viola's unveiling and illustrates again the impulse to rewrite the visual within the textual. In 1850, Walter Deverell engraved the scene for the pre-Raphaelite journal, the *Germ*, in order to take the place of an engraving promised by Dante Rossetti. Like Inchbald's engraving, the etching appears in the context of its facing page, which juxtaposes the text of a poem called "Viola and Olivia" with the image of the same name. This poem, written by John Lucas Tupper, raises the issue of why Viola demands to see Olivia's face and offers its own interpretive possibilities of "whim / Or jealousy or fear" (145).[9] After setting the situation in terms of Viola's request and

Figure 2. Deverell's "Viola and Olivia." Courtesy of the Folger Shakespeare Library.

her motives, the second stanza dismisses the importance of those motives, except to affirm that Viola's request was "natural / As natural as what came next, the near / Intelligence of hearts: Olivia / Loveth." The poet constructs the naturalness of this situation in the juxtaposition of the poem with the etching wherein Viola raises the veil and reaches to Olivia.

Despite the obvious differences between the two engravings in relative height of the figures, body position, placement in the scene, and the actual hand involved in the unveiling, there are significant similarities. In both Inchbald's engraving and Deverell's, Olivia is much more illuminated than Viola, whose face is in the shadow.[10] Moreover, both portray Viola's extended arm in a problematic way. In Deverell's "Viola and Olivia," the hand which lifts the veil suggests one relationship between arm and coat, while Viola's right hand, which also apparently touches

Olivia, seems to emerge from a split sleeve which the other arm does not have. The effect is that the sleeve or folded cloak which hangs down offers one image of where Viola's arm should be while her actual hand suggests another. If it is a cloak rather than a sleeve which so enfolds the top of her arm and shoulder, then the effect is to create an elongated sleeve and a different placement of her arm than the picture suggests on closer examination. The ambiguity concerning what Viola does in extending her arm and hand toward Olivia in the Inchbald engraving recurs in this later etching.

In the *Germ's* poem, this question of Viola's response at this moment is answered by the concluding stanza, which suggests

> That they were married souls—unmarried here—
> Having an inward faith that love, called so
> In verity, is of the spirit, clear
> Of earth and dress and sex—it may be near
>   What Viola returned to Olivia? (145)

The curious question mark and the emphasis on what Viola might be returning to Olivia's love reinforce the notion that what is transpiring in the engraving transcends "earth and dress and sex." Nonetheless, both the poem and the engraving problematize the relationship between the two figures they record. Tupper's narrative of what might exist between them merely exposes Viola's impulsive gesture toward Olivia as an expression of love, a love which is itself unrepresentable.

Given this narrative, it is tempting to "read" Deverell's engraving as the completion of Viola's earlier gesture in the 1808 engraving, to discover in the disturbances of image and text that Viola's transgression of gendered dress has complicated both her gender and her response to Olivia in nineteenth-century representations. Certainly, this is the conclusion which Barbara Melchiori draws when she suggests that "the key to the fondness for this subject [Olivia's unveiling] lies in a curious variant—in the April 1850 issue of the *Germ*, it is Viola herself who raises the veil, and this illustration by Walter Deverell is accompanied by an unsigned Lesbian poem entitled 'Viola and Olivia'" (128). Melchiori offers the engraving *and* the poem as evidence explaining the interest in this scene, ignoring the other evidence of the numerous paintings and etchings which show Olivia raising her veil, as the Inchbald engraving does. The *Germ's* engraving is anomalous, offering a different reading of the scene largely, though not entirely, because of the "lesbian" poem which texualizes the artwork, and this anomalous quality is taken to be a revelation.

Many other etchings of this scene include textual cues; Deverell's etching is exceptional only in the sense that it is at odds with the other depictions of the scene and that its narrative is more thoroughly imagined as extending beyond the scene. The exceptional quality of the etching and the different narrative which it offers (or provokes) together influence the rhetorical use made of the work as evidence—an assertion for which Melchiori's essay may serve as example. According to Melchiori, Victorian illustrators represented Shakespeare for "a novel reading public and shared a preference for narrative rather than dramatic subjects" (128). Her inclusion of this etching and poem, however, constitutes a departure, an exception to her main argument about how the "intensive moralizing and the morbid sensuality" of the Victorian novel influences representations of Shakespeare. For one thing, when she links the image to novels of lesbian friendship which appear late in the 1880s and 1890s, she presents "Viola and Olivia" as a precursor to those novels rather than an effect. More importantly, this image, unlike the others which Melchiori singles out, does not represent a narrative passage but *becomes* a narrative in the hands of those who rewrite the image: John Lucas Tupper, Barbara Melchiori, and now me.

For my argument as well, this etching is an exception. To be sure, the engraving with its accompanying text does underscore my point that visual evidence becomes narrative; moreover, Melchiori's point in approaching these illustrations perfectly accords with my interest in the influence of narrative and text. However, this engraving is much further removed from theatrical practice than any of my other examples. The engraving's notable difference from other images of the same scene and the poem's narrative of diverted love influence the arguments which incorporate either the engraving itself or the poem. This image originates outside of theatrical practice and therefore could not participate in the reconstruction of the performance as event. Nonetheless, as evidence it participates in the cultural negotiations with women's roles in *Twelfth Night* on the nineteenth-century stage. This exception further illustrates how narrative is provoked by images and how the rhetorical force of these provoked narratives extends their influence through those performance scholars, like myself, who use such images.

In some ways the foregoing analyses of the rhetorical positioning in these engravings and the rhetorical features within Hunt's and Oxberry's texts perform the kind of reading which Postlewait advocates for exploring evidence taken from autobiography; my analysis, like his, insists on the context for textual and visual evidence. I have been trying to suggest that this argument can be generalized and extended. First, both intended and unintended rhetorical structures within the textual evidence which we use to reconstruct the past are pertinent, not just for their qualifying contexts but for their own rhetorical approaches to representing performance. I make this assertion not because these rhetorical strategies will reflect performance, but because they will not. Textual constructions will necessarily use narration, description, and dialogue rather than action, visual appearance, and speech.

Moreover, the rhetorical choices within our evidence will influence our own arguments in ways we should analyze. The first section of this essay argued that the effort to represent the actress' performances in review and biography rebounds into familiar discursive practices used to contain female bodies and actions in this period, narratives of the modest self-effacement of the virtuous woman and of the dangerous pretense and acting of the fallen woman. That these two discourses coincide in Tree's case is no surprise, since the actress as a general figure raises the threat that familiar codes of female virtue could be feigned onstage by those not so virtuous (see Tracy Davis). Even the engravings, which seem to capture at least a visual, if static, representation of Olivia's unveiling, are continually positioned in relationship to texts. Like the rhetorical displacements produced by performances as they exceed and elude discursive capture, the engravings' visual representations exceed the texts associated with those images, in their turn provoking more narrative analyses to compensate for stasis and to respond to the images' tensions.

Thus, as we use both textual and visual representations of the performed moment, our arguments, whatever their own agendas, embody and speak the rhetoric of our evidence. As my analysis suggests, embedded evidence does not necessarily lose its rhetorical force when indented or placed in quotation marks. Even if so little of the evidential text is included that discerning its rhetorical features is next to impossible, quotation links the two texts at a juncture which potentially transforms both: the quoted text becomes evidence in relationship to the argument, and the argument comes to partake of the rhetorical flavor of the quoted materials. My purpose, of course, has been deliberately to show these rhetorical influences, most aggressively by juxtaposing

Oxberry's contentious relationship with his evidence alongside my own contentious assertions about evidence and by tracing in my use of the visual and poetic versions of "Viola and Olivia" the same kind of exception that both the image/poem and Melchiori's essay reproduce.

As this essay argues, the consistent, persistent rewriting of the visual and the textual traces of performance never manages to reproduce performance. Acknowledging the differences between text and performance requires that we attend to the rhetoric as well as the context of the textual attempts to capture performance. We need to acknowledge how our evidence informs our own rhetorical practices. Just as importantly, we must remember that performance and its textual and visual traces participate together in material practices which negotiate and renegotiate complex cultural problems, in this case the problematics of female performance. These texts and images, while not able to recuperate performance, participate in and rely upon the discourses which speak through actual performances and performance possibilities.

NOTES

1. Odell, I: 135, 139. Odell quotes the same review of Hunt's about the 1820 production featuring Maria Tree, although he omits elements of the review which most interest me.

2. It is worth noting that Leigh Hunt also wrote for the *Examiner*, though I have found no indication that the review Oxberry quotes is his. In fact, Oxberry does not document his evidence at all—which perhaps offers support for Donohue's insistence on the importance of documentation. For further explorations of Hunt's attitudes toward crossdressing, see Marsden.

3. Oxberry includes no description of this disgraceful attire, underscoring the unrepresentability of visual as well as oral aspects of performance.

4. Winifred Friedman comments on the enormous popularity of this moment for artists (3).

5. Elizabeth Inchbald was a popular dramatist and novelist of the period; her contribution to this edition was limited to writing the introductions for the plays which the publishers decided to include.

6. Yet that gesture is Viola's only response, given that the performance edition cuts the exchange between the two women that follows: "*Olivia.* Is't not well done? / *Viola.* Excellently done if God did all" (1.5.239–240).

7. For a discussion of some of these issues in performance editions, see my essay "The Texts of *Twelfth Night*."

8. Charles Shattuck addresses these and other problems with the promptbooks as resources in his introduction to *The Shakespeare Promptbooks*.

9. Although the poem is unsigned within the *Germ* itself, William Michael Rossetti's introduction to the 1888 third edition clearly identifies Tupper as the poem's author, as does *The P. R. B. Journal*.

10. The emphasis on Olivia's face is all the more surprising, given that the major point of interest in the piece is supposedly Elizabeth Siddal, according to William Michael Rossetti: "'The etching by Deverell, however defective in technique, claims more attention [than the poem], as Viola was drawn from Miss Elizabeth Eleanor Siddal, whom Deverell had observed in a bonnet-shop some months before the etching was done'" (*P. R. B. Journal*, 233).

8

Edwin Booth's *Richard II* and the Divided Nation

Catherine M. Shaw

Late in the evening of April 23, 1879, although it had been somewhat restless up to that time, the audience in McVicker's Theatre in Chicago listened with rapt attention to the greatest voice on the American stage deliver the prison soliloquy from the last act of Shakespeare's *Richard II*. Just as he got to the lines "And these same thoughts people this little world / In humors like the people of this world, / For no thought is contented" (5.5.9–11),[1] two gunshots suddenly shattered the silence of the theatre. After some minutes of panic and confusion, the truth became known—someone in the audience had attempted to assassinate Edwin Booth.

Surprisingly, in all the extensive coverage of this event,[2] there was only one direct statement made of what might seem most obvious—the parallel between the attempt on Booth's life and the assassination of Abraham Lincoln. In an interview with the *Chicago Tribune*, the comedians Stuart Robson and William H. Crane, who were playing in a very successful run of *Comedy of Errors* at the Hooley Theatre, both said that their first thoughts on hearing of the event were of its "realistic bearing on the memorable assassination of Lincoln. . . . It seemed as if someone wished to be avenged" (April 24, 1879).

Why, we might ask, would the press not have made this obvious connection itself? Why did no one seem to notice parallels between the event and the historical substance of the play being produced? Why was there no link made between the name of Edwin Booth's would-be assassin, Mark Gray, and that of John Wilkes Booth?

There are, of course, no verifiable answers to these questions—not any based on "hard" evidence. Nonetheless, by using the kind of sociopolitical and cultural as well as theatrical reconstruction practiced by the modern stage historian, we can compare the interrelationships among actor, play, and venue in Chicago with those in other areas in which Edwin Booth had played Richard II and from those comparisons broaden the scope to suggest that these stage representations and receptions hold the mirror up to national divisions in post–Civil War America. To do this, however, it is necessary to set actor, play, and venues back into their own historical narrative, beginning with the actor himself.

Edwin Booth was not by nature a political man. "The footlight limit is a sealed Greek book to me," he wrote at one point. "I rarely know who's president, and there's a 'muss 'twixt the Turk and the Russ'; therefore my correspondence and conversation must needs be vapid" (Grossmann, 187–188). He did, it is true, vote for Abraham Lincoln in autumn 1864, but it was the only time in his life he took part in a federal election. Although that occasion was important enough to write to his friend Emma Carey, "I suppose I am now an American citizen all over, as I have ever been in my heart" (Grossmann, 12), other matters were occupying all of his time and energy—and understandably so. The 1864–1865 theatrical season was a great one for him. On November 25, 1864, he appeared at the Winter Garden theatre as Brutus in *Julius Caesar*; with him were his brothers Junius Brutus as Cassius and John Wilkes as Mark Antony. The performance was a benefit in aid of a statue of Shakespeare to be erected in Central Park and, although all the seat prices had been raised, the theatre was packed. It was the first (and only) time the three Booths played together, and the audience gave them standing ovations when they first appeared onstage and at each act intermission.

On the following night, November 26, 1864, Booth opened in *Hamlet* and began a run that was to set a theatrical record for a continuous run of a Shakespeare play in New York that remained unbroken for nearly fifty years—one hundred nights. Indeed, for the first time matinées were instituted to accommodate those living outside of the city proper. The press pointed out that the managers of the Winter Garden were swelling their coffers, but there was no doubt that, as one commentator said, "At the rate at which matters are progressing at that establishment,

Hamlet will be got through with about the time the present lessees conclude their lease. We may arrive at Richard the Third somewhere about
the period of Mr. Lincoln's retirement from office. Of course the management are not to blame for this. They have struck a vein and have to
work it. The public are Booth and Hamlet mad" (unidentified clipping,
Hampden-Booth Theatre Collection).

It is perhaps understandable that during this time Booth should admit to thinking about enlarging his repertory to include a lesser-
known Shakespearean hero but one as close to his own temperament as
Hamlet—Richard II. In a letter written to Emma Carey sometime in late
1864, he says, "*Richard II.* I have often thought of doing; it has been a
stranger to the stage since my father's time. I never saw him act in it, but
I am told it was one of his finest interpretations" (Grossmann, 167). Circumstances were such, however, that Booth's *Richard II* was not brought
to the stage until more than a decade had passed.

When *Hamlet* finally closed on March 22, 1865, Booth took up an engagement in Boston, and it was there that he received the news that
stunned the nation a month later—his brother John Wilkes Booth had
assassinated Abraham Lincoln. Although Edwin Booth had the sympathy of some friends, the effect on the Booth family was devastating
and they suffered much at the hands of an angry nation. Thomas Reed
Turner speaks of how they "feared for their lives and faced false accusations of possible involvement in the assassin's deed" (27). He also cites
from *The Unlocked Book: A Memoir of John Wilkes Booth by His Sister
Asia Booth Clarke* her remembrance that "the tongue of every man and
woman was free to revile and insult us" (30). One editor even advised
Edwin Booth "to apply to some legislature to change his name, in obedience to the universal determination of the American public that no one
bearing the name of the assassin should ever again appear on the boards
of our theatres" (unidentified clipping, Hampden-Booth). Before the
year was out, however, he agreed to an engagement at the Winter Garden. His reasons are explained in a letter to Mrs. Richard F. Cary in
December 1865:

> You have also, doubtless, heard that I shall soon appear on the stage.
> Sincerely, were it not for *means*, I should not do so, public sympathy
> not withstanding; but I have huge debts to pay, a family to care for, a
> love for the grand and beautiful in art, to boot, to gratify, and hence my
> sudden resolve to abandon the heavy, aching gloom of my little red

room, where I have sat for so long chewing my heart in solitude, for the excitement of the only trade for which God has fitted me.

(Grossmann, 174)

Once Booth had decided to return to the stage, there was probably no question in his mind (or anyone else's for that matter) that he would do so as Hamlet, the role for which he was most famous. The sensation-seeking *Herald*, however, chose to believe differently. "Is the Assassination of Caesar to be Performed?" was the headline. "Will he appear as the assassin of Caesar? That would be, perhaps, the most suitable character." The unnamed writer goes on: "The blood of our martyred President is not yet dry in the memories of the people, and the very name of the assassin is appalling to the public mind: still a Booth is advertised to appear before a New York audience" (December 24, 1865). The *World* called the piece in the *Herald* "a most brutal attack," to which devotees of the theatre responded by packing the house (January 4, 1866). "Not only was every seat occupied," reported the *New York Daily Tribune*, "but every inch of standing room was eagerly expropriated by the thronging multitude. Seldom, indeed, has any New York theatre been this crowded, and never by an audience of a more intelligent class" (January 4, 1866).

Biographers tend to stress the enthusiasm with which the audience greeted the actor when he appeared in the second scene of the play on the opening night of January 3, 1866. Indeed, *The New York Times* reported that "the applause extended from the parquette to the dome . . . Mr. Booth—as he knows now—has no enemies" (January 4, 1866). Outside the theatre, however, the situation was somewhat different. "The crowd was immense," wrote the *World*, and "a cordon of police appeared at an early hour in the vestibule of the house, and those composing it were placed in various positions by the Captain of the Fifteenth Precinct." It is true that "the unanimity of feeling" of the playgoers prevented any outbreak; nonetheless, there were outside the theatre "ill-disposed persons . . . seeking to create disturbance" (January 4, 1866); the *World* later suggested that they were deliberately stirred up by the *Herald's* continued attack on Booth (January 23, 1866). Even years later, the bifurcation of popular response was recalled. "In the streets," reported *Harper's Weekly*, "as the crowds gathered, angry threats were heard" (June 14, 1891).

This event and the responses to it indicate two of the problems which would ultimately affect Edwin Booth's presentation of *Richard II* and the audience receptions of it. The first was that any association of the name Booth with assassination was bound to give rise to uneasiness, and *Richard II* is an assassination play. The second is the cultural difference between those playgoers referred to above, called at the time of the Macready-Forrest riot the "Silk-stocking Gentry," and those milling about in the street outside the theatre, whose tastes ran more to contemporary melodrama than Shakespeare or, more particularly, to the "Yankee" plays (*The Yankee Jailor, The Yankee Inventor*, etc.) which had proliferated in northern theatres during and after the Civil War.

That Booth was himself conscious of the first, with or without the aid of the *Herald*, is suggested by the fact that he did *not* appear in *Julius Caesar* again until 1871. Even then, however, when the play opened, the *Season*, a publication which Charles Shattuck calls "a scurrilous sheet," was quick to the attack, even though Booth carefully played Brutus as a misguided patriot attempting to save his nation from imperialism. The critic "wondered how Booth could be so morally callous as to stage the 'assassination play'": "How he then could have maintained his composure during the awful scene in which, in mockery, he played the part which John Wilkes Booth played with such dreadful earnestness, no one but Edwin Booth and his God can tell" (December 30, 1871). This attack continued even later in the run when Booth switched to playing Cassius, a role in which he was deemed by the *Herald* to be more successful because it called for "selfish passions": "Envy, malignant hatred, avarice, or cunning, for instance, we should expect him to simulate more effectively than magnanimity or exalted patriotism" (March 5, 1872; Shattuck, 146).

In this instance, however, Booth ultimately won the day. *Julius Caesar*, although originally scheduled for an eight-week run, actually played for twelve: eighty-five performances, a record for that play. I suggest that, having survived one "assassination play" with such success, he felt confident enough to try another. If this is the case, then over the next three years, during breaks from an onerous schedule at Booth's Theatre, he must have given some time to studying and preparing an acting version of *Richard II*.

It is also toward the end of this period that Booth lost what was to have been his greatest accomplishment—his theatre. His reputation as an actor was unchallenged, but his pocketbook was empty. Booth's Theatre had cost him $800,000 to build in 1869; by 1874, when he declared bankruptcy, the house was $200,000 in debt. Thus, in May 1875, when Augustin Daly approached him to appear in an engagement at the Fifth Avenue Theatre, they quickly made a deal from which both hoped to profit. Booth needed the money, and Daly wanted to elevate the status of his theatre by presenting the great tragedian in a number of his best-known roles. "The following," wrote Booth to Daly on June 2, "are the characters which comprise my repertory." In the list is "Richard 2nd," a part in which he had never appeared but which he was clearly prepared to take on. Two days later, Daly agreed to pay Booth "one-half the gross receipts of every performance up to $1500 and two-thirds of all above $1500" and, for whatever reason, suggested a program which included *Richard II*. On September 6, Booth forwarded the promptbooks for the selected plays and, presumably, the company went into rehearsal shortly afterward (Daly, 199–200).

Booth's alterations as recorded in the promptbook held at the Players' Club (Shattuck, 21, 22) serve many purposes, practical, conceptual, and dramatic. They reduce playing time to a comfortable two hours and fifty-seven minutes including intermissions, but they also keep the play firmly focused upon the tragedy of Richard as "an embodiment of afflicted majesty" (*New York Tribune*, November 9, 1875). As both Edmund and Charles Kean had done before him, Booth cut the whole of the Aumerle plot, the lengthy challenges, and most of the list scene. When the Garden scene was also deleted, however, not only did 107 lines disappear but so did testimony to Richard's inadequacies as gardener of the realm.

Still other cuts, of lines rather than whole blocks of text, might imply extradramatic concerns. From the restored 1.2, for example, Booth still omitted the Duchess' lines:

> Ah Gaunt, his blood was thine! That bed, that womb,
> That mettle, that self mould, that fashioned thee
> Made him a man; and though thou livest and breathest,
> Yet art thou slain in him. Thou dost consent
> In some large measure to thy father's death
> In that thou seest thy wretched brother die,
> Who was the model of thy father's life. (1.2.22–28)

This deletion may suggest either a personal sensitivity or a concern for possible audience reaction to any references to a slain brother. The same suggestion might explain the omission of 1.1.102–103, which refer to "a traitor coward, [who] / Sluic'd out his innocent soul through streams of blood."

Another way to render Richard more sympathetic and to strengthen Edwin Booth's interpretation of the king was to remove or lessen some of the sympathy the play accords to Bolingbroke. After the banishments at the end of act I, for example, in Booth's promptbook Gaunt leaves the stage with Richard and his farewell lines to his son are given to Northumberland—a change which alters the whole dramatic effect of the passage. With Bolingbroke's first responses omitted, the sequence begins:

> *North.* Thy grief is but thy absence for a time.
>   What is six winters? They are quickly gone.
>   Call it a travel that thou takest for pleasure.
> *Bol.* My heart will sigh when I miscall it so,
>   Which finds it an enforced pilgrimage.
> *North.* The sullen passage of thy weary steps
>   Esteem as foil wherein thou art set
>   The precious jewel of thy home return.

With the alteration, the dramatic projection shifts from the advice of a concerned father to his "high-stomached" son to a conspiratorial exchange in which a disgruntled nobleman urges a potential usurper to bide his time. The stage is thus set early for the progressive darkening of Bolingbroke and of those who supported him against the King. At the other end of the play, by cutting the whole of the last scene, a deletion much praised by the critics who thought the play was the better for ending with the king's death, Booth removed any suggestion of remorse on Bolingbroke's part and any notion of diminished responsibility. Indeed, after Richard's valiant attempt to defend himself against his murderers, Booth's version of the play ends on an ominous prophecy from which Exton's name (here restored to its proper place) has been deleted: "That hand shall burn in never-quenching fire / That staggers thus my person. Exton, thy fierce hand / Hath with the king's blood stain'd the king's own land"; 5.5.108–110. William Winter, although always somewhat prejudiced in Booth's favor, summed up what he saw as the actor's "embodiment":

> His Richard the Second was suffused with innate goodness, natural
> majesty, and tenderness of grief. He was a noble person, unjustly and

foully treated. The spectator viewed him with affectionate interest and remembered him as the emblem of misfortune, pathetic suffering, and a will too weak to withstand a turbulent world.

(New York Tribune, November 9, 1875)

Winter, however, was really speaking only for himself as spectator. The fact of the matter is that Richard II was not a success in the North.[3] Booth was praised for his acting of the title role, but neither Richard himself nor the play as a whole sat easily with the audience or the critics. The New York Times said that what was defective was the character of Richard himself. Having neither the "clean-cut activity of purpose and of thought" of Richelieu nor "the subjectiveness and melancholy intro- spection" of Hamlet, Richard's "middle ground" offered Booth no op- portunity for "mighty revelations" (November 9, 1875).[4] The Herald critic went so far as to say, "In none of Mr. Booth's parts does he so thor- oughly fill the stage as in Richard II," but added that

> the history of these mediaeval times is dead in this noisy generation. . . .
> There is nothing of the prance and movement of Henry V., where,
> when the play drags, the interest of the audience is kept up by the drums
> and blazonry of war. There is nothing of the terrible personality of
> Richard III., where, in spite of the terrible villainy of the character, we
> never cease to admire the mighty intellect which made even villainy
> tolerable in the eyes of generations.

How can we explain the failure of New York critics to warm to this play, despite all of Booth's theatrical and personal magnetism and the indications from the promptbooks that he designed his production to be a tragedy of a character overwhelmed by adversity rather than of one brought low because of personal inadequacy? Although no clear answer is available, the critic from the Herald suggests that what audiences wanted was positive action and aggressiveness; neither Shakespeare's nor Booth's Richard projected those qualities for them to admire. Nei- ther did the play. On the other hand, Richard's antagonist was a winner who had both of those qualities but was also ambitious and treasonous. This would appear to present the audience with an uncomfortable moral impasse.

We can also speculate about the unpopularity of Booth's Richard II by contrasting it to the success of other plays of Shakespeare. It was Colley Cibber's Richard III and Nahum Tate's King Lear that were preferred in the United States during most of the nineteenth century because, as Lawrence Levine has suggested, they "best fit the values and ideology of the period and the people." *Richard III* agreed closely "with the American sensibilities concerning the centrality of the individual, the dichotomy between good and evil, and the importance of personal responsibility." That Richmond saw the hand of Elizabeth of York as "toil's reward," Levine goes on, "must have warmed America's melodramatic heart as much as it confirmed its ideological underpinnings." As for Tate's *Lear*, Levine offers the comment of a nineteenth-century critic who wrote of Tate's ending for the play, "The moral's now complete . . . [Lear and Cordelia] survive their enemies and virtue is crowned with happiness" (43–44). In the face of such sentiments, we need not be surprised if Booth's *Richard II*—a play in which the hero has no real sense of wrongdoing, does *not* assume his responsibilities, and does *not* survive his enemy and the ambitious antagonist who has shown no virtue whatsoever has his "toil's reward" in the crown of England—failed to appeal to New York audiences.

Michael D. Bristol suggests that America, "lacking depth of cultural tradition," appropriated Shakespeare "as a compact and convenient functional equivalent for tradition in the broadest sense" (123). By the 1870s, however, a strong desire was emerging for cultural independence; this caused still another problem which Booth neither had foreseen nor seems to have registered—cultural nationalism. The *Herald*, not always sympathetic toward Booth, could praise him for bringing to the New York stage a Shakespearean play totally unfamiliar to most theatregoers (September 11, 1875). On the other hand, a critic writing for *Our Sketch Book* about the dashing of Booth's plans for "artistic triumphs" in his own theatre concludes: "Perhaps, if the result had been different, we should see him now, as he ought to be, encouraging the American drama, developing American talent, at the head of the proudest theatre in the world" (no. 14, new series).

One strong exponent of this cultural nationalism was Walt Whitman, who was an ardent theatregoer and admirer of Shakespeare even if somewhat grudgingly at times. Whitman's favorite play was *Richard II*, but his comments about it reflect the same uneasy ambiguity of response to both Richard and his play found in the comments of the New York critics. To Horace Traubel, with whom Whitman was less self-conscious than when he was writing for publication, he explained, "I would buy a cheap second-hand book—tear out the play I wanted [i.e., *RII*]—paste the sheets carefully together—keep them with me" (II: 265). And at another point, holding the home-bound pages of *Richard II* in his hand, he exclaimed:

> Richard: Shakespeare's Richard: one of the best plays, I always say, one of the best—in it's [*sic*] vehemence, power, even it's grace. . . . This Richard—this same Richard. How often have I spouted this—these first pages—on the Broadway stage-coaches, in the awful din of the streets. In the seething mass—that noise, chaos, bedlam—what is one voice more or less added, thrown in, joyously mingled in the amazing chorus?
>   (II: 245−246)[5]

At that moment, Whitman may have had fond memories of mingling Shakespeare's words with "the seething mass," but elsewhere he says, "The Shakespeare plays are essentially plays of the aristocracy . . . [in which] everything possible is done to make the common people seem common—very common indeed" (I: 140−141). This second declaration is much more in keeping with "a preponderant insistence of the poet upon a democratic genius in literature, as opposed to an aristocratic one, and his identification [of Shakespeare] with the latter, and of himself of his ideal with the former" (Harrison, 1203). Even though his close friend William O'Conner wrote to him, "There is nothing more evident to me than what Machiavel in the Prince did for tyranny—i.e. sow death for it by simply showing it up with perfect candour—[Shakespeare] did for feudality" (Traubel, I: 177), there is no evidence that Whitman agreed with him. Rather, much as he loved and was moved by *Richard II*, he judged it dangerous to the new nation. Shakespeare was among the poets who "exhale the principle of caste which we Americans have come on earth to destroy" (*Works*, V: 209; Harrison, 1209).

I am not claiming that the immediate audience for and critics of Booth's productions of *Richard II* consciously reacted to it as strongly as did Whitman, who saw himself as the voice of America. Rather, I am suggesting that the reactions to *Richard II* of poet and theatregoer appear to have significant similarities—at the same time as they were desirous of being "highbrow" by appreciating Shakespeare as a cultural icon, they were asked to applaud a play which presented the downfall of old-world hierarchical order as tragic. The result was discomforting enough to discourage further productions. In both cases, it was the play that caused the problems, not the actor playing the leading role. In the contemporary theatrical world, which tended to be mainly peopled by

New Yorkers, Edwin Booth was America's greatest tragedian and he was theirs. Indeed, having seen him through the terrible months after the assassination, they were almost protective of him. Booth may have been sensitive to what he thought might be touchy issues in *Richard II*, but the problem in the North in 1875 seems not to have been the possibility of political parallels to its historical narrative at all; it was a cultural-ideological alienation that caused the lack of enthusiasm.

The reverse seems to be true when trying to account for the over-whelming response of the Southerners when, at the beginning of the following year, Booth began his first tour south of the Mason-Dixon line since the end of the Civil War. The tour began in Baltimore, by-passed Washington, D.C., a city in which Booth refused to play to the end of his life, and continued through Virginia, South Carolina, Georgia, Alabama, Tennessee, and Kentucky before Booth parted with John Ford, the manager of the southern engagements, and headed north again through Ohio and Illinois. As with my attempt to account for its failure in the North, much of my explanation for the success of *Richard II* in the South is speculative, but let me begin by suggesting that here cultural-ideological concerns mattered less and political correlations a great deal more.

The Southerners, like the Northerners, had a strong self-image, but theirs was a different, even revered image: a vision of a lost Camelot of landed gentry, a softspoken and cultured aristocracy forced by defeat to endure the brashness of Yankee upstarts whom they held responsible for the turpitudes of Reconstruction. The review in the *Richmond Daily Dispatch* on the morning after Booth's opening catches some of the tone of nostalgia for past days and an assurance of cultural solidarity:

> Mr. Edwin Booth appeared last night at the Richmond Theatre for the first time since the war, and under circumstances that brought before the mind's eye in that Temple more of the pomp, grandeur, and mental and social brilliance than has been seen in Richmond since the proud days of drama before the war. . . . There were audiences once met in the Richmond Theatre that will not probably be ever excelled in critical acumen and refinement; but it is due to that which met last night to see the gifted Booth that it appreciated him fully and most delightfully.
>
> (January 18, 1876)

More immediate political concerns, however, influenced the audiences of the Confederate states to find analogies to their own situation in

Shakespeare's *Richard II*. Let's set the stage. The scene is Washington, D.C.; the time early January 1876. It is centennial year, and the nation at large is set to commemorate its first hundred years of existence. All the states are preparing to appropriate funds to finance joint and special celebrations in Philadelphia. At the same time, in the nation's capital, "with the approach of the eleventh anniversary of the war's end a universal amnesty bill which would restore civil rights to all Confederates was before Congress. The country expected its passage" (Strode, 411).

Then a bombshell fell. James G. Blaine, a Republican senator from the state of Maine, proposed a six-word amendment to the amnesty bill— "with the exception of Jefferson Davis." Blaine's motives were clear. Even though he knew his charges against Davis were unfounded, he wanted to be the next Republican president of the United States and was prepared to go to any lengths to gain support even if it meant reopening all the scars of the Civil War in his unwarranted attack upon the former president of the Confederacy. Blaine was, of course, trying to gain support for his candidacy for the presidency, but the central issue for those who supported the Blaine amendment was much more crucial than mere ambitious self-advancement. To restore Davis' rights as an American citizen would make him eligible again for election to public office, and many saw Davis' potential return to Congress as a grave danger to their vested interests. Davis, in other words, represented the same kind of threat to the power bosses in Washington as did Richard to the newly crowned Henry IV. After his capture, Davis had been kept a prisoner in the strongest fortress in the nation. An attempt to convict him of treason, a crime for which he could have been executed, had failed. The next best thing was to assure that he would be kept completely out of the public eye.

The South had called the Civil War the War of Northern Aggression; thus it would not be surprising if southern audiences at Booth's *Richard II* saw in the action of the play a parallel to their own defeat and in its hero a reenactment of the fortunes of Jefferson Davis. Lincoln, like Bolingbroke, had on his side overwhelming odds in sheer numbers and a grim personal determination to prevail; Jefferson Davis, like Richard, had little more than what some would argue as unwritten constitutional right on his. We might also note that in 1881, during the aftermath of the assassination of James Garfield, who, like Lincoln, had denounced secession and advocated force against the South, Booth was pestered by Nahum Cohen for information about John Wilkes. He finally wrote that he had seen little of his brother since childhood. "Professional engagements," he explained, "kept him mostly in the South, while I was employed in the Eastern and Northern States." However, he did give an account of a brief conversation the two had on the occasion of a family gathering. "When I told him," Booth recounted, "that I had voted for Lincoln's re-election he expressed deep regret, and declared his belief that Lincoln would be made king of America" (Grossmann, 227). Such a belief was not exclusively John Wilkes Booth's. Among southern contemporary writers, J. B. Jones wrote in *A Rebel War Clerk's Diary* that Davis had referred to Lincoln as "His Majesty Abraham the First" (Bryan, 384), John S. Wise in *The End of an Era* that "Lincoln incorporated to us the idea of oppression and conquest" (quoted in Francis Wilson, 301).[6] Such sentiments could provide still another connection between Lincoln and Bolingbroke, another would-be king, in the minds of southern audiences.

That the title role was played by a Booth delighted the Southerners further. They not only welcomed Edwin Booth, they lionized him so much that even the northern newspapers took notice. People from miles around, reported the *New York Daily Tribune*, flocked into centers where he was to perform. The reviewer singled out one play from the repertory: "His personation of *Richard II*, it is important to record, was a genuine success, particularly in Baltimore, Richmond, Charleston, and Savannah, which places are understood to be unusually exacting in critical views of the acted drama" (March 8, 1876). The *Louisville Courier-Journal*, on the other hand, referred to less charitable northern papers. A feature called "Small Talk" noted that "every time Edwin Booth makes a Southern tour the Northern Republican papers which talk about 'reform within the party' reprint this: 'Edwin Booth is making a professional tour through the South, exciting great enthusiasm and making a great deal of money. Everybody will be glad of it, though it is said that it is the brother of John Wilkes Booth quite as much as the actor which attracts such large and applauding audiences'" (March 13, 1876).

There can be little doubt that Booth's presence conjured up the ghost of the brother whose words as he slew Lincoln, "Sic semper tyrannis," are also the motto of Virginia, the first state to rescind its centennial appropriation in retaliation for the Davis rider attached to the Amnesty Bill. Indeed, on the very page on which the *Richmond Dispatch* printed its tribute to the Booth family (including John Wilkes) and its welcome to "the most gifted man on the stage in his day," the editorial condemned Blaine for his revival of "war-rancors" (January 15, 1867).

Since he was up to his ears in debt, Booth wanted this tour to be a financial success, but the onus for deliberately playing on the name of John Wilkes Booth must fall on John Ford, who, it will be remembered, had owned the theatre in which Lincoln was shot and who was now managing the tour for Edwin. He arranged that the names "FORD" and "BOOTH" would jointly appear in the largest print at the head of all advance publicity notices. Ford could not have foreseen, of course, the revival of "war-rancors," but he was as quick then as he was later to take advantage of the ambivalent southern attitude to Lincoln's assassin.

The press must also share the blame for cheap sensationalism. At the same time as it mocked the northern Republican papers, even the *Courier-Journal* was quick to pick up and print an article, "Graves of the Booths," which had been circulating ever since Edwin Booth had successfully petitioned for his brother's remains and buried them in the family plot. Happy as he was with the success of the tour and particularly of *Richard II*, Booth, who was not a man easy to anger, sent a copy of what he called the "ghoul-feast" to William Winter because, he wrote,

> I want you to see what I have to endure in the midst of my "glory." . . .
> All through the South,—from Balto. to this place [Louisville] I have
> been greeted with disgraceful anecdotes about my Father (all in the
> main false or exaggerated), and the flaunting in my face of buried cere-
> ments—raked up by these hyenas. . . . Tho' I have recd. much to be
> proud & grateful for at the hands of the Southern people . . . I sincerely
> hope I shall not be invited South again. (Watermeier, 58–59)

Of course he was invited to the South again, and he went, but he did not take *Richard II*. Whether he was conscious that the play struck close to southern sentiments is difficult to say. He certainly never mentions such particularities in audience response in his letters. It may be that the play was just too expensive to carry in his repertory for occasional performances in select locations. The tour, however, became another item for theatrical history in the United States. At his death, an event for which the press coverage in New York was greater than it had been for Abraham Lincoln, the *Morning Advertiser* wrote that when Booth went to the South in 1876 "the people swarmed to see him. It was by long odds the most brilliant tour the actor ever played in this or perhaps any country. Not a box office was open during this trip, all seats from pit to gallery being sold out weeks in advance" (June 7, 1893). The fact remains, however, that *Richard II*, overwhelmingly successful in cities

where it played to southern audiences, just could not earn its keep in
the northern metropolitan centers of New York, Boston, or Philadelphia,
and in 1879 it disappeared again from the American stage for more than
a half-century.

I have tried to explain the different receptions accorded Booth's
Richard II in terms of the different cultural and political contexts within
which the play was produced. Audiences in New York and throughout
the North, who were strongly pro-Union in their sympathies but had
no particular love for Lincoln,[7] continued to show their great admiration
for Edwin Booth even though they rejected the play as out of touch
with their own aggressively entrepreneurial energies. The South, which
could hardly be pro-Lincoln, considered the Booths "theirs" because the
family were Marylanders. Their great admiration and applause, however, extended to Booth's production of *Richard II* as well, a play which
I have suggested they found both politically and culturally compatible.
But there is little or no hard evidence to support such an explanation;
I can find no newspaper review, editorial, or political commentary which
states out-and-out that the circumstances which I have outlined led to
the play's reception in either venue. To be sure, the play's general stage
history tends to provide broad support for the explanation I have offered
here. Specific productions of the play can be shown to have been deliberately political (e.g., Nahum Tate's adaptation banned in 1681), but even
others without such overt designs tended to take on political and cultural coloration from the particular times in which they were produced.
As Andrew Gurr says in his introduction to the New Cambridge edition,
"Politics, whether open or subterranean, have always influenced attitudes to *Richard II*" (45). Moreover, the absence of politically centered
commentary is not surprising at least in the South, since the federal
government took control of the major newspapers at the end of the war
and military occupation did not end until 1876. I want to suggest that
the absence of evidence to support the view I have developed here may
actually strengthen the case. Let me try to explain this claim by returning to the place of the performance from which I began and offering another analogue.

Chicago was in the midwestern enclave of Free States and also in the
heart of Lincoln country: not only did the audience there reject the
play, but one of their number gave the actor a reception he remembered
the rest of his life. Booth had first played Richard II in Chicago during
the last leg of the tour that had taken him through the South. Even then,

the play had not been popular for reasons which were akin to the criticism it had received in New York. It lacked action; it was "too refined and spiritual" for "the city of the big shoulders" (*Chicago Tribune*, April 11, 1876). This time, however, the interest of the media was not in the play but in the attempted assassination, although in retrospect the comments seem to take on a personal focus as if the actor were not any more popular than the play in which he appeared.

Stuart Robson, for example, the comedian at the Hooley who had made such an astute observation on the shooting, could not seem to resist turning the potentially disastrous event against the actor himself. Although quoted as saying that had the attempt culminated in tragedy the actor would have been "terribly lamented by the American people," Robson nevertheless felt obliged to add that, as comedians, he and his partner recognized that the situation also had a "ludicrous side"—such "good advertisement" could turn the "poor house[s]" at McVicker's into a financial bonanza for Booth. "It was a new role for Booth—this target act." Implying that the whole business was a hoax, he even suggested that he should "hire some one to shoot at Crane" to ensure continued full houses at Hooley's. This insult to his integrity caused Booth much pain but, as a letter to William Winter shows, Robson and Crane's making light of the event "as an advertising dodge" was not his main concern. "Think of my poor mother," he wrote, "with all the horrible Past recalled so vividly by this newly adverted horror!" (Watermeier, 127).

What might be called the official attitude of the *Chicago Tribune* toward the attempt on Booth's life appeared in an editorial two days after the shooting (April 25, 1879). In the first quarter of the piece, Edwin Booth is praised not only as an eminent actor but also as a modest, retiring man of exemplary character. Look, however, at the description of the attempted assassination:

> Yet he suddenly becomes an innocent, unsuspecting, and helpless target for a man who seeks to kill him, who selects an elevated front seat in the theatre at close range, and who fires twice while Mr. Booth is sitting alone on the stage under the glare of a limelight, thrown by a window in the scene, and making him literally a "shining mark."

Eyewitness accounts of the shooting printed in the *Tribune* and in the *New York Times* (April 24, 1879) give quite a different scenario. Mark Gray was not sitting in "an elevated front seat" but to "the extreme left of the balcony"; he did not fire "at close range" but from the gallery;

and, although it is true that simulated moonlight came through a grating, "the stage was quite dark, and it is probably owing to this fact that the assassin missed in his aim, and the bullets, instead of entering the person of the actor, penetrated the scenery and buried themselves in the stage floor."

The *Tribune* editorial is not recreating an image from Chicago's McVicker's Theatre at all but one which recalls the horror of an event which took place, almost to the day, fourteen years earlier in Ford's Theatre in Washington, D.C. The similarity between the two events is so uncanny that there should be little wonder that in the editor's theatrical reconstruction from his mind's eye the "shining mark" seated in an "elevated front seat" in the glare of the stage footlights and "at close range" for his assassin became Abraham Lincoln rather than Edwin Booth, the bearer of a name particularly odious. Three days later (April 27, 1879) and for no apparent reason, the same newspaper picked up what might be construed as the whole midwestern, pro-Lincoln, anti-Booth reaction to the attempted assassination. The *Cleveland Leader*, wrote the *Tribune*, thinks " 'Edwin Booth will learn after a while to stay away from Chicago' "; and then added, "What! and go to Cleveland! 'Hardly ever!' "

The Lincoln legend, says Richard Hofstadter, came "to have a hold on the American imagination that defies comparison with anything else in its political mythology" (92). How much more so might this be true in Chicago, where Lincoln was considered a native son; where the "log cabin to White House" part of the American dream had its beginnings; how much more understandable an unwillingness to play gracious host to one whose very name was an anathema.

The Chicago newspapers made nothing of the fact that *Richard II* is an assassination play, that Mark Gray had a copy of *Richard II* in his hand during the performance, or that he attempted to end the actor's life during the scene in which the King is assassinated. In fact, the main interest both in the press and in the courtroom appears to have been whether or not Gray was insane. That question was quickly decided in the affirmative on May 10. This does not mean that the Midwest was necessarily totally unsympathetic to Edwin Booth, took vicarious pleasure in his misfortune, or consciously wished him any ill, but rather that the whole matter was dangerously unsettling. As a result, when the shooting that threatened to bring to the surface anger and hatred best left buried was quickly brought to a close with the verdict that Mark Gray was mad, it was as if the deep national division in the American psyche caused by the Civil War and the assassination which followed was swept under the carpet. Perhaps, for different reasons it is true, Mark Gray if kept in the public eye was as unsettling a figure as Jefferson Davis—each a grim reminder of dangerous political tensions.

In investigations like this, theatre historians are like juries in that they try to reconstruct past events in order to come to some form of judgment. When hard evidence exists, the task is fairly straightforward. When such evidence does not exist, the law allows some leeway and circumstantial evidence, if enough of it points in one direction or another, becomes admissible as providing probable cause. In this case, by reading between the lines of the available research materials, by using what might be called "soft" evidence, I am suggesting that the probable reason why a cloak of silence dropped about Mark Gray and the connections between the murder of Richard II, the slaying of Lincoln, and the attempted assassination of Edwin Booth is that they were just too painful and dangerous to consider. So were the obvious political and cultural links between Jefferson Davis and the South to the historical substance of Shakespeare's play. Even in New York, least threatened by whatever there was in *Richard II* that made its audiences uneasy and where Booth was himself and not his brother's brother, commentators on the southern tour, on the injustices to Davis, and on the attempted assassination in Chicago were remarkably circumspect.

By what I am suggesting was a significant silence the national unrest of the few decades after the American Civil War was kept under wraps; the potential for renewing "war rancors" by bringing out into the open the reasons behind the divided attitudes toward Edwin Booth himself and toward his version of Shakespeare's *Richard II* was thwarted. The scars of Civil War were not obliterated; it was a case of pretending they were not there. Only during the Spanish American War at the end of the century, which Secretary of State John Hays called "a splendid little war," in which, as Richard Mansfield rhapsodized, the two cubs of the lion (North and South) fought side by side, "staunch and valiant and free and strong,"[8] was any real sense of national unity achieved.

NOTES

1. All quotations from *Richard II* are taken from *The Riverside Shakespeare*.

2. There were eight full-length columns on the front and second pages of the April 24 edition of the *Chicago Tribune* from which details were picked up by every major newspaper in the country.

3. Originally, Booth was to play at Daly's for six weeks, during which *Richard II* was to play five nights and a matinée in the fifth week. However, the engagement was cut to four when Booth's recuperation from an accident took longer than expected. This may also be the reason for shortening the number of performances of *Richard II*. On the other hand, the play's dismal financial showing might also suggest that Daly persuaded Booth to substitute *Hamlet* to help bolster their profits. Joseph Frances Daly says:

> It will be interesting to know the pecuniary results of this, one of the most important of Booth's engagements in New York: *Hamlet* was played nine times to an average of $1855; *Iago* three times to an average of $1696; *Richelieu* three times to an average of $1675; *Shylock* once to $1503; *Othello* once to $1446; *King Lear* three times to an average of $1436; *Pescara* four times to an average of $1125; and *Richard II* four times to an average of $731. The largest receipts of the engagement were at the two matinées in which Miss [Fanny] Davenport played with Mr. Booth—"The Lady of Lyons" drew $2176 and "The Stranger" and "Katherine and Petruchio," $2152. (205)

The Shakespearean plays with which Booth could still fill the house were those for which he was most famous, and certainly *Richard II* was not one of them—not in New York and not in other large northern cities. After the disappointing reception of the play in 1876, when Booth included it in a return engagement at the Boston Theatre in the following year, the managers balked. "The picayune management of this shop," he wrote to William Winter, "don't want to do *Richard II* although it is announced and as I get a *certainty* (not daring to trust the sharing system, from past experience) I cannot well insist on doing what they think will not draw." A week or so later from Pittsburgh, he complained again, "I really cant judge how many [prompt]books could be disposed of—I have fears for *Richd 2*. The d——d managers fight against it & plead for other plays." However, on April 7, 1878, he crowed, "I have settled the *Lear* & *Richard 2* business with Ford— I shall do both!" (letters 266, 269, and 273 in the Folger collection). Nevertheless, the writing was on the wall for *Richard II*. Booth had played Richard in New York on February 15, 1878, and again in October it was scheduled once during a five-week engagement at the Fifth Avenue Theatre. Finally, having failed to arouse sufficient interest either in the audience or with the theatre managers, Booth appeared in *Richard II* for the last time on November 19, 1879.

4. Booth's portrayal of Cardinal Richelieu in Edward Bulwer-Lytton's play was one of his most popular and acclaimed roles.

5. "A copy of *Richard II* which answers this description is among the treasures presented by [Thomas] Harned to the Library of Congress" (Harrison, 120n6n10).

6. Recent historians have seen Lincoln's behavior as ambitious (Hofstadter, 133) and his "extraordinary use of executive power" as tending to what we now call the "imperial presidency" (Fehrenbacher, 212), or what Davis and others at the time perceived as quasi-monarchial.

7. In May 1860, much to the chagrin of the powerful contingent from New York and their highly qualified candidate, William Henry Seward, Abraham Lincoln had won the Republican nomination for president in a shady political coup which involved bargaining Pennsylvania's votes for a cabinet post for their candidate, Simon Cameron. An example of how long it took for the myth of Lincoln to emerge after his assassination and how much New York loved Booth can be seen in the fact that when Edwin Booth died in 1892, the press coverage and public mourning in New York were greater than they had been for Lincoln twenty-seven years earlier.

8. This is the refrain in Mansfield's poem "The Eagle's Song," quoted by Wilstach (297–298). Also interesting in Mansfield's poem is the acknowledgment of innate differences between the North and the South. Stanzas 3 through 5 read (emphasis mine):

> Two were the sons that the country bore
> To the Northern lakes and the Southern shore,
> *And Chivalry dwelt with the Southern son,*
> *And Industry lived with the Northern one.*

> Tears for the time when they broke and fought!
> Tears for the price of the union wrought!
> And the land was red in a sea of blood,
> Where brother for brother had swelled the flood!

> And now that the two are one again,
> Behold on their shield the word "Refrain!"
> And the lion cubs twain sing the Eagle's song,
> "To be staunch and valiant and free and strong!"

9

Theatre Archives at the Intersection of Production and Reception: The Example of Québécois Shakespeare

Leanore Lieblein

The reconstruction and analysis of Shakespeare theatre productions, whether they be current or in the recent or distant past, depend upon archival materials.[1] However, the material that survives in theatre archives comes from a variety of sources and was produced for a number of different purposes. In consequence, because such documentation is far from disinterested, its evidential authority is often regarded with skepticism. Nevertheless I would argue that theatre archives cannot and need not be disqualified as a source of information, even though it is important to be aware of the ideological and other investments that produced the materials the archives contain.

The nature of the evidence available to document theatre productions is related to the nature of the theatre event itself. Archival materials are produced by individuals: directors, designers, actors, publicists, and spectators (including reviewers), among others. All of these individuals bring with them cultural assumptions and vested interests, sometimes shared, sometimes not, and the Shakespeare they stage and see may or may not be for each of them the same. The archive collects what they imagined, or planned, or expected, or experienced; in sum, what they saw—or foresaw. But that is all that remains. As Thomas Postlewait notes, quoting the historian Carl Becker, "The [theatre] historian 'cannot deal directly with the event itself, since the event itself has disappeared. What he [*sic*] can deal with directly is a *statement about the event'* " ("Historiography," 160). In other words, the theatre event as written about is never present, but always elsewhere. It leaves its trace in the notations of the promptbook, in the sketches of the designers, in the promises of the publicity and the photos of the press package. It survives as well in the memory of the spectator and the descriptions and judgments of the reviewer, the journalist, or the critic.

When each of these accounts tells a different story, which account does one privilege? Postlewait's use of the term *event* is important, and the theatre historian's choice of word may be contrasted with the terminology of the performance critic, for whom the theatre production or performance is a *text*.[2] Given the necessarily local, partisan, contingent, and contradictory nature of reviews, programs, and other such documents, one may question whether it is possible to reconstruct a single "performance text," which may in fact be inaccessible. I would like to suggest, however, that for the discussion of performance as event—for which I follow Barbara Hodgdon's definition of "a series of readings produced by individuals from an encounter with a text within a particular social situation" ("Splish Splash," 29)—it is precisely the diversity of viewing positions and agendas that make such documents a rich source. While it is important to recognize that the provenance of different types of documentation implies different vested interests, it is equally important to welcome, even rejoice in, the diversity of interests they represent, because this diversity helps us to contextualize the theatre event through what it has seemed to mean and seemed to be to a variety of people.

Traditionally theatre historians faced with a multiplicity of documents have attempted to produce a synthesis—a single internally coherent account that effaces inconsistencies while it accommodates the broadest range of evidence—that comes to "stand for" the performance. They have found their inadvertent allies in those theatre artists for whom the creative act is "intuitive" and "spontaneous" and killed by reflection. However, a quest for the performance as a single entity is neither realizable nor desirable. It violates the very nature of the theatrical event, which, because it results from a multiplicity of investments and viewing positions, is itself mediated and multiple. Further, our only access to the event is through its representation, reception, and interpretation by its various constituencies, including its producers and audiences. We can try to disentangle the viewing positions represented in theatre archives, not in order to abstract them into a coherent integrity, but rather to view theatrical performance as a network of relations.

The information that actually comes from a company's archives varies. The material traces of the production itself—things like the promptbook, designs, notes, and letters—I do not intend to discuss in this essay,[3] because I am focusing on the way a company represents its work to its external audience. I am interested, however, in the contents of the "dossier de presse," which these days even small companies seem to be quite good about collecting, keeping, and making available. Items like press releases, programs, and publicity (including photographs, posters, ads, and so on) are acts of communication, designed to represent the production to the public. Reviews, eyewitness accounts, and journalistic or scholarly articles, if they exist, constitute the documentation of reception. Falling between reviews, at one end of the spectrum, and publicity at the other, are interviews, promo pieces, and reports of press conferences, in which a critic or journalist represents the production from the point of view of the producing artists or companies, but frames or mediates that representation by posing the questions, selecting the details to be included, and making (or being constrained by) choices of things like diction, tone, and style. Taken together this material constitutes the discourse generated by the production.

Needless to say, this discourse is neither disinterested nor unaffected by other discourses, and the motives that generate it may vary enormously. The description of a production cooked up by the publicist of a large commercial theatre will be different from the discussion for the program created by the dramaturge of a regional repertory theatre. Two reviewers of a single production, one writing for a large-circulation daily newspaper and the other for a weekly with a narrowly targeted audience, will be addressing very different readers, and the expectations and interests of those same readers will change when they read a review of the same production in a specialized theatre review.

There is a notable amount of resistance to the very kinds of materials that I am proposing we need to take seriously. The documents generated to represent the production to its public tend to be cited gratefully by theatre historians hungry for traces of performance, but are often resented at the time of their issue as attempts to tell critics and audiences what to think. Supposedly, documents such as press releases, posters, and programs are meant to attract attention and/or provide information. But they do other things as well. As Ann Wilson has shown, in the case of a recent production of *Hamlet* the program was also designed to make the audience "feel comfortable in the theatre" ("Starters," 52) and to "direct an audience's reception of the play" (49).[4]

Analysis of documents like programs and posters, I would argue, contributes to our insight into the nature of the performance event. But it is precisely because items like programs do not (cannot) leave an audience totally to its own devices that documentation emanating from a theatre company itself has been viewed with suspicion. Particularly in the Anglo-American theatre tradition, the play—or the performance—has been taken to be "the thing." It is presented as an unmediated artifact that is expected to "speak for itself" and be understood "in its own terms." The Broadway tradition of a single program for all shows being performed in a given week (which may include a vast range of musical comedies, tragedies, classical and recent revivals, etc.) is ostensibly a refusal to come between the play and its audience (although that refusal is part of its representation of itself).[5]

The resistance to extraperformance communication with an audience by some theatre artists is related to the still asserted (in some places) notion that the creative act results from "inspiration" and that its authenticity is guaranteed by spontaneity, is contaminated by reflection, and is unchanged by the nature of its audience or the context of its production; in other words, that it is unchangeable and unchanging. This view further implies that the creative act results in a transparently readable artifact that is diminished by explanation. If communication does not take place, it is the spectator who has failed. The view is exemplified in the response of director Michael Bogdanov to a student question during a postperformance discussion of his RSC touring-to-schools production of *Macbeth* at the Cottesloe Theatre in 1983. Asked about an interesting and unusual treatment of the witches, he shrugged: "I don't know; it just happened." It is also seen in the half-serious response of Terry Hands as artistic director of the Royal Shakespeare Company to a question about dramaturgical work at the RSC: "Dramaturgy," he wrote, "grows out of an intellectual tradition; we have no intellectuals."[6]

Such comments are disingenuous in their implication that a performance has "no message" and that it "speaks for itself." In contrast to the conviction that conceptualization and discursive intervention corrupt the purity of artistic invention is the attitude more prevalent in northern and eastern Europe, influenced probably by the German tradition and practice of dramaturgy that goes back to G. E. Lessing in the eighteenth century. It is the sense that the production *is* an act of interpretation and a product of analysis and reflection, as seen in the archival traces of the preliminary research and discussion that lead up to a production as well as in the public communications that follow. Press releases, programs, interviews, etc., in this tradition often contain an account of how a particular production evolved, what precipitated it, what issues were involved, and why they were interesting enough to be explored.

To some this tradition smacks of a preemptive strike: it is too much like telling an audience what to see and how to respond. Others are particularly sensitive to its potential for abuse, precisely because they may have experienced firsthand the interference of autocratic regimes in the operations of the arts. Thus Antoine Vitez, of Russian origin and director general of the Comédie Française before his death, thought of dramaturges, who in eastern European national theatres were responsible for generating this kind of interpretive material and were after all (like other artists) government employees, as "thought police" (Badiou, 14). Others would argue that telling people what one is doing represents honesty, communication and dialogue, sharing the process, and making oneself accountable.

But the biases and the insights of the discourses of production are not necessarily mutually exclusive; it may be *in* the biases that we find the insights, as in many of the early Berliner Ensemble productions. And if the cumulative record of a production's view of itself must be read with a healthy skepticism (but read!), the same is no less true of the documents of reception.

For example, everyone loves to hate the critics (Wilson, "Deadpan"; Prosser, 17), but as theatregoers and as theatre historians, we find ourselves dependent upon them (Saddlemyer, 136). We know the limitations of theatre reviews: they tend to be hastily written, often contain errors of fact, are frequently edited into incoherence, and occasionally have axes to grind. Reviewers seem to be more comfortable writing about things like acting (and hence character) and often ignore things like lighting, sound design, and use of space. At their worst theatre reviews may be written by people who know little, and couldn't care less, about theatre, and who work for people whose prime interest is to sell newspapers (Wardle).

Nevertheless, a review does what its name implies: it re-views, however partially, a performance. Even when to other viewers it may seem most unsatisfactory as a *record* of performance, it remains extremely interesting as a *reading* of a performance. Since the performance as a single transparent entity, an idealized authentic original, may, as I have been suggesting, be inaccessible anyway, the record of performance is made up of such readings. However idiosyncratic they may be, they in fact contribute not only to the climate of reception but also to the shaping and promotion of the theatre event itself.

Clearly the documentation of both production and reception has its value, even if it also has its limitations. More importantly, I would like to suggest that the visions of the producing company and its audiences are not mutually exclusive: rather, they are in dialogue with one another and inevitably intertwined. In fact, I would argue that a consideration of both is necessary in order to take the measure of the theatre event.

Media relations, as we shall see, provide one example of a point of intersection. That the language of a production's press release often shows up in the reviews of that production is a demonstrable fact. It does not follow, however, that this echo proves the co-optation of the critic. While it may be that the independence of the critic has been compromised, it may also be that the critic and the show's producers are in agreement or, quite simply, speak the same "language." Rather than discredit documents that promote productions and documents that respond to them, I would suggest that the following guidelines may help us to use them:

The more views of a theatre event, the better.

An account originating with a producing company is not necessarily more (or less) useful than the account of a reviewer or any other account.

One's own recollections or responses are neither more (nor less) valuable than someone else's.

Favorable views (or reviews) are no more (or less) useful than unfavorable views or reviews.

Mutually exclusive or contradictory views are important to consider in relation to one another.

In the remainder of this essay I implement these guidelines in a discussion of recent French-language productions of Shakespeare in Québec. I hope to show that a single script, its words unchanged, may change its significance over time, that a single production may be variously described to different audiences, and that members of the same audience may represent constituencies that perceive a supposed same production

differently. Once again, my interest is in the different particular circumstances that constitute various theatre events, in contrast to some gener-
alization about a single performance text. An examination over time of
the rhetoric produced by companies to promote their plays and by critics
to respond to them helps us to understand theatrical performance as a
social and political event which can be illuminated by conjunctions and
disjunctions in the discourses of production and reception. Finally, it
helps us to understand that the production of Shakespeare in French in
Québec is an "event" that is produced by the readings it generates.

Shakespeare performance in French in Québec, especially in the latter
half of this century when issues of political and cultural independence
have been a major preoccupation, has traditionally had two functions,
the legitimating and the parodic. As at Stratford and elsewhere in Canada, the performance of Shakespeare, the central text of the dominating
power, has been taken to be a sign of cultural seriousness and maturity.
However, Québec's relationship to British colonialism is complicated by
a sense of oppression by and alienation from English Canada. The ability
to deform or treat Shakespeare with irreverence (in what Brisset, 115,
has called "la traduction iconoclaste") has been an important liberating
gesture, as seen in the grotesque *Lear* of Jean-Pierre Ronfard (1977), in
Jean-Claude Germain's *Rodéo et Juliette* (1970), and, most famously, in
the political allegory of Robert Gurik's 1968 *Hamlet, prince du Québec.*
In Gurik's play King Claudius was associated with "l'Anglophonie," the
Queen with the church, Polonius with Prime Minister Lester B. Pearson, Laertes with Pierre Elliott Trudeau, his minister of justice who was
to succeed him as a strongly federalist prime minister, Horatio with the
pro-independence party leader René Lévesque, and "le Spectre paternel"
with Charles de Gaulle, while Hamlet's "To be or not to be" soliloquy
was rendered as "To be or not to be free" ("Etre ou ne pas être libre," 73).
As an example of a text whose significance as perceived by both the
producing company and its audience has changed with time, we may
look at Michel Garneau's translation of *Macbeth.* The publication and
performance in 1978 of a *Macbeth* "traduit en québécois" by Michel
Garneau was experienced as a politically significant act (Dassylva). In
1978, two years before the anticipated referendum on Québec sovereignty, a translation into "québécois," which was clearly meant to be
distinguished from "français," affirmed that Québec had a language of

its own that was worthy of even "le grand Will" (Lévesque, "Asselin"; Gélinas, "La Fête"). As the authors of an article in *Cahiers du théâtre jeu* wrote at the time, "Just as Shakespeare, through his work, gave poetic status to a language that did not yet have it, Garneau wishes to demonstrate the richness of the Québec language and place it on equal footing with other languages" (Andrès and Lefèbvre, 84).[7] Garneau himself explained that his translation affirmed the right of Quebeckers to the masterpieces of world dramaturgy in their own language, rather than in, say, contemporary European French (Larue-Langlois).

Garneau's Québécois, with its deliberate archaisms, functioned not only to retrieve the Edenic language of "our great grandfathers" (Talbot; Brisset, 235), but explicitly to serve as a "langue légitime" (Thaon, 207), "the language of a people, and not the anemic instrument of an oppressing elite" (Larue-Langlois). In a recent study of theatrical translation in Québec, Annie Brisset goes further to demonstrate how the Garneau translation explicitly conflated the Scotland of *Macbeth* with the New France of Québec history and refigured the struggle to overthrow the tyrant Macbeth as a struggle for the national liberation of "not'pauv'-pays" (193–251). Clearly Garneau's text inscribed itself in the separatist political discourse in circulation at the moment of its creation and publication, and his own representation of it in interviews was echoed in analyses and reviews.

Fifteen years later, in 1993 to be precise, this translation, along with two others by Garneau (of *Coriolanus* and *The Tempest*), was performed in a *mise-en-scène* by Robert Lepage in Montreal at the Festival du Théâtre des Amériques. This time "traduit en québécois" meant something else. In fact Shakespeare was no longer translated but, according to the Festival brochure, "réinventé." Garneau the translator was linked with Lepage the director in a "rencontre de deux magiciens" or, in the words of the English version of the same text, "a tour de force of linguistic and theatrical alchemy" (5). The emphasis therefore was no longer on the translation's relationship to the political and cultural agenda of the community for which it was translated; rather, it was on the verbal calisthenics of the translator. *Coriolanus*, according to the brochure, is translated into an "international Québécois" (6), *Macbeth* into "a harsh, sensual French similar to that spoken in Québec during the 17th century" (7), and *The Tempest* into "'classical' Québécois" (8). The politics and cultural agenda of Garneau's translations had changed.

The Québécois of *Macbeth*, in 1978 for Garneau the language of a potentially independent Québec, in 1993 takes its place in a historically
defined evolution: it has its source in a seventeenth-century "français
rude et sauvage" (7) but, in a Québec ready to participate in the world's
theatre, is capable of incarnation as both a "classical" and an "international" language.

I leave it to others to reflect upon the definition of a classical and of an
international Québécois, though their very appellation invokes a disem-
bodied sense of language. But I suggest that the invitation to experience
Garneau's *Macbeth* in 1993 is very different from that extended in 1978
and that, as I have been suggesting, the play the audience is invited
to experience is no longer the same, even if the script has not changed.
In an international theatrical arena, as part of a "Cycle Shakespeare"
unified by a single director and a single translator, the language of Garneau's translation is now related to the language of the other plays rather
than to the issues of its own play and promoted as an accomplishment in
itself rather than as an instrument: "It is to a journey in the evolution of
a language that the Théâtre Repère invites you" (brochure, 5).

The array of linguistic registers was alluded to by all seven journalists
reporting on Lepage's April 7 press conference and became a truism of
many of the reviews that followed. It is interesting by way of contrast
that the press release for the Festival d'Automne (1992) production in
Paris gave a different emphasis. The very same linguistic "nuances" and
"distinctions" (quotation marks in the original) were described as tren-
chant mirrors ("miroirs incisifs") that could reflect "the origin of our
common language and, beyond it, of language itself."

In addition, the Paris press release also spoke of the three plays as a
journey into the innermost depths of the European experience, a reading
that was nowhere offered in the documentation for the Québec performance and that, had it been, would have been unlikely to resonate.
Clearly, a production takes place in specific geographic, historic, social,
and other contexts. If, in its most negative construction, a press release
is an attempt to "manipulate" an audience, it cannot do so without first
seeing that audience and making an informed assessment about the
terms to which and in which it is able to respond.[8]

Thus is it no surprise that Robert Lepage's 1992 production of *A Midsummer Night's Dream* for the Royal National Theatre in London dif-
fered radically from his *Songe d'une nuit d'été* discussed below. Even so,
reviews of the London *Dream* suggest that British audiences and the

Théâtre Repère drew upon different theatrical traditions to make different assumptions about performing Shakespeare.[9]

Even locally, however, a single production may find more than one audience, more than one community of reception. Thus, while the discourse of production may match one community's discourse of reception, it may be refused, contested, or ignored by another. This happened in Montreal in 1988, during what was variously called "le printemps shakespeare," "un printemps shakespearien," or "l'événement Shakespeare," when Shakespeare was "l'enfant chéri de la scène montréalaise" (Camerlain, 5). The Shakespearean spring featured well-received productions of *The Tempest* (dir. Alice Ronfard, Théâtre Expérimental des Femmes at l'Espace GO), *A Midsummer Night's Dream* (dir. Robert Lepage at le Théâtre du Nouveau Monde), and the plays of Shakespeare's second tetralogy (done as *Le Cycle des rois*, dir. Jean Asselin, Omnibus, at l'Espace Libre).

What was remarkable about the discussion surrounding all three 1988 productions, in contrast to the politicized Shakespeare of the 1970s, was the almost total absence of political analysis or of context-specific reading. Rather, the language of promotion (in programs, press releases, interviews) and the language of reception (in reviews, citations, and critical articles)—and they were in agreement—reveal that, in spite of what could be read as postmodern and dislocative performance, the productions of all six plays (or five, since the two parts of *Henry IV* were compressed into one) were framed by an essentializing discourse that emphasized the greatness, the universality, and the timelessness of Shakespeare and resulted in productions that, by taking their own theatricality as their subject, would be able to speak not only to their Québec audiences but to audiences elsewhere, especially abroad.[10] The exception was the anglophone critics. As we shall see, they continued to produce context-specific readings which addressed and commented on local political issues.

Over and over again, in both publicity and reviews, the greatness of Shakespeare was affirmed. For critic Robert Lévesque, Shakespeare was "the most famous playwright in the history of theatre" ("Quand Shakespeare"); for director Jean Asselin, he was "the theatre's mentor and its greatest author" (St-Hilaire, "Le Printemps"). Actor Robert Gravel concurred: "I don't think there exists a greater author than he" (Choquette). In a headline in *La Presse* (March 12, 1988) *La Tempête* was described as "the testament of an eternal author" ("Le Testament"). And director

Robert Lepage said in an interview in *Le Devoir*, "I have the sense that Shakespeare will always be there to relaunch us [pour nous relancer]" (Lévesque, "A Montréal").

In addition to his celebrated greatness, Shakespeare is now no longer seen as the vehicle of cultural nationalism but as the most universal of writers. According to Lepage, "He doesn't belong to the history of theatre, he belongs to that of humanity" (St-Hilaire, "Le Printemps"). Clearly "humanity" in this statement transcends the local and temporal in which the *history* of theatre is mired. Shakespeare is severed from the history of theatre in order to enable theatre to transcend history and embody the ostensible timelessness and universality of human nature. Not only is *The Tempest* "a play on the human condition," but, according to a press release, "Prospero's island is, in a way, the world of the theatre." Similarly, Lepage, speaking of the rotating platform on which *A Midsummer Night's Dream* was performed, writes in the program notes, "The island is either the world or the stage," reminding us that "for the Elizabethans [and by implication for us] . . . the stage was the world and the world the stage."[11]

There was a direct relationship between the implications of this essentialist view and the *mises-en-scène* of the plays. The productions themselves strove to embody the timelessness claimed for Shakespeare by the directors—a claim accepted by the reviewers. Sharing the view of Alain Pontaut on *Le Cycle des rois* in *Le Devoir*, they showed "the desire of Shakespeare to attach himself to the theatrical universe rather than to historical truth."

To begin with, all three plays used sets that resisted historical or geographical reference. Prospero's island, we have seen, suggested the world of the theatre and the theatre of the world, but, as *La Presse* pointed out, did not represent a particular country (Beaunoyer, "'Le Songe'"). Similarly, though in a program note Robert Lepage compared the wood of *A Midsummer Night's Dream* to Shakespeare's island England, he too concluded, as we have seen, that the island was the world and/or the stage. Almost no critics mentioned that the platform was in the shape of "l'île britannique," and one of the two who did made no use of the point in his reading of the production or response to it (David; Ackerman, "French Theatre's Love Affair"). Even the set of the Henriad, though its angles evoked for some the polygons of the Elizabethan public theatre, suggested to most an image of its world as a stage. Although the reflecting surfaces multiplied the actors' images and gave back to the audience images of itself, nobody spoke of the dislocations this multiplication of images might bring about.

Costumes too defied periodization. The costumes of *The Tempest*, for example, were described by Daniel Guérard in a radio broadcast as "timeless, completely outside of time." Meredith Caron's very baroque and highly praised costumes for Lepage's *Midsummer Night's Dream* contained suggestions of an Elizabethan silhouette, but were deliberately and grotesquely overdone to suggest that these were "play-acted" Elizabethans (who were playing Athenians). It was the costumes of *Le Cycle des rois* by Yvan Gaudin (who received for them the prize of the Association québécoise des critiques de théâtre) that drew the most comment. They were built from materials gathered in the secondhand shops of the poor quarters of Montreal, the hand-me-downs of twentieth-century urban living. $9,000 worth of old clothes, curtains, bric-a-brac, and disused household appliances were transformed into costumes for 130 characters (Lévesque, "Le Prix"); an old birdcage became a crown, a discarded film reel the spiraling top of a bishop's crook. This was a theatre made in and of its time, but no more representing its own time than it represented the Elizabethan period.

The blend of the Elizabethan and the modern suggested the continuity or interchangeability of different historical periods, and the lavishness and theatricality of all three productions elicited substantial comment for their own sake. Alice Ronfard drew much attention for her extensive use of video screens and synthesized music. Even her use of space was considered "luxurious" ("Un Printemps"). As the press release made clear, the audience had to compete with the set: "The stage invades nearly all the space. . . . Only 100 seats are reserved for the audience."

Robert Lévesque in *Le Devoir* associated the scale and scope ("démesure," with its implication of recklessness, and "générosité" were his words) of the Shakespearean productions with a general tendency in Québec theatre of the 1980s toward "entreprises au long souffle" ("Robert Lepage"). Others, however, pointed out that its inspiration was far from local. Pat Donnelly in the *Gazette*, under a headline that alluded to "Songe's mix of Oz and Cats," suggested that the production "owe[d] as much to Andrew Lloyd Webber as it does to Shakespeare." And in a radio broadcast René Homier Roy described the same play as "quasiment Broadway et très Paris en tous cas."

This theatricality, which was an end in itself, was thematized in each of the three productions. In the case of *The Tempest*, it was emphasized through the doubling of the role of Prospero with a figure in modern dress called "The Actor," whose presence encouraged "reflection upon the theatre as the locus of the Other" (David). The three video screens also promoted a sense of the theatre as a site of image-making. On them were projected images of the action taking place before the eyes of the audience, but also of action being performed live offstage, as well as footage prerecorded for this production and sometimes, as in the case of a sinking battleship in the storm scene, archival footage. In *A Midsummer Night's Dream*, the dizzying turns of events were literally generated by Puck and the other actors who got down from the platform and pushed it to make it rotate. Even the conspicuously local origins of the semiotic richness and splendor of *Le Cycle des rois* drew attention to its own theatricality. It spoke not of the poverty suggested by the second-hand stores from which its material elements had come, but of the ingenuity of the designer in transforming them. The fact that, in spite of being recognizable as contemporary objects, they could be made to represent the England (and France) of Shakespeare's text worked to assert twentieth-century Québec's closeness to what was fantasized to be Shakespeare's world rather than its distance from it.

In *Le Cycle des rois*, fourteen actors played over 130 roles with little attempt to hide their own identities in order to show "the interchangeability of roles and destinies" (Ouaknine). This breaking down of the boundaries of social and gender identity was also present in Lepage's exploration of androgynous, ungendered sexuality (Barbe; Boulanger). But the most explicit unlinking of sexuality from gender and gender from character and historical context came in the casting of Françoise Faucher as Prospero in *The Tempest*.

While it is far from surprising that a production of the Théâtre Expérimental des Femmes cast a woman as Prospero, it is at least somewhat surprising that everyone commenting on the fact insisted that doing so be seen as neither political nor feminist. Pat Donnelly in the *Gazette* wrote of Françoise Faucher's "unisex interpretation of Prospero" ("Brilliant Tempête"). On the radio Daniel Guérard said, "She doesn't play a transvestite. . . , it's without sex." [12] And an article in *La Presse* assured readers, "Contrary to rumor, this is not a feminized Shakespeare. . . . If Françoise Faucher plays Prospero, it is first and foremost to go beyond the sexes" ("Le Testament").

Prospero is not a sexual being, he is a human being—so went the refrain. Françoise Faucher confirmed in numerous interviews that this indeed was how she saw the role: "I don't feminize Prospero, and I don't masculinize myself; I just play Prospero, a human being, that's all" (Lévesque, "Françoise"; Lefèbvre; Gélinas, "Françoise"). Like Shakespeare, in this discourse, human nature is timeless, universal, and transcendent, independent of time and place and political construction.

But this universalizing tendency was not without at least one exception—interestingly enough, in the response of the anglophone critics. Though no less enthusiastic about the three productions than their francophone counterparts, they experienced them, especially the second tetralogy, much more ironically. For example, Marianne Ackerman pointed out that the Théâtre Omnibus triumph with "the greatest dramatist in the English language" took place "while language politics, that ongoing and often tedious local squabble, continued to make headlines this week" ("Bard"). Pat Donnelly in the *Gazette* ("Shakespeare") couldn't resist the "delicious irony" of the parting lines of banished Mowbray in *Richard II* "at an experimental theatre in the heart of 'Ne touchez pas la loi 101 country' ":[13]

My native English, now I must forgo . . .
What is thy sentence [then] but speechless death,
Which robs my tongue from breathing native breath?
(1.3.160, 172–173)

Matthew Fraser wondered in the *Globe and Mail* "if the director had seized upon these plays to make a statement about Canadian federalism" and noted "similarities between the battle of Agincourt and the French defeat on Québec's Plains of Abraham." "Of course, they were, in a way, the same battle," director Jean Asselin was quoted by reviewer Donnelly as saying. But Asselin went on to add: "We never even thought about the sociopolitical aspect of playing Shakespeare here" ("Shakespeare").

Jean Asselin's astonishing indifference to sociopolitical issues in 1988 would have been to most anglo-Quebeckers as inconceivable as an equivalent indifference on the part of Michel Garneau would have seemed, had he displayed it, to his Québécois audience in 1978. But "l'événement Shakespeare" of 1988 is marked by its contradictions. It created recognizably postmodern productions which displayed fragmentation, rupture, and discontinuity, and read them as humanist, essential-

ist, universalist, and transcendent. It also produced the resistant readings of anglophone critics whose political situation led them to create
and experience it as a quite different event.

As we have seen, the study of theatre archives enables us to examine
the readings produced by individuals from their encounter with a text
within a particular social situation—Hodgdon's definition of the theatre
event. At times the theatre event is constituted by a consensus in the
community of theatre artists and spectators, as in the case of Garneau's
1978 *Macbeth*. When this is replaced by a different consensus, as during
the 1992–1993 productions of the same script, what is created is not a
different version but another event. When, as in the 1988 *Cycle des rois*,
an audience consists of different constituencies by whom the production
is experienced differently, the event is comprised of their different readings. The script participates in its multiple incarnations, but there is no
"authentic original" which stands apart from and transcends the "readings" of the producing company and the readings of their audience. It is
the very "interested" nature of archival documentation of production
and reception that makes possible the apprehension of the theatre event.

NOTES

1. I wish to thank the Centre des Auteurs Dramatiques (CEAD) and the
theatres and companies about whose productions I write, especially l'Espace
GO, le Théâtre du Nouveau Monde, le Théâtre Omnibus, and le Théâtre
Repère, for their helpfulness and generosity with archival materials.

2. The performance text, in the terminology of theatre semiotics, includes the scripted text (lines that are spoken, stage directions that are—or
are not—followed, etc.) but is not identical with it (Ubersfeld, 17).

3. The availability of such materials varies. The Royal Shakespeare Company, to take an example of a large subsidized institution, has a policy, a library, and a staff, and makes its resources totally available. In Québec,
where people are very sensitive about issues of creative property, such material may seem too personal or too potentially stealable to release.

4. Carlson, 90–95, in addition to discussing theatre programs, considers
the consequences of a mismatch between audience expectations as prepared
by the publicity and the audience's actual experience of the production.

5. Regardless of the play, Broadway programs for the week are identical in cover, in feature articles which tend to promote the "industry" via its stars, institutions, and events, and in ads and differ only in such details as title, author, production team, cast, and playing time.

6. Personal communication, September 23, 1988. Of course the RSC makes available (for sale) beautifully designed and informative programs. But comments by the director, designers, actors, etc., are significantly few. The programs tend to consist of things like performance history, period woodcuts and engravings, selections from critical writings, and attributed quotes, the effect of which is to provide either "background" or an "image" that is an extension of the production. The collage style of the programs leaves it to the audience to synthesize the varied materials and seems at all costs to avoid suggesting that the production is a reading or interpretation of the play from a particular point of view.

7. All silent translations from the original French are my own.

8. In addition to Montreal and Paris, the "Cycle Shakespeare" was performed in Maubeuge, France, as well as in Germany, Holland, Switzerland, Japan, and England.

9. Hodgdon finds crucial in both Lepage's interviews and the discourse of the reviews the opposition of "seeing vs. hearing; body vs. voice" ("Splish Splash," 32). She explains this as a difference in national theatrical cultures: hearing is etymologically central to the word *audience* in English, whereas the source of the French word *spectateur* is the sense of sight. However, speaking (and hearing) the words is no less important to the French theatrical tradition than to the English. I would argue that it is specific traditions of Shakespeare performance, so central to British national culture, whose violation is transgressive. This is equally true in postcolonial Canada. For example, a number of reviews of the 1988 Québec Shakespeares discussed below described the productions as anti-Stratfordian (cf. Ackerman, "Bard"; St-Hilaire, "Le Printemps"), though the allusion was to Stratford, Ontario, as much as to Stratford-upon-Avon.

10. The reasons for this change are beyond the scope of this paper. Possible explanations range from increased European interest in Québec culture and a consequent increase in international touring to Marianne Ackerman's suggestion that by the end of the 1980s francophone Quebeckers had tired of political questions: "As metaphors go, the island is a good one for Québec in the 1980s. After a period of creative self-absorption, actors are keen to see the world, make a splash abroad, and gain inspiration from over the horizon" (Ackerman, "French Theatre's Love Affair").

11. In contrast, as Hodgdon suggests, Lepage's 1992 production of *Dream* at London's Royal National Theatre foregrounded materially mired physical bodies.

12. The word *gender*, as used in English to signify the socially constructed component of sexual identity (as distinct from biological sexual identity), does not exist in French.

13. Bill 101, known as "the language law," outlawed the use of English on public signs in Québec, defined the conditions of accessibility to education in English, etc. "Ne touchez pas la loi 101" was the slogan of the campaign to resist attempts to change it.

10

"Here Apparent": Photography, History, and the Theatrical Unconscious

Barbara Hodgdon

Were it not here apparent that thou art heir apparent . . .

1 HENRY IV, 1.2.52−53

           Summer 1992. In a long glass case in the atrium of the Shakespeare Centre Library in Stratford there is a photograph; an accompanying notecard tells viewers that it represents Richard Burton as Prince Hal in a 1951 Festival of Britain season production of 1 *Henry IV* (figure 1). One of many photographs in an exhibition memorializing Angus McBean's long-term relationship with the Shakespeare Memorial Theatre, Burton-Hal's image appears alongside others linking actors to roles—Anthony Quayle as Aaron, Charles Laughton as Bottom—as well as studio portraits of actors (several of Vivien Leigh) as their (glamorized) "selves." Arrested by Burton's photograph, I buy two postcards: one I send (I have seen this; it is to be shared); the other I keep—a habit-forming kind of consumership which blurs the distinction between seeing Burton play Hal (I never did) and wishing that I had. With my purchase, I acquire the quotation (if not the trace) of a theatrical event; I possess Burton's Hal as image, information, (mock) memory. It is the eyes that trap my gaze, the face sculpted by chiaroscuro to reveal a double self which emerges in curious contrast to the patently theatrical crowned helmet and chain-mail collar. What is captured here? The desire for a representational past, for the *idea* of painting, not painting itself. Yet even though there is no attempt, here, to exorcise the specter of art history but rather to retain it, the photograph touches that history only

Figure 1. Richard Burton as Prince Hal. Shakespeare Memorial Theatre, 1951. Angus McBean, photographer. Courtesy of the Harvard Theatre Collection, the Houghton Library.

through theatre (cf. Barthes, *Camera Lucida*, 31). It is the photograph's status as palimpsest that intrigues me: conventions drawn from High Renaissance portraiture (Titian, Rembrandt) written over by those of a Cecil Beaton Hollywood star shot (I search the shoulder of Hal's cloak for, but do not find, traces of Burton's signature).[1] Looking at the image brings Kenneth Tynan's review to mind: "Burton is a still, brimming pool, running disturbingly deep; at twenty-five he commands repose and can make silence garrulous. His Prince Hal is never a roaring boy; he sits, hunched or sprawled, with dark unwinking eyes; he hopes to be amused by his bully companions, but the eyes constantly muse beyond them into the time when he must steady himself for the crown" (Tynan, 11–12).

Tynan's words recall another, equally familiar McBean photograph of *2 Henry IV*'s so-called crown scene (figure 2). Here my eye travels first to Burton's face, spotlit by a bright triangle that draws attention to the uplifted gaze of this smooth-faced boy (no pores discernible here to mar Hal's youthful purity and spirituality) absorbed in what lies beyond the frame. His fingers hold the crown as though it were made of glass—a tentative gesture that reveals both his desire for and hesitancy about the hallowed (hollow?) object, which seems to have been bestowed from above. Caught between an invisible godly father and the obviously stagy figure of Harry Andrews' Henry IV (the heavy makeup exaggerating his age; the wig and beard so obviously false), Burton's Hal takes on a presence that exceeds representation: rising out of his father's form, his image resurrects "theatre" as "the real."

In the volume memorializing the 1951 Festival of Britain where I first saw this photograph, a caption ties the image to Shakespeare's text—

Figure 2. Richard Burton as Prince Hal; Harry Andrews as King Henry IV. Shakespeare Memorial Theatre, 1951. Angus McBean, photographer. Courtesy of the Harvard Theatre Collection, the Houghton Library.

"My due from thee is this imperial crown"—and asserts an interpretive frame—"On Bolingbroke's deathbed, the prince comes face to face with his destiny" (Wilson and Worsley, 42). But if I read beyond the textual, critical, and cultural codes endowing this theatrical moment, this once and future king, with mythic import (Barthes' *studium*), what I hear is Burton's Hamlet, a decade or so later, throwing away "To be or not to be" like a used shopping list. And what I see, through an accident of knowing that cuts through my experience of the photograph (Barthes' *punctum*) is Burton's ravaged Antony, the man who will marry Elizabeth Taylor.[2] What Walter Benjamin called the optical unconscious is not, I think, revealed through photography; if it can be spoken of at all as externalized in the visual field, that is because it is constructed there by the photographer, by the viewer (cf. Krauss, 178–180; Solomon-Godeau). In these mutations of reading (cf. Barthes, *Camera Lucida*, 49) do I construct a theatrical unconscious?

If this obviously Barthesian meditation on looking maps some parameters of my own experience as a collector and consumer of theatrical photographs, it also introduces, even as it papers over, some of the questions and issues I wish to raise about categorizing such photographs as "evidence." By bracketing the term, I mean to destabilize its privileged epistemological status: evidence of what? for whom? and in what contexts? Normative protocols governing the use of theatrical photographs bear an uncanny resemblance to those used by editors to establish a stable or "true" Shakespearean text, protocols in which terms such as "actor's corruption," "compositor error," and "theatrical transmission" have traditionally served to taint certain texts and privilege others.[3] Thomas Postlewait writes, for instance, of how extraneous as well as extrinsic causes may modify, limit, or distort a document's use value for reconstructing the history of a particular performance. Setting his comments on photographic reliability within archaeological paradigms for deriving cultural meanings based upon material, formal, efficient, and final causes, Postlewait argues that when a photograph's final cause is a publicity shot or its formal cause the aesthetic principles of a portrait its status as a mediated document is further subverted ("Historiography," 169). Similarly, Dennis Kennedy cites the compromising conditions under which McBean produced his photographs—a half- or full-day photo call, imported studio lighting, prearranged poses determined by McBean himself that often improved upon whatever stage pictures emerged in a performance.[4] Nonetheless, he adopts a more inclusive attitude toward admitting such mediated, and mediating, images as evidence of theatrical truth (my oxymoron, not his), advocates exercising care in their use, and argues that the full-stage photograph showing relationships of actors to setting is the most accurate index (a term that invokes Hamlet's problematic "mirror") of performance conditions. Even so, he maintains, accepting a photograph as documentary evidence requires corroborating it with other available records, such as designs and video recordings (20–24).

Although such cautionary advice seems eminently sensible, Kennedy's procedure strikes me as somewhat suspect, for it risks repeating pat formulations based on unexamined perceptual and methodological paradigms, all of which require further interrogation. After all, the monitoring practices to which he refers may, or may not, establish "what really occurred." Theatre is a stream of moving images, each successive one canceling, replacing, and sometimes recalling its predecessor; the photographic still (that which makes "theatre" collectible by tourists, specialist spectators, or archives) aches with absence even as it stakes out some sort of talismanic claim on the "theatrical reality"—a phrase which, in this connection, takes on the status of "the author." The problems surrounding the status of theatrical stills appear more clearly when set in relation to the legal use of photographs—the *only* pictorial evidence routinely admitted into courtrooms. Despite knowledge of the ability of photographer and photographic processes to alter or disturb traces of documentary reality, and however obvious it may be that all photographs are put under the pressure of both the photographer's and the viewer's ways of seeing, "reasonable accuracy" remains the flexible standard for photographic evidence in legal protocols.

Seen through such a lens, both the documentary status Postlewait would so severely limit and Kennedy's more generous embrace of a photograph's evidentiary value emerge as a self-regarding discourse bent on enclosing the aesthetics of performance and production exclusively within theatrical culture. Yet both Postlewait and Kennedy would, I think, agree that it is often on the basis of photographs that a production, or an actor's performance, takes on meaning, position, and import—in *cultural* as well as theatrical history. Certainly, Kennedy's scenographic history, *Looking at Shakespeare*, depends on the premise that readers and viewers will accept the "truth," as well as the cultural import, of the theatrical events he analyzes based, in large part, on the photographs chosen for and reproduced in his book.

I position my own enquiry, then, at an angle to these practices, which erect disciplinary boundaries around the theatrical still. Within the common practice of marking the theatrical photograph as a factual "proof-text" or "document," the notion of "documentary" needs to be reconsidered as a *historical* rather than an ontological category. I want first to insist on the *event status*[5] of the photographic image as it is constituted in the concrete, historical conditions of its viewing within what Henry Giroux and Roger Simon call "a discursively saturated materiality" (98)—conditions which, in this case, extend beyond the boundaries of the frame, beyond actors' performances, scenography, lighting design, beyond the production. How, I want to ask, can the photograph as event be thought: what ideological work does it perform? Such an enquiry invites questions about how theatrical images are *taken* (an operative term), mediated, and circulated, about how knowledges are constructed, and about the intersections between theatrical culture and other cultural realms. I view theatrical photography as a practice, a particular mode of textual signification which, when placed within systems of display, distribution, and engagement, helps to constitute or reconstitute a sociocultural imagination. My interest is with how photographic images invite viewers to invest in and translate them and with how such processes intervene in narratives about performed Shakespeare— especially, given the range of my examples, in narratives of "Shakespeare history." And within this framework, I also want to explore how the theatrical photograph becomes implicated in processes of subject formation, how it produces and smooths over forms of cultural self-representation constructed within dominant historical, hierarchical, and representational systems (cf. Giroux and Simon).

Returning to McBean's Burton-Andrews crown scene can localize these concerns further. Earlier, I catalogued that photograph as a picture at an exhibition, as a tourist souvenir or fetish, and, by attaching somewhat idiosyncratic meanings to it, suggested how language, in some form, consistently invades the photographic image (cf. Mitchell, 282). Yet that private meditation bears traces of other, more public reading practices which activate its meanings—that is, the captions accompanying the photograph anchor it to the Shakespearean *logos* ("My due from thee is this imperial crown") as well as to a body of Shakespeare criticism ("On Bolingbroke's deathbed, the prince comes face to face with his destiny"). Together, these practices validate and categorize the photographic object, emplot it (to use Hayden White's useful term) within institutionalized reading formations that mediate the photographer's as well as the viewer's understanding and permit a stable, even *naturalized*, meaning to emerge, the result of complicity between "author" ("Shakespeare," the photographer), performance, and reader.[6] Although McBean's photograph represents a *pose* and thus may not capture an *unmediated* moment of performance, it aligns with the Tillyardian premises driving the 1951 *Henriad*, which accentuated the coming-on of the idealized monarch. Indeed, I would argue that it is precisely because the photograph is a pose that it responds so effectively to these premises, for by recording the mythical, transparent idea of succession ("The king is dead. Long live the king"), it makes visible the theatrical embodiment of a historical and critical trope.[7]

McBean's crown scene, in other words, becomes an event that makes the act of reading "Shakespeare *as* performance"—and as ideology—possible. If, as Susan Sontag writes, "Having a photograph of Shakespeare would be like having a nail of the True Cross" (154), McBean's image represents the next best alternative to such a fantasy. No gaze at performed Shakespeare without "Shakespeare"—or "his" interpreters. Mining the photographic archive, one searches for the image that will validate one's own thesis; the relation between picture and discourse can be understood, as W. J. T. Mitchell writes, as a relation of power (6). And what makes this particular photograph matter is that something like the "look of Shakespeare" leaks into the image, validating it as a subproduct, however remote, of an "authentic" encounter with the "author," constructed as a flexibly fictive presence who regulates meanings and whose identity merges, through the photograph, with that of the actor-in-the-role. This is not to say that "Shakespeare" emerges simply and unproblematically; rather, it simply points to how the myth of his authorship becomes netted into processes of cultural reproduction and consumption.

Consider, next, this photograph's reincarnation in another context: a 1967 volume, *Shakespeare Play by Play*, that summarizes the plots of Shakespeare's plays and provides line drawings of major characters. Representing a kind of quick-study guide, this volume illustrates the *Henry IV* plays with three images—Anthony Quayle's Falstaff, cup in hand; the Boar's Head tavern, featuring Pistol with his drawn sword

Figure 3. From Stephen Usherwood, *Shakespeare Play by Play*, copyright © 1967 by J. M. Dent & Sons Ltd. Drawing by Raymond Piper. Courtesy of Hill & Wang, a division of Farrar, Straus & Giroux, Inc.

surrounded by a group of laughing observers; and the crown scene—each "taken" from McBean's photographs (figure 3).[8] As the crown scene reappears, returned to and refigured as historical portraiture, any link to the photographer, the 1951 Shakespeare Memorial Theatre production, and its actors disappears. With their identity and locale so erased, the images escape one history to serve another: an eternal present where the drawing of Burton seems to offer evidence of what Shakespeare's Prince Hal "really looked like." No matter how curious and devious (yet this is, after all, a *theatrical* enterprise), that statement can be said to be "true." How can we think about this moment when a photograph, assuming other representational conventions, becomes an ahistorical synecdoche for "Shakespeare's *Henry IV*," gets caught up in memorial survival, and acquires a pedigree not unlike those accorded to canonized texts?

Beyond noting this peculiar traffic in images, we can ask what happens when the McBean photograph is set in relation to later photographs of the crown scene. How is each remapped, revised, implicated in viewing circumstances that give a broader historical dimension to this particular instance of a theatrical—and political—unconscious? Here, it is useful to turn to T. S. Eliot's formulation of the nature and operations of literary canonization, perhaps the most influential statement of its kind: "What happens when a new work of art is created is something that happens simultaneously to all works of art which preceded it. The existing monuments form an ideal order among themselves, which is modified by the introduction of the new (the really new) work of art among them . . . whoever has this idea of order . . . will not find it preposterous that the past should be altered by the present as much as the present is directed by the past" (109).

Appropriated to serve my purposes, Eliot's "Great Tradition" aligns with Tillyard's reading in that it imposes a profoundly conservative model for perceiving, and monitoring, a past visual heritage. Although new (really new?) photographs will change the parameters of looking that pertain to those taken earlier, they also enable coherent and sequential processes of reevaluation in which like enhances like, in which similarity and complementarity affirm, over time, the cultural limits, theoretical borders, and dominant ideologies within which representations of the crown scene are or can be produced (cf. Sontag, 141–142; Giroux and Simon, 103). This is especially pertinent in the case of Shakespeare's English histories, at least in Britain, where theatrical reproductions consistently tend to emphasize the word *in* the visual sign and so to become folded within particular economies of truth, value, and power. What keeps *Shakespeare's* "Great Tradition" in flux, constantly being re-newed, depends in part on how the theatrical photograph records a sequence of rediscovery of the same that monitors the taste for and accords value to those particular scenes and moments which make demands for intelligibility. And what is equally important is to reveal the complexity and density of such discursive practices as a set of determinations, insofar as they are conceived in accordance with existing traditions but capable of being modified, retooled, and reformulated (cf. Foucault, *Archaeology*, 208–209).

An archive. Even as they sublimate "Shakespeare-history" into the theatrical real by means of photography's empirical claims, two other crown scenes taken from productions directed by Trevor Nunn (1982) and Adrian Noble (1991) make a history of the Royal Shakespeare Company's succession (figures 4 and 5). In these images, nothing survives of McBean's painterly desire to enhance one form of representation with another; each is firmly situated in photography as a recording art—the dominant twentieth-century mode of seeing; only costume silhouettes signify a historical past being recuperated and interpreted by the designer for the theatre. Not only do these images seem to efface any Tillyardian aura but the photographer's presence (as a controlling authorial eye/I) is masked by the seeming materiality of the photographic sign. No marks of swooning mysticism here; instead, these images map a trajectory that demystifies the crown's exchange. Although that *textual* subject clearly organizes each photograph and accords the two commonality, the codes each cultivates are premised on the expressive body, channeling the viewer's interest toward how each pair of actors guides meaning toward—what? An "ideal" of performed Shakespeare, imprinted upon the human figure? The power of political and cultural institutions (the crown, the theatre) to discipline the body? Strikingly, each floats the actors' presences free of any encompassing *mise-en-scène*: poised against dark backgrounds, these figures seem to be present in a nowhere that, by concealing the theatrical "in" the photograph, enables reading these encounters as transhistorical. Yet the still photograph does not escape history entirely, for each refers to the *idea* of the Brechtian gest, which bears the weight of a social history (cf. Barthes, "Diderot," 73–75): immobilized, this crucial instant of the crown's passage, seen dispersed across mutable subjectivities, makes canonical history both intelligible and desirable and locates "character" as its product.

Here, then, is a visual history of theatrical succession. In 1951, Burton's purity, simplicity, idealism, his desire for the crown. After 1951, no desire, no heroes; instead, signs of struggle. As though quoting McBean's photograph, 1982's crown scene replaces Burton's exalted look with that of an angry, determined Hal, and the crown itself sits uneasily, almost anachronistically, on Gerard Murphy's tousled head. In 1982, this image appeared in at least five major newspapers' first-night reviews, a choice (from among other press-packet photographs) that perhaps served less to mark the moment's ideological significance than to commemorate "the new"—the opening of the Barbican, the RSC's London home, Trevor Nunn's choice of Murphy to play the role, and Murphy's perfor-

Figure 4. Gerard Murphy as Prince Hal; Patrick Stewart as King Henry IV. Royal Shakespeare Theatre, 1982. Chris Davies, photographer.

Figure 5. Michael Maloney as Prince Hal; Julian Glover as King Henry IV. Royal Shakespeare Theatre, 1991. Donald Cooper, photographer. Courtesy of Donald Cooper, Photostage.

mance itself, which went against the grain of previously "heroic" Hals.[9] In 1994, however, that context, as well as the shock-value of Murphy's presence, competes with and is somewhat blurred by the aura surrounding Patrick Stewart's image. For many will view his sleeping form, not as Shakespeare's Henry IV but as *Star Trek*'s Jean-Luc Picard, and so will read this image through their memory of another father figure who stands at the center of a mass-culture narrative, one which often draws its themes and its language from "Shakespeare," whose words, placed in "alien" mouths, offer proof of their "humanity."[10] And by 1991, in a still which reverses the (canonized?) positions of king and son, Henry IV forces the crown down onto the head of Hal, who cringes beneath its weight. Discipline and punishment: forty years ago, the reigning sovereign jamming the crown on the reluctant or naughty heir's head would have been unthinkable. If such an image had emerged in a performance, *it would not be taken*, much less marketed and given value. But in the nineties, with Britain's monarchy in crisis and become a daily tabloid topic, the theatrical photograph moves against the grain of interpretive history to endow the actor's sovereignty with the form and pressure of his time.

Contexts. The image representing the 1982 crown scene appears in the souvenir program for Adrian Noble's 1991 *Henrys*, where it becomes part of a découpage which shapes the plays' theatrical past and narrates the Royal Shakespeare Company's history, in which the *Henry IV* plays have served as a touchstone for the theatre's own celebratory discourse about itself (see Hodgdon, *Henry IV*, 17, 90–92). In that archive, the principle of succession—monarchical, performative, empirical, phenomenological—is relentlessly male (figure 6). According to this visual account, Roy Byford's Falstaff (1931) and Randle Ayrton's King Henry (1932) sire a heritage which is then represented by two photographs each from 1951 (Burton and Andrews; Burton with Anthony Quayle's Falstaff, Alan Badel's Poins, and Heather Stannard's Doll), 1964 (Ian Holm and Eric Porter as Hal and Henry IV; Patience Collier as Quickly, Hugh Griffith as Falstaff), 1975 (Alan Howard's Hal with Brewster Mason's Falstaff and Emrys James' King), 1980 (Alfred Marks as Falstaff; Bernard Lloyd as King Henry, David Rintoul as Hal at Shewbury), and 1982 (Gerard Murphy's Hal with Joss Ackland's Falstaff and Patrick Stewart's Henry IV).

Functioning much like review discourse, these photographs work to construct (even, perhaps, to alter) the viewer's subsequent experience of

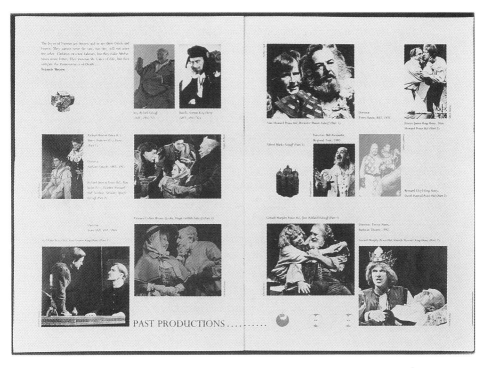

Figure 6. Royal Shakespeare Company souvenir program. *Henry IV, Part 1* and *Part 2*, 1991. Courtesy of Kathy Elgin, head of publications, Royal Shakespeare Company.

Noble's production by mooring it to the ceremonial presentation of actors in roles. Although the presences of various actors call attention to distinctions between them, the layout and choice of similar images erase that difference. Moreover, what seems ephemeral also acquires a certain degree of fixity, especially from 1975 onward, where juxtaposed stills repeat the triangulated relationship of Hal, Falstaff, and Henry IV. By showing who and what the characters once were and what the spectator should remember about them, the sequence of images becomes an effective means of programming popular memory (cf. Foucault, *Foucault Live*, 91–92) and of establishing performance traditions. Both determine not only what spectators see but also what photographers allow themselves to see as they *take*, and so form, a "fixed" pictorial record.

Who and what is speaking here? Although captions identifying actor and character distinguish the two by typeface, no comma separates them, suggesting that one fades into or merges with the other. Any further rupture—as in Brechtian distanciation or even voguing, in which an appearance gets layered onto the "self" (cf. Phelan, 92–111)—disappears or is healed over: the "star" reconfigures both the "I" of the character and the eye of the viewer, whose gaze is directed to the character's "humanity" and, beyond that, to a comfortable reassertion of Shakespeare's reputation as a humanist playwright. Although recent theory and Shakespearean criticism has paid little attention to characterology—in what appears to be a protest against A. C. Bradley—character (especially as a neo-Freudian or Lacanian construct) becomes reinstalled within the frame of the theatrical photograph, where the close-up (the space of interiority) can enlarge and make visible its "effects."[11] In this lexicon of images (moments to look *for* as well as to retain), the photograph becomes a site where the discourses of "stardom"[12] and humanist individualism converge and become implicated in proposing, if not achieving, an intimate relation between theatrical subjects and viewing subjects. And as though to sustain such processes, what also determines seeing is an excerpt from a Francis Bacon essay: "The Joyes of Parents are Secret; and so are their Griefs and Feares; They cannot utter the one, nor they will not utter the other. Children sweeten Labours, but they make Misfortunes more bitter; They increase the Cares of Life, but they mitigate the Remembrance of Death" (Bacon, 23). By linking this array of images to generational parables, Bacon's text commemorates a time-honored strategy for reading the *Henrys* as a father-son narrative; moreover, the photographs not only confirm "history" as an encounter between men but even make visible the joys, griefs, and fears Bacon claims to be secret, inexpressible.

Yet another company publication further enforces an imaginary synchrony between authorial presence, performance, and the photographic object. Available for purchase at the Royal Shakespeare Theatre's bookstalls is a sixteen-page booklet of (mostly) color photographs of Noble's *Henrys*, a memorial trace of the production which neatly accomplishes the work of collecting theatre. An updated substitute for the *RSC Yearbooks*, no longer published, this slick photographic essay, enclosed by two images of Shrewsbury (Hal bending over Falstaff's "corpse" on the front cover, a partial tableau of massed bodies and a chivalric banner on the back), maps the narratives of both plays, beginning with an image of Julian Glover's Henry IV seated on the throne and holding the crown; marching in order through the play's main events; and ending with one of Michael Maloney's Hal, crowned and all in white, looming up behind Robert Stephens' Falstaff, a shadowy foreground shape. Here, as in the souvenir program, images are (lovingly) cut out, as for a scrapbook, and further cropped and shaped in order to display actors' performances and, in the occasional tableau, Noble's neopictorial style. Throughout, the dramatic is further dramatized by the didactics of layout and montage.

Whereas the souvenir program permits a sixteenth-century text to manage a viewer's seeing, here the actors' words, offering responses to reading and playing their roles, gloss their respective images. Appropriately, Glover takes a CEO's perspective: "Working on the Henrys is like trying to climb a mountain, only to find at the peak that there's another one before you; but my God, the views are spectacularly worth the effort"; and Owen Teale, speaking of Hotspur as "the personification of the theme of honour," maintains "it isn't just a characteristic you can hang on the role, everything stems from it . . . lead[ing] him like a death-wish." As for the tavern inhabitants, Stephens considers Falstaff to be "hard as steel, totally unsentimental and keenly intelligent . . . even . . . when Hal turns him away, he regards it as a kind of triumph; . . . the culmination of all he has taught him in preparing for kingship"; and Linda Bassett, noting that Quickly lives in a land threatened by Falstaff's misrule, observes the irony of her imprisonment for resisting Doll's arrest "when the Prince becomes King and imposes his new rule of justice. But she'll survive . . . , as people who have a reckless trust in humanity generally do." Finally, Maloney, speaking "beside" his image as the newly crowned Henry V, categorizes "Shakespeare-history": "These plays are not historically accurate . . . they were never intended to be. While every audience is fascinated by the dark side of human life, ultimately Shakespeare's work is about the heroism of the human spirit in whatever guise."

As I have argued, collusion always marries text to the theatrical still, and this instance is no exception. While such a captioning practice opens up a dialectic between the two, it can also counter or resist conventional interpretive frames or reading formations, as in some of the actors' accounts of their work in *Players of Shakespeare 1, 2,* and *3.*[13] But that is not the case here, where what is on sale, after all, is a version of national history. What does seem entirely possible, however, is that the RSC's publicity staff, aware of such booklets' broad-based appeal, has deliberately issued a fan's "popular" alternative, one in which the actors, by

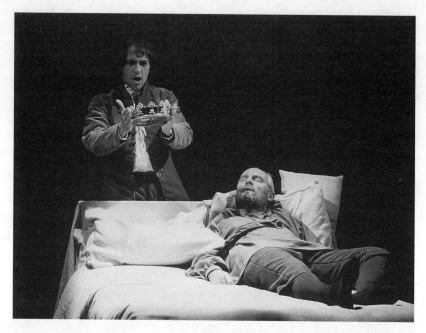

Figure 7. Michael Maloney as Prince Hal; Julian Glover as King Henry IV.
Royal Shakespeare Theatre, 1991. Donald Cooper, photographer. Courtesy of
Donald Cooper, Photostage.

Figure 8. Michael Maloney as Prince Hal. Royal Shakespeare
Theatre, 1991. Donald Cooper, photographer. Courtesy of
Donald Cooper, Photostage.

playing Shakespeare, not only imagine themselves as conflated with and ventriloquizing "his" characters but have internalized the mainstream myth of his "greatness" and become subjected to its ideology.

If it proves pleasurable (at least to women viewers) to hear Linda Bassett speak for Quickly, it is also not surprising that the photographs selected favor male performers and marginalize women. Among thirty-two images, two feature Sylvestra de Tousel's Lady Percy, showing her in relation to Teale's Hotspur; three are of Bassett's Mistress Quickly, again posed as an adjunct to male performers (Stephens' Falstaff, Albie Woodlington's Pistol), where she becomes an item of local color at the Boar's Head Tavern; and one portrays Joanne Pearce's Doll, seen slightly behind Falstaff, whose laughing face occupies the center of the photograph. Certainly, however, the choices for the brochure's front and back covers invite reading Shrewsbury's battle (an exclusively male enterprise) as the event that grounds the story—a move that (at least for a spectator who has not yet seen the production) "gives away" or heightens anticipation for one of the production's major set pieces or tableaux. Moreover, the cover image of Hal and Falstaff directly echoes the relationship of Hal and Henry IV in earlier representations of the crown scene, a featured attraction which, on the booklet's inside pages, appears in three photographs: first, an image of the sleeping King, Hal standing above him, holding the crown; next, a shot of Hal setting the crown on his head (unlike the others, this image is severely cropped, as though to exhibit his figure for "pure" contemplation); and, finally, the already familiar image of Henry deliberately weighting his son's head with the crown (figures 7, 8, and 5).

When one looks at the first two images—and especially at the second—it is hard not to conjecture that Maloney or Donald Cooper, the photographer, had seen McBean's photograph of Burton, for whether through mere iconic accident, deliberate memorial recall, or both, Maloney's hands repeat, as though apprenticed to a past gest, Burton's carefully delicate grasp on the crown. Visual tradition, it would seem, not only informs but recuperates something like Eliot's individual talent in a process which marks the actor's body as a site of departure and return, a medium of exchange for a "fixed" fiction of the crown scene.

I have been referring to this booklet as a photographic essay, a label that would align its "documentary" project with classic examples of this form, such as James Agee and Walker Evans' *Let Us Now Praise Famous Men* (1939).[14] Yet since it reverses the dominant textual strategy that incorporates photographs as evidentiary or illustrative examples to insist that image *is* text, it would not only be more accurate but also more appropriate to call it a *phototext* or, even better, a *photoplay* (cf. Mitchell, 288). Insofar as that rubric alludes to the title of a moving-picture fan magazine, it seems especially apt, for if this magazine represents the RSC's knowledge that the images produced in its theatres are collectible commodities, the strategy they adopt to market them is precisely analogous to those the cinema employs to advertise its products. Not only do some of these same images appear in a magazine sent to members, where they function, like a cinematic preview, as a teaser for the production, but the very existence of the souvenir booklet acknowledges that theatre's pictures exist in competition with other, often cheaper, moving images.

Certainly, in what Guy Debord calls "the society of spectacle," circulating such images occludes Shakespeare's *written* text and replaces a culture of reading with a culture of spectatorship. And, although copies of that text are also available in the theatre's bookstalls (those mini-museums of words and images), the photoplay—as though aware of its status as an object that displaces the word—bears the same title and (more or less authentic) authorial ascription: "*Henry IV Parts 1 and 2* by William Shakespeare." What is most intriguing, however, is that the magazine includes a 23 1/4 × 16 2/3 fold-out color page of the crown scene (figure 5)—an "art" reproduction (an imitation painting?). At least within the contexts I have been developing, such an enlargement does more than simply give McBean's photograph of Burton and Andrews another face, a Hal and Henry IV for the nineties. Blown up into poster art, the crown scene becomes suitable for framing—or perhaps for tacking up beside, say, the celebrity icons of rock stars or sports heroes.

If this image represents Maloney and Glover as raptly absorbed in the fiction (but also presenting themselves to spectators they know are there), the obverse of the large color insert reveals that fiction being constructed. Here, ten black-and-white photographs document moments of *Henry IV Part One* in rehearsal, supposedly laying bare what goes on behind the scenes.[15] Aside from a pensive still of Noble and Bob Crowley, the designer, in conference and one of Stephens taking a rehearsal break, posed against a wall papered with costume sketches, the photographs focus primarily on disciplining (male) actors' bodies in preparation for combat: two shots, for example, illustrate building—and

tearing down—one of the pyramid-like battle set pieces. What is prof-
fered here is akin to televised documentaries on the making of films,
which not only serve to hype spectators' interest but provide voyeuristic
perspectives on the theatrical event in process: wrote Brecht, "this is not
magic but / Work, my friends" (425). Here a viewer may search these
image-texts for traces of collaborative "invention" caught in process and
compare what appears both as playful improvisation and as directorial
fiat with "actual" moments of performance, reading one through the
other. Capturing moments of "text" as "work," these pictures visual-
ize/make visible Barthes' notion of text as "play, activity, production,
practice" ("Work to Text," 155–164),[16] offering spectators a formal imitation of insider knowledge, a mediated view of "truth" behind the theatrical facade, but one nonetheless susceptible to the reading protocols
governing any photographic still. Significantly, however, these images
do not interfere with the narrative being laid out in the photographic essay proper. They remain hidden—one has to unfold and turn over the
large color insert in order to discover them—a perfect trope for the
manner in which rehearsal work, displaced through performative practice, becomes consumed by and translated into a final product, the performance text.

So far, I have been narrating a history of the photographic still that is
embedded exclusively in the institutional practices of the RSC, where it
serves in an adjunct capacity to market theatrical products. I also have
been placing considerable ideological weight on the crown scene, almost
turning it into a fetish-object, the emblem of a cultural legacy. Certainly
one way to account for its continuing reappearance has to do with
configuring the *Henrys* as Bildungsroman, an interpretation sustained
and enforced by literary and theatrical reading formations alike. Indeed,
what a photograph of the scene seems intent on recording—a moment
when Hal is "becoming" someone else—serves as a trope, one might
say, for the theatre itself. Especially for British viewers, however, such
images may well perform a more crucial role by grounding a larger cultural narrative in which a nostalgic desire for a lost, supposedly "authentic" past becomes mapped onto the idea of the crown itself. And
insofar as the theatrical still mobilizes such desires and affective investments, the theatre (and its products) becomes entirely complicit with
confirming national ideologies by means of photographic "truth."

But consider another instance, one occurring outside the RSC succession narrative and its reproduction practices, that takes my history into

Figure 9. Michael Pennington as Prince Hal; Patrick
O'Connell as King Henry IV. English Shakespeare
Company, 1987. Laurence Burns, photographer.

a different kind of archive.[17] In this image of the crown scene from
the English Shakespeare Company's 1987 *Henrys*—a 2 1/2 × 3 7/8
snapshot-proof (not even yet a "photograph") found among a pile
stacked, willy-nilly, in a corner of the company's offices ("take what you
want")—there is nothing remarkable (figure 9): no mystification (1951),
no determined resolve (1982), no rehearsal of past images only to move
beyond them (1991). Rather, a somewhat mundane image which, although it opens both actors out to the camera's eye, records little else except, perhaps, a gesture in the making—an image-text recording work.
Never circulated, either in stills posted in theatre lobbies or in the book
commemorating the ESC and the productions' history (Bogdanov and
Pennington), this discarded image apparently lacked value as a theatrical
record. Instead, the range of photographs the ESC used to signpost their
work—ones signaling a scenography of difference, a neo-Brechtian,
eclectically postmodern collage—called attention to deliberate ruptures
of traditional interpretive schemes and countered a nostalgic politics
of looking. Yet when the production reached Toronto, the *Kitchener-
Waterloo Record* for May 25, 1987, printed, alongside its review, a more
canonical image of Hal snatching the crown from a sleeping Henry IV.
Attributed not to Laurence Burns, Michael Bogdanov's official produc-

tion photographer, but to "Canadian Press," this image imposes hegemonic meanings on a production which sought to interrogate such meanings. Curiously enough, the photograph's caption, which reverses the
actors' names, offers the only index of this misidentification (and mis-
representation), for the review text assures readers that, despite "innovations," the production makes Shakespeare's genuine presence available.[18]

If this frisson between discarded and reproduced images points to
how the theatrical still is subjected to protocols of selection that may
contest, translate, or renegotiate the premises of particular productions,
similar protocols police the image and its selection in other publishing
practices as well. Among the nine photographs (eight "paired" images
and one cover image) I sent to Manchester University Press to accompany *Henry IV Part Two* for the Shakespeare in Performance series, I
juxtaposed the 1951 and 1982 crown scenes in order to illustrate how an
ideologically significant moment of performance had remained the same
(the relative physical positions of king and heir) and, simultaneously,
been refigured. My choice for the cover, a "star shot" of John Woodvine,
the ESC's Falstaff, as a present-day ad-man dressed in combat fatigues
and hawking the virtues of sherris-sack, signaled my argument, which
downplayed the play's royal narrative and attempted to reinstall Falstaff
as the fictional "other," and *theatrical* center, around which that narrative revolves. Yet the press, claiming preference for a "full-stage picture" (and apparently having misplaced the ESC photograph), was about
to go to print with the RSC's 1982 crown scene in its stead. Without my
intervention, the book's cover would have featured an expectational image totally at odds with the text, one which would not only foreground
the RSC's mainstream Shakespeare but also insist on royal history, with
the crown scene as its symbolic capital, as the imaginative center of the
play's theatrical and cultural history.

Appropriately enough, I want to conclude with a picture about an
ending, one that will permit me to question my own reliance on the
fugitive testimony of theatrical photographs. Other reasons prompt this
choice as well. Like the image with which I began—McBean's portrait of
Burton—I have a personal investment in this one, for it not only illustrates my penchant for collecting closural images but suggests how such
final events, condensed into tableaux, attain the fixity of a theatrical
still and can be retained, filed away in a spectator's memory.[19] My case
in point is the image on the back of the dust jacket for yet another

Figure 10. Alan Howard as King Henry V; Brewster Mason as Falstaff. Royal Shakespeare Theatre, 1975. Joe Cocks, photographer. Courtesy of the Shakespeare Centre Library.

commemorative enterprise, the publication of the "working text" for the RSC's 1975 centenary production of *Henry V*, directed by Terry Hands (see Beauman). An image cut out from Falstaff's rejection, it pictures the king's imperial presence, a golden-masked icon of power who imposes his will on the kingdom's most unruly subject (figure 10).

Representing "the end" (or close to it) of *2 Henry IV*, this image occurs literally beyond the ending of the book, marking its enclosure. Moreover, its placement in relation to the image on the front of the dust jacket—a Rembrandt-esque portrait of Henry as military hero, a sword crossing his torso, his head encased in a crowned helmet, his brightly lit face traced by a half-exalted, half-anguished gaze—narrates the hidden history of the fully formed royal subject. Given its context, this image of the rejection makes sociopolitical and psychological meaning available as *theatrical* meaning. Seen as a channel through which the political unconscious merges with the theatrical unconscious and becomes intelligible, the two images offer a perfect icon for the dialectic I have been exploring, that between theatrical stills that privilege "character," registering emotional interiority or "individuality" as the actor's province, and those that reveal a full stage picture, capturing an illusory instant of the social. Representing radically distinct ideological frames, each is photographed differently and mediated differently; each bespeaks different values, which compete for authority.

I want to pursue this point a bit further and ask how it is that an image like this one of Falstaff's rejection is thought to offer the most authentic testament to and evidence of performance. To begin with, it incorporates and mimics a spectator's position and gaze: taken from a slight high angle, it produces the illusion of a seemingly objective, "God's eye" view that seems to escape mediation and capture the "truth" of the theatrical event, as though from a preferred seat in the dress circle. Put in more theoretical terms, the image combines spectacle with surveillance—according to Mitchell, the "soft" and "hard" technologies for the formation of subjects in our time. Evoking Debord, he writes, "Spectacle is the ideological form of pictorial power, and surveillance, its bureaucratic, managerial, and disciplinary form" (327; see also Debord, par. 215). Significantly, then, such a still embodies a double perspective, not only by capturing theatre's laudatory monologue about itself but also by offering viewers the pretense of intellectual control over the theatrical event—as in Brecht's epic theatre, where, as Barthes writes, "the

Figure 11. Alan Howard as King Henry V; Brewster Mason as Falstaff. Royal Shakespeare Theatre, 1975. Joe Cocks, photographer. Courtesy of the Shakespeare Centre Library.

tableau is offered to the spectator for criticism, not for adherence" (cf. Debord, par. 24; Barthes, "Diderot," 71). But to what extent does the metatext of theatre appear "in" and frame this, or any other theatrical still? As reproduced, this image has "lost" some part of its photographic status, both through cropping and because the borders framing it as a mechanically reproduced object have been erased.[20] Thus blurred, it seems to offer access to a transparent reality in which the stage becomes the world and both can be seen as "pure" image.

Particularly, though not exclusively, because of its appearance on the dust jacket of a widely read book, this rejection scene has, like the crown scene in other contexts, become a synecdoche for Hands' neoformalist style, in which physical relationships between characters clearly define their sociopolitical roles, further enhanced by costume. As reproduced in two contexts—Kennedy's cultural history of scenography, my study of closure in the histories (Kennedy; Hodgdon, *End*)—this moment has particular value for explaining the relations between spectacle, ideology, and theatrical cultural capital. But intriguingly enough, in documenting Hands' production and his distinctive style, neither Kennedy nor I chose to reproduce this dust-jacket image. Instead, we both selected another, one taken from another angle which captures a moment just prior to that memorialized on the book jacket and also reveals a balcony jutting out over the stage in the upper left corner—an element of the photograph blurred in both instances by the size and quality of the (black-and-white) reproduction (figure 11). Kennedy's caption constructs his own aura of intelligibility around the photograph: " 'I know thee not, old man': a golden Hal (Alan Howard), brilliantly lit and treading on rushes, mechanically and ritualistically turns away from Falstaff (Brewster Mason), dead branches in the background" (249). Tying the image to the text (although the line has not yet been spoken, it tropes the scene), he then singles out actors, lighting, blocking, and a scenographic emblem, further authenticating the still's position in his history, investing it, as I argued earlier, with language. For my part, I chose this photograph rather than the one that appears on the dust jacket, which emphasizes the robot-like king and represents Falstaff as his subjected subject, because it locks into a moment *before* all is "fixed," over, ended—one where Falstaff's face is visible (as it is not in the dust-jacket still) and which captures his glow of anticipation. Once again, something like Barthes' *studium* and *punctum* guided my viewing politics.

What is equally pertinent here is that, in the particular archive available to us both, other images compete with this one for attention: Joe Cocks' proof sheets contain more than ten shots of the scene. (Did the photographer know this moment was coming, suspect it would be "memorable," and so attempt, as though turning the camera into a video-recorder, to show the entire process?) Curiously enough, theatrical photographers tend to remain somewhat marginal until the moment of obtaining permission to reprint: selecting photographs always requires a return to their "author," the inescapable link in the chain of representation and commodification. Before making my choice, I purchased copies of six stills: in each, the angle of vision shifts slightly, registering the photographer's movement, the apparent desire to frame the most compelling perspective. Viewed in sequence, they narrate the unfolding process of the performance's final moments: the first shows Falstaff alone, stage-center, framed by the tavern crew; three others trace the changes in blocking which occur as the king enters with members of the court and Falstaff moves toward him and the subsequent rejection; a fifth stop-frames the mechanized king turning on his heel to exit, stage-right; and the last documents onstage observers on the balcony watching the arrest of the tavern crew, as Falstaff, again at stage-center, starts to walk slowly toward the dead branches on the back wall and an upstage-centre exit[21]—a move that will eventually leave Prince John and the Lord Chief Justice alone on the white-carpeted stage, the rejection's aftermath and the beginning of the closing tableau.

Although only one of these could be reproduced (one can always collect more images than current publishing budgets allow for), my text turned the photographed sequence into language, decoding it back, one might say, into its original medium—a process through which the theatrical still itself becomes a specter, the basis for writing another text. Even more to the point, however, is that several of the images I have been describing reveal the framing edge of the proscenium arch, the lip of the raked platform as it juts toward the auditorium seating, the overhead lighting rig, and, at the left downstage corner in the final shot, an array of other lighting instruments. That is, these images not only reveal "theatre" in its operational mode; they also clearly define the edges marking off the stage reality from that of the spectator. Yet in making choices for publication, I rejected all these in favor of the image of a "perfect instant," at once totally concrete and totally abstract, in which the historical as well as critical "essence" of the represented action can be read at a single glance—what Lessing called "the pregnant moment" (quoted in Barthes, "Diderot," 73). In spite of paying lip service to documenting theatre, both Kennedy and I selected an image that, by erasing all evidence of the theatrical apparatus, serves to mark director and scene designer as co-authors of a (transparently) "Shakespearean" spectacle—the master-fiction which grounds, sustains, and enjoins their collaborative activity.

Where, then, have we been led, taking up the threads of this web of Shakespeare's looking relations? Traditionally, an essay should end with a picture of the overall argument. Yet throughout, this one has been compiled much in the manner of a photograph album—one that both supports and belies those mythical adages "Seeing is believing" and "One picture is worth a thousand words." Nonetheless, some precepts emerge as (dare I say it?) self-evident. Whatever forms of belief the theatrical photograph-as-event gives rise to are firmly tied to the historical circumstances of viewing, which are themselves framed by a whole series of practices that appropriate images to ground and replicate critical as well as cultural narratives. We show ourselves pictures in order to live; the history of the theatrical still constructs a critical practice which enables cultural recovery.[22] How might that history be modified or rewritten to reassess the status of the photographic document? What publishing and marketing practices might question, even reform, dominant visions? What images taken, circulated, and displayed would contribute to a critical approach to these questions and issues?

With the increasing availability of and advances in digitizing technologies, the status of the theatrical still is likely to change dramatically—either by becoming obsolete or, more probably, by being incorporated into new forms of *critical* work that support or counter current reproduction practices, both institutional and ideological.[23] One might mention that, of the photographs reproduced here, not one represents the work of a woman photographer.[24] And, like Buggin' Out in Spike Lee's *Do the Right Thing*, one might ask for images other than these to share positions of honor on a Wall of Fame. If "presentation" denotes gift giving, then "representation"—in this case, taken as referring to the theatrical still—encompasses the idea of giving back the theatrical event, of acknowledging that it is caught up in systems of public as well as private ownership.[25] So resituated, it need not be governed exclusively by Kennedy's terms, or thought of as a narrowly confined set of indexical, iconic, and symbolic signs that corroborate documentary protocols for establishing "accurate" evidence. Rather, since sightseeing is always a paradoxical enterprise, the photographic image can be thought of in terms of the cultural work it performs within particular networks of viewing relations. Finally, then, I want to argue for a materialist poetics of photographic evidence that reenvisions how the theatrical still, embedded within a series of authorized and authorizing institutional practices, participates in a whole range of uses which "dirty" the pictures.

NOTES

1. For an account of McBean's work, see Woodhouse. McBean's theatre photographs and glass negatives are at Harvard; some holdings are also in the Shakespeare Centre Library, Stratford-upon-Avon.

2. For the terms *studium* and *punctum*, see Barthes, *Camera Lucida*, 26–27, 51.

3. Such traditional practices are, of course, currently in dispute and, to a large extent, are being displaced by editorial protocols which acknowledge and attempt to account for the distinctions between multiple texts.

4. Comments about McBean's photo calls come from conversations with Maurice Daniels, who was present at many of them.

5. The idea of the photograph as an event is adapted from de Certeau's discussion of "events" as a structuring foundation for historiographical writing, xiv–xv, 81.

6. For the notion of reading formations, see Bennett, 206–207.

7. See Tillyard; Wilson and Worsley. For an account of the relationship between Tillyard and the 1951 Festival of Britain productions, see Hodgdon, *Henry IV*, 18–43.

8. See Usherwood, 43. My thanks to Jonathan Shectman for calling this volume to my attention.

9. Reviews featuring the crown scene appeared in the *Times* (June 4, 1982), *Sunday Times* (June 13, 1982), *Daily Telegraph* (June 11, 1982), *Financial Times* (June 10, 1982), and *What's on in London* (June 18, 1982).

10. For an account of similar popular reading formations, see Bennett, 206–207, 218–220.

11. For an analysis of how the practice of close reading produces character, see Hodgdon, "Critic," 263–272.

12. For important studies of star discourse, see Dyer, *Stars* and *Heavenly Bodies*.

13. See Brockbank, *Players*; Jackson and Smallwood, *Players 2* and *Players 3*. For an excellent analysis of how, in these volumes, character becomes appropriated by the actor, see Worthen ("Staging 'Shakespeare' ").

14. On Agee and Evans, see Jefferson Hunter.

15. While the photoplay's color photographs are the work of Donald Cooper, the black-and-white stills, including the rehearsal photographs, were taken by Richard Mildenhall. For whatever reasons (the availability of both photographers, for instance), the booklet thus represents more than one perspective or "viewing eye."

16. See also Worthen, "Staging 'Shakespeare,' "; Hodgdon, *The End Crowns All*, 263–265.

17. Archives and their curatorial practices also need further study, especially in terms of their functions in circulating and producing knowledge.

18. This instance engages with a larger issue: the relations between Canadian and British cultures and, more especially, the relation between Canada's Stratford Festival productions and "English" Shakespeare. My thanks to Denis Salter for calling these issues to my attention.

19. On tableaux, see Barthes, "Diderot," 69–78. On Diderot, see Fried.

20. For a practice which insists on calling attention to the status of an image-text as still photograph, see Thompson and Bordwell, in which cinematic frame stills and production stills are surrounded by a black border. See also Bordwell, in which the corners of each frame or production still are rounded and blurred. My thanks to Richard Abel for calling this to my attention and for reading and commenting on drafts of this essay.

21. This last image has an even more complex status, in that Falstaff's upstage move cites, raids, and pays homage to Orson Welles' 1965 film, *Chimes at Midnight (Falstaff)*.

22. I play here on "We tell ourselves stories in order to live" from Didion, 11. The idea of cultural recovery is adapted and extrapolated from Giroux and Simon, 97.

23. I am thinking particularly of current work at MIT's Shakespeare multimedia hypertext project. See, for example, Donaldson, "Ghostly Texts" and "Books in Bits."

24. On the gender politics of documentary photography, see Rosler.

25. These definitions of presentation and representation are adapted from Mitchell, 420.

Invisible Bullets, Violet Beards: Reading Actors Reading

W. B. Worthen

In the past decade or so, "text-and-performance" criticism of Shakespearean drama has been able to draw on a new resource: books and essays on Shakespearean performance written by actors. Unlike the occasional remarks on a given role that might be gleaned from an actor's memoirs or journalistic reviews of a given performance, books like the *Players of Shakespeare* series, Carol Rutter's *Clamorous Voices*, Antony Sher's *The Year of the King*, and Simon Callow's *Being an Actor*, among others, have enabled actors to describe the specific challenges posed by Shakespearean acting and to position their process within the entire ensemble of a production's work. Written with an eye to changing how Shakespearean drama is taught and understood, such books often speak to a still-embattled sense of the authority of performance—as interpretation, as criticism, and as a site for the cultural production of "Shakespeare." Surprisingly enough, this anxiety about the location of a legitimate "Shakespeare"—in the words on the page or in their embodiment on the stage—persists in a climate in which the "poetic" Shakespeare of the New Criticism has been largely displaced by the "theatre poet" of performance criticism, and—not incidentally for a poet writing in the overdetermined idiom of staged behavior—by a writer whose fullest reach is said to appear neither in textual nor in theatrical poetics, but in the larger space of the poetics of culture.[1]

Who speaks for "Shakespeare"? This crisis of legitimacy is in many ways the inevitable outcome of conceiving the meanings generated by stage production as *opposed* to those generated when the text is produced in other ways—as reading or criticism, for example.[2] For neither *text* nor *performance* points to a stable identity; each term marks out an arena of shifting practices of production and reception, where signification is imbricated in a close-grained fabric of values, attitudes, identities, and desires, in ideology itself. Indeed, the intensity of the "text vs. performance" skirmishing suggests that the stakes are mainly ideological, having less to do with Shakespearean drama than with how competing visions of culture are sustained by a "legitimate" vision of "Shakespeare."[3] When Robert Smallwood introduces the third volume of the *Players of Shakespeare* series by citing A. C. Bradley's introduction to *Shakespearean Tragedy* as a decisive "stage in the educational establishment's appropriation for the classroom and lecture hall of Shakespeare the writer for the popular theatre" (*Players*, III: 1), we can see claims about an essential Shakespeare (popular and theatrical, not effete and literary) being used to mark stage production as the natural venue of authentic "Shakespearean" meaning. In this view, "the actor's professional disciplines" provide insight not only into the acting process itself, but also into the innate and timeless features of Shakespearean drama, the vision of ethics, morality, and behavior—the "properties of being human"—said to lie at the heart of Shakespeare's greatness as a playwright (Brockbank, "Foreword," ix; "Introduction," 1). To read the *Players of Shakespeare* volumes is to enter a zone of "purely" theatrical interpretation, where decisions are held to be "instinctively made, perceptions unconsciously arrived at, fine discriminations mysteriously achieved" (Brockbank, "Introduction," 3).

Yet despite repeated efforts to distinguish their process from criticism as such, the actors' readings help us to locate the interface between the interpretive priorities of scholarship and those of the stage. At first glance, the essays in *Players of Shakespeare* seem remarkably insulated from the concerns driving much of Shakespeare studies today. While the actors variously allude to Coleridge and the Lambs, Muriel Bradbrook, Nevill Coghill, Wilson Knight, Jan Kott, F. R. Leavis, Kenneth Muir, Marvin Rosenberg, Edith Sitwell, and Dover Wilson, other names more representative of the state of contemporary critical thinking about Shakespeare—say, Catherine Belsey, Jonathan Dollimore, Stephen Greenblatt, or Stephen Orgel—are absent.[4] To be sure, citation of schol-

arly authority is precisely beside the point in a series of essays devoted
to the pragmatic ways and means of acting. What this metonymy reveals is a particular kind of rupture between the actors' sense of the purpose of "scholarship" and the issues and practices animating academic
Shakespeare studies today. This has little to do with the innate propriety
of either old or new critical approaches or with the inherent adequacy of
either theatrical or scholarly conceptions of "Shakespeare."[5] For read as
a whole, these essays reveal a consistent body of interpretive practice,
strategies for reading Shakespearean drama that produce a palpable vision of what counts as "Shakespeare" in the theatre and in modern culture. Actorly reading is notably trained on questions of "character," the
integrated, self-present, internalized, psychologically motivated "character" of the dominant mode of modern theatrical representation, stage
realism. And although recent stagings of Shakespearean drama have
often engaged the "themes" of gender, class, race, and empire, such the-
matics are conceived as ways of exploring—rather than unseating—
conventional conceptions of "character." Where scholars and performers seem at the moment most opposed is in their understanding of
"character," of what and how the roles of Shakespeare's plays signify.
These brief essays on Shakespearean performance are evidence of the
different strategies of reading practiced in the institutions of the academy and the theatre. They record the shifting ways that "Shakespeare"
is made to mean, and the different visions of culture that "Shakespeare"
appears to authorize.

One of the challenges shared by both actors and scholars has to do
with the historical remoteness of Shakespearean drama. The plays arose
in circumstances quite different from our own, and those differences
must be acknowledged; at the same time, both performance and scholarship are involved in making the plays speak to us today. This engagement with history provides one way to mark the interpretive work of
performance, and the way it both invokes and produces a particular vision of "Shakespeare." In the *Players of Shakespeare* series, the politics
of interpretation emerge in the ways performers understand and represent "character." Despite the British theatre's reputation for being less
involved in an explicitly Stanislavskian tradition than the American
stage, the *Players of Shakespeare* essays are informed by notions of a
coherent and internalized characterization fully consistent with Stanislavskian mimesis. Granted, Gregory Doran, describing his preparation
for Solanio in Bill Alexander's 1987 production of *The Merchant of*

Venice, is one of the few actors to allude directly to a "Stanislavskian search for detail . . . the tentative extrapolation of arguable subtextual hints into quintessential radix traits" (Jackson and Smallwood, III: 72).

Nonetheless, throughout *Players of Shakespeare*, actors conceive of "character" as an entity whose "radix traits" can be discovered in the text and used to motivate a single spine of action, the actor/character's "journey" through the play. Philip Brockbank attributes the "journey" metaphor to Peter Hall's influence ("Introduction," 2), and its effects are apparently pervasive: actors learn to resolve the fragmentary and inconsistent signals of the role into the continuous "experience" of a discrete, individual subject. As Roger Rees discovered when working on Posthumus in *Cymbeline*, the "journey" and the centered "self" are reciprocally defining terms: he attributes his difficulty seizing on Posthumus' "journey" to an inability to find "Posthumus's true centre" (Brockbank, I: 142, 147).[6]

In her recent book on Shakespearean acting, Meredith Anne Skura remarks that in "an era mistrustful of 'presence,' drama maintains a convincing illusion of immediacy, resistant to postmodern technology and fragmentation" (29). But the actors' essays suggest that this "presence" is actually implicit not in the drama but in the actors' ways of reading it, their trained approach to translating the text into embodied action. In some respects, the actors' performance occupies a familiar postmodern position, the unstable terrain where personal and cultural history and identity meet in the register of representation: the terrain of *pastiche*.[7] Translating the Stanislavskian superobjective into the metaphorical "journey" involves the actors in a dual engagement with history: with the "past" traced in the text (the play's given circumstances, the eccentricities of "character" drawn from an era so removed from our own, their necessary effort to write a motivating personal history for the role) and with the "present," the moment of performance, which necessarily decenters, occludes, or displaces the authority of the text. What is surprising is that the actors understand their interpretive practice less as a mode of self-authorized creation than as a mode of fidelity to "Shakespeare." Conceiving Shakespearean "character" as an organic whole, the actors stage a Shakespeare closer to Henrik Ibsen or Eugene O'Neill than to Heiner Müller or Anna Deavere Smith.

The actors' use of history to open and sustain their readings of Shakespearean "character" dramatizes these interpretive priorities and situates them in a clear contrast to recent critical practice. The actors use historical research to help them enter the imaginative space of the role, to identify and particularize the odd quirks and edges of a dramatic style and sensibility so removed from a contemporary idiom. But the ultimate purpose of this historical inquiry is usually to deny history, to achieve an interpretation that *is* properly Shakespearean precisely because it denies the difference of the past. The actors' principal mode of engagement with the past concerns the need to develop a biography for the role, a "past" to motivate the character's present actions. This act of biographical invention serves much the same function it does for Stanislavski: it enables the actor to produce the illusion of a single, whole, coherent "character" whose behavior flows from a concrete past into a determined present. Donald Sinden's approach to playing Malvolio—"What kind of man is Malvolio? What is his background?" (Brockbank, I: 43)—is fully reminiscent of Stanislavski's similar question of the role of Roderigo: "What is the *past* which justifies the *present* of this scene: Who is Roderigo?" (131).[8]

Moreover, in devising this motivating "history" of the role, the actors of *Players of Shakespeare* frequently resort to historical materials in order to specify and concretize the "character," to make it respond to the "given circumstances" of Shakespeare's era. In most cases, this research confirms the "reality" of the character to the actor (and eventually to the audience), by confirming that people *then* were pretty much like people *now*.[9] Ralph Fiennes, playing Henry VI in Adrian Noble's 1988 adaptation of the first tetralogy, *The Plantagenets*, "read a bit about the 'real,' the 'historical' Henry VI" and was pleased to find

> some historians' assessments of him to coincide very much with Shakespeare's plays, not so much in terms of dates and accuracy of events, but in essence, as it were. The character they described fitted very much with the character I found myself playing: someone obstinate, certain of their faith, wishing to appease people through granting favours, talking them into loyalty, into peaceful ways of conducting their affairs, but, on finding himself crossed, as Henry is by Suffolk, passionately decisive, however unwise the actual decisions may be.
>
> (Jackson and Smallwood, III: 113)

Shakespeare responds to history by catching the essence of the man; the modern actor responds to Shakespeare by transmitting that recognizable essence to us. More often, however, "history" serves an almost purely instrumental function: to render the illusion of a consistent, coherent "character." For example, when Tony Church compared his Polonius (in Peter Hall's 1965 *Hamlet*) to Lord Burghley, he was able to cast several parallels between Burghley and Polonius into his performance. Nonetheless, he admits that the historical evidence for such a comparison is inconclusive and that the figure of Burghley functioned for him "in *character*, and as a fertilizer for the actor's imagination" (Brockbank, I: 105).

Of course, the "historical" character of the actors' work is evanescent in performance, traced only in the vision of character, action, and culture that is encoded in their behavior onstage. Though absent in performance, this sense of history provides one of the conditions from which the performance emerges. The actors' "historical sense," like T. S. Eliot's sense of poetic tradition, is a sense "not only of the pastness of the past, but of its presence," a sense of history in which the "temporal" is ineluctably troped by the "timeless" (49).[10] The actors use history to confirm this "traditional" sense, to confirm a continuity in the "radix traits" of a stable human nature between Shakespeare's era and our own.[11]

Working on Portia for Bill Alexander's 1987 *Merchant*, for example, Deborah Findlay remembered

> reading a court ambassador from Spain or Italy of the period who wrote home about this passionate, volatile English nation. He spoke of our forebears in terms which we would reserve, suppressed as we now are by Puritanism and Victorianism, for the hot Latin temperament. It was my ambition to catch some of this full-bloodedness and for us all to embrace characters who could hate and love, and feel joy and sorrow, passionately. (Jackson and Smallwood, III: 53)

The Spanish ambassador's portrait of the volatile English first enables Findlay to distance herself from the modern English character and to justify her sense of the play's surprisingly passionate energy. At the same time, however, this portrait also seems to confirm Findlay's stereotype of the rambunctious "nature of the Elizabethan man and woman," a full-blooded passion that Findlay implies might still flow through "us all." The ambassador's letter enables Findlay to annihilate the historical difference it appears to summon between fiery Elizabethans and repressed moderns, for in the end Findlay's romantic attraction to this "full-blooded" sensibility is what attracts her to Portia and helps to forge her identification with "the vibrant, excellent person that she is" (53, 52).

Gregory Doran's brilliant essay on playing Solanio in the same production is more notable in this regard. Solanio is a small and thankless
part, but Doran worked to render it with a fine clarity of persuasive
detail, work that clearly paid off in Salerio and Solanio's brutal treatment
of Antony Sher's Shylock. As a role in the play, Solanio's function in the
plot clearly predominates over his individualized "character," and Doran
worked hard to find ways to make the part concrete, individual, and
his own:

> In researching the period I discovered that the young Henry III of France
> had visited Venice on his way back from Cracow, where as a young gen-
> eral he had won the throne of Poland. When he returned from Venice,
> however, he was a different man. The court was stupefied to see him
> caked in powder, hung with precious stones, and surrounded by a flock
> of parrots and little dogs. He began to hold fêtes in the royal parks,
> decked out in a pink damask dress embroidered with pearls, emerald
> pendants in his ears, diamonds in his hair, and his beard dyed with
> violet powder. . . . Adreana Neofitou, the costume designer, drew the
> line at the violet beard powder, but created a very dashing outfit for
> Solanio, in russets and umbers, with a splendid orange panache, and
> for further ornament I added an ostentatious pearl rosary, commas of
> rouge on the cheeks, kohl on the eyes, and a pickadevant beard and
> moustache. All this gave plenty of scope for Solanio's "outward show"
> to fall apart as the first half progressed, and pull himself together by
> the trial. (Jackson and Smallwood, III: 71)

Needless to say, Henry III has little to do with Solanio, *The Merchant of
Venice*, or Doran's performance, for that matter. What does function
here is the image of Venice as the site of elaborate ostentation, reduced
to a significant detail—the violet beard—which, though finally absent
from the production, specifies the kind of display animating Doran's
Solanio. The violet beard epitomizes Solanio, centers the "character" in
Doran's imagination, and enables him to discover a "journey" through
the fragmentary Solanio scenes. Though Doran's wished-for violet beard
is perhaps an extreme example, it precisely dramatizes the function of
"history" in the *Players of Shakespeare* volumes: a soup of nuance, image, and detail internalized toward the production of "character," usually in ways that claim to reveal the human essence of recalcitrant classical characters and so to enable their intrinsic "properties of being
human" to speak again to today's public.[12] Reading for "character," the

actors use a kind of historical bricolage to assimilate the centrifugal energies of the role to the modern demand that their performance incarnate a single, undivided, modern subject, a readable "self."

This (promiscuous, inspirational, what you will) use of anecdote to
situate an unfamiliar discourse (the behavior of Shakespearean roles) in
relation to a familiar one (the modern "self") may not seem entirely unexpected; the actors' practice almost parodies the new historicist penchant for "episodic, anecdotal, contingent, exotic, abjected, or simply
uncanny aspects of the historical record" (White, "New Historicism,"
301).[13] This likeness is more than a glancing one. To seize on an eccentric yet dramatic detail drawn from the character's period and make it
signify in an apparently remote discourse has more in common with the
practices of contemporary new historicism than with traditional "historical" representation in the theatre. For while Victorian actors like
Charles Kean and Henry Irving would work to produce a play like *Macbeth* or *King Lear* in its appropriate historical "period," the practice of
contemporary actors resonates with the eclecticism of contemporary
staging, which tends to strike a more overt (and often unstable) relationship between the play's historical setting, the period of the play's
composition, and other periods signaled by costume and set design.[14]

New historicism—with its often shrewd tension between excavating
the otherness of history and revising the present by revising the past—
has a similarly "eclectic" feel, claiming likeness between historical eras
in terms of their internal symbolic and representational dynamics rather
than in the narrative, linear causality of more conventional historiography. Much as new historicism is criticized for removing "facts," events,
or texts from their original context to make them signify in other, surprising (or eccentric) registers, so it might be argued that the *Players of
Shakespeare* actors develop history in a similarly anecdotal fashion, deploying details in ways that register the contingency of terms like "past"
and "present." Does Solanio's violet beard work (on us, on the contemporary audience) like the invisible bullets of Stephen Greenblatt's seminal (and much revised) essay, providing a way both to "other" the past
and to suggest the continuities between some of its ideological categories
and operations (character, subversion, and containment) and those of
the present day? Is it possible that in their strategies of reading Shakespeare, and reading history, the actors are in some unacknowledged way
more Greenblatt's contemporaries than Dover Wilson's?

It is notoriously difficult to generalize about new historicism, which (like acting) can seem like a practice—or aggregate of practices—in search of a theory or method. Nonetheless, new historicist inquiry has, by now, come to have a recognizable shape. The term and the practice of new historicism have been variously challenged and contested; here I am using "new historicism" merely to label a familiar body of work (mainly in Renaissance literary studies) and a familiar set of controversies surrounding the interpretation of "history" in the reading of "literature." As historical/critical practice, new historicism is urgently differential, engaged in the intense scrutiny of the local specificity of Renaissance literature as a means of distancing it from us, rendering the text as the register of the particular and local, rather than the essential or universal. Arguing, for instance, for a political analysis "which examines how Shakespearean texts have functioned to produce, reproduce, or contest historically specific relations of power (relations among classes, genders, and races, for example) and have been used to produce and naturalize interested representations of the real" ("Introduction," 3), Jean E. Howard and Marion F. O'Connor position this historical practice in opposition to the "Shakespeare" of the liberal humanist cultural and intellectual tradition, in which "Shakespeare has been used to secure assumptions about texts, history, ideology, and criticism" rather than interrogate them, a tradition in which Shakespeare functions "as a kind of cultural Esperanto, a medium through which the differences of material existence—differences of race, gender, class, history, and culture—are supposedly canceled" (4).[15]

Yet while it weaves literature deeply into the rhetoric of its originating culture, new historicism also claims its inquiry into the past as an inquiry into the circuits of power in the present as well. This conception of history departs from an inert Eliotic tradition, however, in which the categories of the "timeless" and universal constitute a "simultaneous order" informing the categories of contemporary experience. Instead, as Louis Montrose has elegantly argued, this sense of history is powerfully dialectical and

> necessitates efforts to historicize the present as well as the past, and to historicize the dialectic between them—those reciprocal historical pressures by which the past has shaped the present and the present reshapes the past. In brief, to speak today of an historical criticism must be to recognize that not only the poet but also the critic exists in history; that the texts of each are inscriptions of history; and that our comprehen-

sion, representation, interpretation of the texts of the past always proceeds by a mixture of estrangement and appropriation, as a reciprocal
conditioning of the Renaissance text and our text of the Renaissance.
Such critical practice constitutes a continuous dialogue between a
poetics and a *politics* of culture. (24)

This understanding of the function of texts in history engages those
involved in reproducing Shakespearean texts—critics, actors, readers—
in a complex enterprise. For as Montrose argues, in "its anti-reflection-
ism, its shift of emphasis from the formal analysis of verbal *artifacts* to
the ideological analysis of discursive *practices*, its refusal to observe strict
and fixed boundaries between 'literary' and other texts (sometimes including the critic's own), the emergent social/political/historical orientation in literary studies is pervasively concerned with writing, reading,
and teaching as modes of *action*" (26). This approach to history blurs or
erases the boundaries between the literary and the nonliterary, under-
takes a determinedly antiauthorial understanding of the production of
textual meanings, and is concerned not only with the ways in which
texts signify in the era of their initial production but with the interested
ways they continue to be appropriated and reproduced in subsequent
history. As a result, many critics argue as Jean Howard does that "the
analysis of Renaissance culture can be made to speak to the concerns of
late twentieth-century culture," particularly if we conceive of "our own
historical moment as the post-humanist epoch in which essentialist notions of selfhood are no longer viable" ("New Historicism," 5–6).

Like some critics, many actors may appear to "eschew overarching
hypothetical constructs in favor of surprising coincidences" (Veeser,
"Introduction," xii).[16] Yet while the explanatory power of new historicist argumentation relies on the contested assumption that "any social
practice has at least a potential connection to any theatrical practice"
(Cohen, 34), this sense of the interplay of cultural discourses in Shakespeare's era is sharply different from ways contemporary actors sample
history. For the actors' commitment to "character" suggests a fundamental resistance to the kind of discursive interplay typical of new historicist inquiry, in which the subject itself is conceived less as an "identity" or "self" than as a shifting site where the claims of competing
discourses—of the state, religion, the economy, class, gender, sexuality,
and so on—are registered. Despite an analogous commitment to seeing
Shakespeare in the past and in the present, actors' engagement with

history reveals strikingly different commitments, which really become visible in how they conceive of Shakespeare's commentary on the *present*.

One way to phrase this distinction would be to say that actors are (paradoxically enough) interested in what "Shakespeare" *is* rather than what "Shakespeare" can be made to *do*. The use of historical detail in actors' preparation, geared as it is to the service of character, locates "meaning" in the text (or, much the same thing, in an ineffable "Shakespeare") rather than in its *use*; performance turns out to be a vehicle for representing the naturalized truths of an Eliotic tradition—cultural Esperanto—rather than contesting them, or even showing how such "truths" are our own creation as well as Shakespeare's. This tendency is particularly evident in plays where Renaissance and modern sensibilities are clearly misaligned; *The Merchant of Venice* provides one telling example. Writing about his 1978 Shylock, Patrick Stewart notes that because "of the Nazis' Final Solution and six million deaths, those passages of anti-semitic expression in *The Merchant* will reverberate powerfully for any audience in this second half of the twentieth century." Yet Stewart is concerned that the play's significance will thus be read too narrowly by modern audiences, who will miss its larger—indeed, its justifying—frame of reference.

> But however important Jewishness and anti-semitism are in the play they are secondary to the consideration of Shylock, the man: unhappy, unloved, lonely, frightened and angry. And no matter how monstrous his cold-blooded attempt on Antonio's life, it is the brave, insane solitary act of a man who will defer no more, compromise no more. Taking Antonio's life is his line of no retreat and, although justified on commercial grounds, this murder is also, therefore, symbolic. Perhaps this makes of Shylock a revolutionary in modern terms. Certainly, when as Shylock I stood in the court and said "my deeds upon my head," I felt closer to *all* those oppressed and abused who stand up in the face of a hostile and powerful enemy. This was not one Jew, but all victims who turn on their persecutors. (Brockbank, I: 19)

Stewart's redemptive reading of Shylock resonates with a theatrical tradition extending at least to Henry Irving's tragic *Merchant* (in which the solitary exit of Irving's Shylock ended the performance), and with familiar modern critical attitudes as well: the sense that Shakespeare's values are essentially humane and that Shylock's claim to an essential humanity ("Hath not a Jew . . .") points to the play's desire to claim an underlying humanity uniting the variously (class, gender, ethnically, sexually) identified castes of the play. Yet to make Shylock a universal victim, Stewart must self-consciously generalize the explicit function of Shylock's ethnicity in the play, the specific terms in which his identification as a Jew enables the romantic Christians to stage antisemitism as the sign of mercy rather than oppression. As Frank Whigham argues, Shylock demonstrates that Venetian society's "oppression of one . . . reveals its oppression of many"; unlike Stewart, however, Whigham sees the victimization of Shylock as a function of the abstract and universalizing rhetoric the Christians use to destroy him. Where Stewart makes of Shylock a symbol of oppressed humanity, Whigham sees the generalized category "humanity" as part of the self-interested "ideology of universal harmony" that the play opens to demystification (108–109).

It should be clear that I am not attempting to choose between Stewart's reading—which, after all, promoted a moving and complex performance—and Whigham's, but am instead trying to elaborate the continuities and discontinuities between two representative ways of reading the text. Stewart's assumptions about Shakespearean meaning are grooved on the theatre's belief in Shakespearean morality: although Shakespeare's plays represent profoundly disturbing evils—the blinding of Gloucester, Macbeth's cancerous imaginings, Leontes' engulfing jealousy—"Shakespeare" finally stands for a just vision of human nature and action. If critical reading evokes a hermeneutic of suspicion, the sense that Shakespearean drama negotiates (and is sometimes betrayed by) its densely ideologized theatrical, political, and cultural milieu, reading for the theatre appears to involve a hermeneutic of transcendence, the belief that the values asserted most positively in the play express its core meanings, the meanings that speak equally to Renaissance and modern audiences.

Portia's treatment of Shylock in the act 4 trial scene throws these divergent perspectives into sharp relief. Like Patrick Stewart, Deborah Findlay, Portia in Bill Alexander's 1987 *Merchant*, takes "racism" as "an element of the play, but not the main one. It is encompassed by the broader debate about mercy and justice, about commitment and loyalty, about the nature of choice and its consequences, and most broadly about how we should treat each other" (Jackson and Smallwood, III: 56). Contemporary critical practice, as we have seen, tends to see the "debate about mercy and justice" as an ideological screen that normalizes and naturalizes the play's antisemitism. And yet there is a striking symmetry between Findlay's sense of Portia and critical accounts of the role's ideological functioning in the play. In a provocative reading of Shakespearean set speeches, Thomas Cartelli develops Whigham's sense that the play's characters—Bassanio and Portia in particular—slip "into a stylized rhetorical mode that foregrounds a set of abstract values," which are often taken as identical to the play's—or Shakespeare's— meaning; yet, Cartelli continues, this rhetoric "simultaneously embodies the speaker's most personal projections" (16), which reveal the speaker's complicity in the play's ruling order. Though "innocent of consciously employing the mercy speech as an ideological weapon against Shylock," Portia's speech on mercy registers her immersion in the dominant ideological discourse of Venice: she is instrumental to Shylock's scapegoating (17). For "the mercy speech is an unanswerable proposition that gilds its speaker in the trappings of all things bright and beautiful" (17), offering the bright horizon of a fantasy or utopia clearly detached from the play's actual politics, which repeatedly insist on the rule of a law that lies in the hands of its social elite. So, once Shylock refuses to cooperate, mercy is withdrawn, and the terms of the law are shown to be infinitely fungible.[17] As Cartelli concludes, "Portia's initial insistence on mercy resonates with the mercilessness of her ensuing treatment of Shylock in such a way that it renders the very concept indeterminate and her unqualified hold on its validity tragic, insofar as it radically distorts her consciousness of things as they are" (20).

Deborah Findlay's response to playing Portia resonates eerily with Cartelli's description. Director Bill Alexander and Antony Sher—her Shylock—"wanted an idea of ritual sacrifice in the trial scene," emphasizing the "Christian-Jewish conflict" by having "an image of Antonio strung out on a cross" and by "having Shylock perform an improvised ritual before he kills Antonio. The ritual included spattering blood on a sheet before Antonio's prostrate body and he suggested that this would be a marvellous way for Portia to get the idea of 'no drop of blood'" (Jackson and Smallwood, III: 63). Findlay found the complexity and power of this conception disorienting and sensed that Portia must be "in control of the scene from the moment she enters." Bringing Portia into the center of the scene, Findlay also makes her the register of the play's dominant ideology, in ways that seem to echo Cartelli's and Whigham's readings:

Far from being vindictive, she follows a simple rule of thumb: mercy, or justice. Having learnt about the nature of choice and its consequences from the caskets, Portia brings this wisdom to the trial and seeks to educate everyone there. It is her only option. . . . She has only that logic and her wit to see her through. She holds scrupulously to the letter of the law, since that is what Shylock has chosen. . . .

Portia gives Shylock as many chances as she can to choose mercy, but once he has made his choice (for me when Tony produced his knife) she follows the consequences through to their final terrible conclusion. Hers is an act of strict impartiality, explaining the law to everyone present. If you reject human mercy then there is only the implacable face of justice to fall back on. If you seek to pervert that, chaos follows. (64)

But of course chaos doesn't follow, only the seizure of Shylock's property and his brutal conversion to Christianity. What's striking about Findlay's nuanced account of her playing is that it confirms Cartelli's sense of Portia's "innocence" and of the dramatic (and practical) effect of that innocence, an unknowing that enables both Portia and Findlay to act as though the only alternative to Shylock's "mercy" is his "implacable" ruination. Addressing her reading to the lineaments of "character" alone, Findlay duplicates the character's immersion in the play's ideological "given circumstances": Portia could wish for no better defense of her "innocent" implementation of Venetian hegemony. To play the character's "journey" from the character's perspective, freighted with the weight of Shakespeare's transcendent morality, is to reproduce the ways the play naturalizes the character's behavior to its larger suasive purposes, its attempt to achieve the effect of the "real." In succumbing to the "vibrant and excellent *person* that she is," Findlay succumbs to the play's larger designs (52, emphasis mine).[18]

Although Cartelli and Findlay agree about the content of Portia's speech, they differ sharply on its effect and its relation to the play's larger concerns; this difference marks a larger divergence between how scholarly and theatrical institutions regard the purpose of interpreting Shakespeare. If recent scholarship tends to regard the play's manifest assertions as the mask of a concealed ideological complicity with various modes of hegemony, actors tend to regard these assertions as the play's essential meaning, what makes the play continue to speak to modern audiences. This attitude comes into view in the ways actors understand the plays to comment on contemporary life. Writing of his fascinating performance as Thersites in Sam Mendes' 1991 *Troilus and Cressida*, Simon Russell Beale recalls acting "*Troilus and Cressida* in Stratford on the night that war was declared in the Gulf, and I was powerfully aware then that Thersites's despair was shared by everyone in the theatre. Shakespeare's discussion of institutionalized machismo seemed more powerful and more relevant than ever, and I was reminded that it was an enormous privilege to have a part in presenting this great play and this extraordinary character" (Jackson and Smallwood, III: 173). In a similar vein, Brian Cox suggests a variety of historical parallels that have rendered *Titus Andronicus* an important play in the twentieth century:

> In our century the context for this play has never been more powerful.
> When Peter Brook produced it in 1951 the shadow of totalitarianism
> was very much upon us: Stalinism and the purges of the thirties, Hitler's
> Germany and the subsequent revelations of the Nuremburg [*sic*] trials.
> And now we have the rise of Islamic fundamentalism, the breakdown of
> social units, the mindless violence of soccer hooliganism, the sectarian
> violence of Northern Ireland, the disaffection of individuals within soci-
> ety resulting in mass murder sprees, not to mention the ever-increasing
> rise in rape crimes over the last forty years.
>
> This may seem an over-generalized spectrum of events relating to
> just one play by Shakespeare, but every one of those incidents has its
> parallel in *Titus Andronicus*. (Jackson and Smallwood, III: 176)

In these performances, as well as in Roger Allam's account of *Measure for Measure*—where in the city scenes, the "grey cut-away coats and knee-breeches of the court gave way to outrageous cycling shorts and Doc Marten boots. Most of our whores were rent-boys, run by Pompey, working a gents' toilet that rose from the floor" (Jackson and Smallwood, III: 27)—reference to a contemporary setting, and to contemporary politics, is taken to "de-anaesthetize" the plays "and thus shock and awaken our audience anew to the meaning of the scene" (27). Remarkably, these accounts cast performance as a parasite on the text: modern settings find "parallels" but don't produce new meanings, new Shakespeare, anti-Shakespeare. In all three cases, the "meaning" of the Shakespearean original is seen to be constant, despite the many—and contradictory—"parallels" that can be drawn to contemporary life through felicitous and imaginative design and direction. Putting "Shakespeare" on the modern stage may give us insight into our condition, but it doesn't change "Shakespeare"—it just dresses him in new clothes.

While critical activity locates the rhetoric of Shakespearean drama in its ideological milieu, in performative accounts (and, surprisingly, in academic "performance criticism") "Shakespeare" remains a point of repair, a touchstone of value beyond the actions and events the plays criticize. Much as *Merchant of Venice* is taken to be about antisemitism but not to participate in it or produce it (as it evidently did throughout its first two or three centuries onstage), so *Troilus*, *Titus*, and *Measure for Measure* are shown to criticize from the timeless Shakespearean perspective those temporal elements of social life which parallel meanings already somehow "there" in the play. To engage contemporary culture more critically, Shakespearean production—and Shakespearean acting—will have to engage the rhetoric that reproduces that culture more directly. Such a strategy would demand a more self-evident decentering of the privilege of "character" and a more skeptical regard for how Shakespearean "nature" is produced and implemented.

Brian Cox' account of his performance in Deborah Warner's 1987 *Titus Andronicus* points—at least momentarily—in this direction. Describing the production's brilliant finale, Cox notes how the play deliberately unmoored its audience from a conventional position of tragic judgment, an unmooring to which *Titus* is perhaps particularly well suited. Not parody, not irony, not Brechtian alienation, Warner's *Titus* seems to have released other, alternative ways of responding to the play. Cox recalls how Titus and his attendants entered, whistling "the *Snow White* dwarves' song, 'Hi-Ho'" as they set the table for Tamora:

> And then, in full starched white chef's garb, I came in, leaping over the table, with the pie. The world had gone crazy; the audience's embarrassment about serving the boys in the pie was released in laughter—but laughter from which you could cut them off. You could allow another laugh in the welcome:
>
> > Welcome, my lord; welcome, dread Queen;
> > Welcome, ye warlike Goths; welcome Lucius;
> > And welcome, *all* . . .
>
> —the last words addressed to the pie. (Jackson and Smallwood, III: 187)

Cox is right to see the tension between horror and laughter as akin to the way violence is represented in more recent plays. He suggests that Warner's scene, and Shakespeare's play, "out-Bonds Bond. It is a cruel play, deliberately cruel." But for all the didactic energy of Bond's prefaces and other writings, Bond's plays tend not to present violence as the human condition or an inevitable expression of human nature. Indeed, the overwhelming brutality of Bond's plays stems from the voluntary quality of their violence, the fact that characters (and audiences) choose violence when they are *not* tragically compelled to do so. Warner's playful horror seems directed toward this end, recomposing the play's violence away from key of high tragedy and toward something else, perhaps that "free-floating and impersonal," affectless euphoria typical of postmodern aesthetics.[19] It might be argued that this pastiche of Seneca, Shakespeare, and Disney represents an effort to decenter the constitutive "subjects" of the play: "Shakespeare," Titus, the actor, the ineffably self-present spectator. Perhaps—but the recuperative power of hegemonic ideologies is considerable, and in Cox' view *Titus* ultimately tells a different story: "The way human life is prized, the value of man and of his destiny—these things have never been as severely under question as they are now. *Titus Andronicus* examines the values by which we live" (188).

Comparing *Titus* to Bond, or as he might have done, to Peter Barnes or Howard Barker, Cox opens another way of conceiving the scene, a more problematic one. The use of Shakespeare to comment on the contemporary horizon almost always assumes that the conditions of Shakespearean production are themselves outside that horizon, that "Shakespeare" articulates a moral critique of contemporary life through his native language, the timeless language of the stage. The stage is often said to apply the "test" of performance to critical readings of Shakespeare, a "test" that screens out "meanings" unsuitable to the rhetoric of contemporary performance as innately illegitimate, un-Shakespearean. But there is no way to "translate" between different modes of producing the text; acting practice and critical practice remain in dialogue precisely because they are incommensurable.

By situating actors' reading in dialogue with scholars' reading, we make it possible to denaturalize the practices of the contemporary theatre, to ask how the practices of putting "Shakespeare" onstage resonate not only with contemporary theatrical conventions, but with the larger beliefs and attitudes that inform the wider reproduction of culture. Is there a way, for instance, in which the "intensities" of Warner's spiky, untragic *Titus* are, say, reminiscent of the "Singing in the Rain" scene from Stanley Kubrick's *A Clockwork Orange*, more a part of our cultural condition, representing and reinforcing it, than a critique of it? To ask how contemporary performance practice—how actors learn to read Shakespearean drama and rewrite it in the text of stage behavior— might respond in its own idiom to the more alienated perspective of contemporary criticism is to ask how Shakespeare in the theatre can become our contemporary in a very different sense than the one imagined by Jan Kott: not because he mystically anticipates our trials, or merely reflects the deeply ideological contours of our sense of "human nature," but a "Shakespeare" whose production is involved in our own deceptive and slippery rhetoric of self-fashioning.

NOTES

1. On "theatre poet," see Hapgood.

2. I have addressed some of these issues elsewhere; see Worthen, "Deeper Meanings" and "Staging 'Shakespeare.'"

3. See, for example, Buzacott.

4. See Brockbank I: 131, 153, 155; Jackson and Smallwood II: 15, 138, 181, 192; Jackson and Smallwood III: 22.

5. The scholars I have listed here are in fact immediately occupied with the signifying capability of Shakespeare's theatre; some have been criticized for not respecting the text of Shakespeare's plays faithfully enough.

6. For actors' use of the "journey," see Brockbank I: 2, 142, 159; Jackson and Smallwood II: 55 ("voyage of discovery"), 56; Jackson and Smallwood III: 41, 52, 113. Carol Rutter also notes, describing her plans to inteview five Shakespearean actresses for *Clamorous Voices*, that she "wanted them to follow the journey their character makes through the play" (xv).

7. I am thinking here, of course, of Fredric Jameson's use of *pastiche* as one of the identifying markers of postmodern representation.

8. "What kind of man is Malvolio? What is his background? I see him as a military man; unpopular at school, he joins the army and, while he displays no quality of leadership, he is so damned efficient that he now finds himself, at forty-five, a Colonel in the Pay corps, embittered, with no prospect of further promotion. He has bored every woman he has met and he stays unmarried. A certain widowed Count I suppose needed a major-domo to manage his Mediterranean estate, and who better than this totally efficient and honest teetotaller?" (Brockbank I: 43). Compare Stanislavski: "What is the *past* which justifies the *present* of this scene: Who is Roderigo?

I imagine that he is the son of very wealthy parents, landowners who took the produce of their village to Venice and exchanged it for velvet and other luxuries. These goods were in turn shipped to other countries, including Russia, and sold at great profit. But now Roderigo's parents are dead. How can he manage such a tremendous business?" (131). These are Stanislavski's notes for Roderigo's first entrance in the play.

9. Geoffrey Hutchings (Lavatch in Trevor Nunn's 1981 *All's Well That Ends Well*) notes that setting the play in 1910 helped to focus the "importance of class in the play and the emergence of women in society," as well as justifying a kind of military enthusiasm not imaginable in "our sophisticated world of nuclear and anti-nuclear warfare" (Brockbank I: 83).

10. Eliot's well-known passage reads, "The historical sense, which is a sense of the timeless as well as of the temporal and of the timeless and of the temporal together, is what makes a writer traditional. And it is at the same time what makes a writer most acutely conscious of his place in time, of his contemporaneity" (49).

11. Roger Allam, the Duke in Nicholas Hynter's 1987 *Measure for Measure*, describes reading Richard Sennett's *The Fall of Public Man* and Quentin Skinner's *The Foundations of Modern Political Thought* "in a quite dilettantish way to stimulate my imagination" while playing Brutus in *Julius Caesar*. This reading, a visit to Pentonville prison, Michael Ignatieff's *A Just Measure of Pain*, and Ignatieff's television series *Voices* blended together in a "varied soup of thoughts and experiences I brought in at the start of rehearsals to begin the more practical task of finding some sort of character for the Duke" (Jackson and Smallwood, III: 23, 24–25). "Historical" research, in Allam's practice, ameliorates the difference between a "character" whose mode of being seems remote and strange and the assumed sensibility of a contemporary audience.

12. See also Tony Church's comments on his "oppressive Victorian-style paterfamilias" Polonius in 1980 (Brockbank, I: 107); and Geoffrey Hutchings' reading of "the metaphysical poets" and "poems about war" for his 1981 Lavatch (Brockbank, I: 83).

13. On the function of such anecdote, see the openings of each chapter of Stephen Greenblatt's *Shakespearean Negotiations*, including chapter 2, "Invisible Bullets." Yet as Jean Howard has asked, "But again, as with Greenblatt's use of the illustrative example, one wants to know more about the process by which disparate phenomena are chosen for juxtaposition and discussion; the juxtaposition can seem arbitrary to those reared on the notion of 'coverage,' that is, on the idea that all the texts and all the documents need to be surveyed before one can say with confidence that any two stand

in a pivotal cultural position. Greenblatt's practice implicitly challenges this mode of thinking, but one wishes for an overt articulation of his oppositional point of view" ("New Historicism," 31).

14. For example, the American Repertory Theatre's 1994 production of *Henry IV, Parts 1 and 2* created the court "with images from the American Civil War, while Falstaff's tavern world is very much of the 1990s, with a punk Prince Hal (Bill Camp) and his biker buddies. Some critics found such anachronisms distracting but [director Ron] Daniels maintains that his interpretation is by no means cynical. 'This is an interpretation of integration—of how this young man is very cleverly synthesizing within himself the feminine and masculine principles. The interesting thing about the play is the way it brings the warring aspects of a nation together through the person of the new king, who is himself a synthesis of these opposing forces'" (Tropea, 41).

15. It should be noted that Howard and O'Connor, with their emphasis on material history, sit somewhat uneasily within the general rubric of "new historicism," as do nearly all of its practitioners; see also Howard, "The New Historicism in Literary Studies" for a critique of the practice of new historicism.

16. Veeser's remark in its entirety reads, "Suspicious of any criticism predetermined by a Marxist or liberal grid, New Historicists eschew overarching hypothetical constructs in favor of surprising coincidences" ("Introduction," xi–xii).

17. As Whigham argues, when Portia "finds no mention of a jot of blood, she reveals the language of the law as infinitely interpretable, as the ongoing creation of its native speakers, who maintain their power precisely by 'ad libbing' with it. Portia discovers the necessary escape clause in the white spaces between the lines, where no strict construction is possible" (110). For a position that questions this use of ideology, see Ferber, 462.

18. Cartelli remarks that "for Brecht in our own time, a set speech (or 'set song') occasions the alienation (understood by Brecht as the enhancement of self-consciousness) of both actor and audience by explicitly illustrating the actor's movement from his role as character to his role as commentator or spokesperson, and by conjoining this movement to the play's corresponding shift from presentation to proselytizing" (16–17). It is precisely this movement that is impeded by a conception of the character's "journey" through the play.

19. I am thinking here of Fredric Jameson's discussion of the relationship between postmodern art, the death of the subject, and what he calls "the waning of affect" (15).

Contributors

Michael D. Bristol, professor of English at McGill University, is the author of *Carnival and Theatre: Plebeian Culture and the Structure of Authority in Renaissance England* and *Shakespeare's America, America's Shakespeare*. His current research is concerned with Shakespeare's long-term cultural authority.

Alan C. Dessen, Peter G. Phialas Professor of English at the University of North Carolina–Chapel Hill, is the director of ACTER (A Center for Teaching, Education, and Research) and the editor of the "Shakespeare Performed" section of *Shakespeare Quarterly*. He is the author of six books on Shakespeare and English Renaissance drama, including *Elizabethan Stage Conventions and Modern Interpreters* (Cambridge University Press, 1984) and *Recovering Shakespeare's Theatrical Vocabulary* (Cambridge University Press, 1995).

Barbara Hodgdon, Ellis and Nelle Levitt Professor of English at Drake University, is the author of *The End Crowns All: Closure and Contradiction in Shakespeare's History* (Princeton University Press, 1991), *Henry IV, Part Two* in the Manchester Shakespeare in Performance Series, and *Restaging Shakespeare's Cultural Capital: Women, Queens, Spectatorship*, forthcoming from the University of Pennsylvania's Cultural Studies series. She is the editor of *The Taming of the Shrew* for Arden 3.

Leanore Lieblein, chair of English at McGill University, has published articles on medieval and Renaissance drama in performance and has directed medieval, Renaissance, and modern plays. She has been associated with the Centre de Recherches sur la Renaissance of the Université de Paris–Sorbonne and done archival research at the Théâtre Nanterre–Amandiers and other European theatres. She has co-translated *Les Esbahis* (*Taken by Surprise*) by Jacques Grévin (1561).

Kathleen E. McLuskie, professor of English at the University of Southampton, has written *Renaissance Dramatists* (Humanities, 1989) and *Dekker and Heywood: Professional Dramatists* (Macmillan, 1994). She is currently editing *Macbeth* for the Arden 3 edition and working on a book about the commercialization of drama in early modern England.

Laurie E. Osborne, associate professor of English at Colby College, is the author of *Twelfe Night, or what you will (F 1623)* in the Shakespeare Originals Series (Harvester, 1995) and *The Trick of Singularity: "Twelfth Night" and the Performance Editions* (University of Iowa Press, 1996). She has also written essays on Shakespearean film, theorizing the Renaissance female audience, and alternative editorial traditions of Shakespeare.

Edward Pechter, the author of *Dryden's Classical Theory of Literature* (Cambridge University Press, 1975) and *What Was Shakespeare? Renaissance Plays and Changing Critical Practice* (Cornell University Press, 1995), is professor of English at Concordia University.

John Ripley, Greenshields Professor of English at McGill University, is a theatre historian, actor, and director. His publications include *"Julius Caesar" on Stage in England and America 1599–1973* (Cambridge University Press, 1980), *Gilbert Parker and Herbert Beerbohm Tree Stage "The Seats of the Mighty"* (Simon and Pierre, 1987), and essays on Shakespeare in performance and Canadian theatre. His stage history of *Coriolanus* is forthcoming.

Catherine M. Shaw, of the English Department at McGill University, is the author of *"Some Vanity of Mine Art": The Masque in English Drama* (1979), *Richard Brome* (1980), and numerous essays on Shakespeare. She has published critical editions of Middleton and Rowley's *The Old Law* (1982) and Cokayne's *The Obstinate Lady* and is at present writing a collection of essays on Shakespeare's histories in performance.

Robert Weimann is professor of drama and performance theory at the University of California, Irvine. In Berlin, he headed a research group on English and American literature in the Zentralinstitut für Literaturgeschichte from 1976 to 1991 and co-chaired Forschungsschwerpunkt Literaturwissenschaft from 1992 to 1994. He served as president of the German Shakespeare Society in Weimar (1985 to 1993), and has held visiting professorships at major universities in North America. He is currently completing a two-volume study of authority and representation in early modern discourse.

W. B. Worthen is professor of English and theatre and director of the interdisciplinary Ph.D. in theatre and drama at Northwestern University. He is the author of *The Idea of the Actor: Drama and the Ethics of Performance* (Princeton University Press, 1984), *Modern Drama and the Rhetoric of Theater* (University of California Press, 1992), and articles on Shakespearean performance and performance theory. He is past editor of *Theatre Journal* and editor of *The HBJ Anthology of Drama* and *Modern Drama: Plays/Criticism/Theory*. He is currently completing a book on textuality and authority in modern Shakespearean performance.

Works Cited

Achinstein, Peter. "Concepts of Evidence." In *The Concept of Evidence,* ed. Peter Achinstein, 145–174. Oxford Readings in Philosophy. Oxford: Oxford University Press, 1983.

Ackerman, Marianne. "Bard Well Served in East End Cycle." *Montreal Daily News,* April 1, 1988.

———. "L'Evénement Shakespeare." *Canadian Theatre Review* 57 (Winter 1988): 81–85.

———. "French Theatre's Love Affair with the Bard." *Montreal Daily News,* March 19, 1988.

———. "Lepage's Bard: Thoroughly Modern Willie." *Montreal Daily News,* April 16, 1988.

———. "Shakespeare? Oui!" *Saturday Night,* October 1988, 107–108.

Agee, James, and Walker Evans. *Let Us Now Praise Famous Men.* 1939. Rpt. Boston: Houghton Mifflin, 1980.

Allen, Guy Pierce. "Seven English Versions of the Coriolanus Story." Diss. University of Toronto, 1978.

Andrès, Bernard, and Paul Lefèbvre. " 'Macbeth/Théâtre de la Manufacture." *Cahiers de théâtre jeu* ll (1979): 80–88.

Archer, Ian W. *The Pursuit of Stability: Social Relations in Elizabethan London.* Cambridge: Cambridge University Press, 1991.

Ayres, James B. "Shakespeare in the Restoration: Nahum Tate's *The History of King Richard the Second, The History of King Lear,* and *The Ingratitude of a Common-wealth.*" Diss. Ohio State University, 1964.

Bacon, Sir Francis. "Of Parents and Children." *The Essayes or Counsels, Civill and Morall,* ed. Michael Kiernan, 23–24. Cambridge, Mass.: Harvard University Press, 1985.

Badiou, Alain. "L'Etat théâtral, en son état." *L'"Art du théâtre"* 8 (1987): 13–26.

Barbe, Jean. "Les Fées ont soif." *Voir,* April 7–13, 1988.

Barker, Howard. "Conversations with a Dead Poet." In *Arguments for a Theatre,* 25–28. Manchester: Manchester University Press, 1989.

Barroll, J. Leeds. "A New History for Shakespeare and His Time." *Shakespeare Quarterly* 39 (1988): 441–465.

Barthes, Roland. *Camera Lucida: Reflections on Photography* (1980). Trans. Richard Howard. New York: Hill and Wang, 1981.

———. "Diderot, Brecht, Eisenstein." In *Image/Music/Text,* trans. Stephen Heath, 69–78. New York: Hill and Wang, 1977.

———. "From Work to Text." In *Image/Music/Text,* trans. Stephen Heath, 155–164. New York: Hill and Wang, 1977.

Bazin, Germain. *Baroque and Rococo.* Trans. Jonathan Griffin. London: Thames and Hudson, 1989.

Beauman, Sally, ed. *The Royal Shakespeare Company's Production of Henry V for the Centenary Season at the Royal Shakespeare Theatre.* Oxford: Pergamon Press, 1976.

Beaumont, Sir Francis. *The Knight of the Burning Pestle.* In *The Dramatic Works in the Beaumont and Fletcher Canon,* ed. Fredson Bowers, vol. I. 10 vols. Cambridge: Cambridge University Press, 1966.

Beaunoyer, Jean. "Pour en finir avec Shakespeare." *La Presse,* April 21, 1988.

———. "Un Printemps shakespearien." *La Presse,* March 12, 1988.

———. " 'Le Songe . . .' une pièce violente traitée par un homme très spécial." *La Presse,* March 12, 1988.

Beckerman, Bernard. *The Dynamics of Drama.* New York: Knopf, 1970.

———. *Shakespeare at the Globe, 1599–1609.* New York: Macmillan, 1962.

———. "Theatrical Plots and Elizabethan Stage Practice." In *Shakespeare and Dramatic Tradition: Essays in Honor of S. F. Johnson,* ed. W. R. Elton and William B. Long, 109–124. Newark: University of Delaware Press, 1989.

———. "The Use and Management of the Elizabethan Stage." In *The Third Globe: Symposium for the Reconstruction of the Globe Playhouse,* ed. C. Walter Hodges, S. Schoenbaum, and Leonard Leone, 151–163. Detroit: Wayne State University Press, 1981.

Bélair, Michel. "St-Tite à Terre des hommes." *Le Devoir,* July 16, 1970.

Benjamin, Walter. *The Origin of German Tragic Drama.* Trans. John Osborne. London: New Left Books, 1977.

Bennett, Tony. "Texts, Readers, Reading Formations" (1983). Rpt. in *Modern Literary Theory*, ed. Philip Rice and Patricia Waugh, 206–220. London: Edward Arnold, 1989.

Bentley, Gerald Eades. *The Jacobean and Caroline Stage.* 7 vols. Oxford: Clarendon Press, 1941–1968.

Berger, Harry, Jr. *Imaginary Audition: Shakespeare on Stage and Page.* Berkeley: University of California Press, 1989.

Bernard, Jami. Review of *Hamlet*, dir. Franco Zeffirelli. *New York Post*, December 19, 1990.

Berry, Herbert. "The Globe Bewitched and El Hombre Fiel." *Medieval and Renaissance Drama in England* 1 (1984): 211–230.

Bevington, David. *From "Mankind" to Marlowe: Growth and Structure in the Popular Drama of Tudor England.* Cambridge, Mass.: Harvard University Press, 1962.

Bogdanov, Michael, and Michael Pennington. *The English Shakespeare Company: The Story of "The Wars of the Roses" 1986–1989.* London: Nick Hern Books, 1990.

Bordwell, David. *Narration in the Fiction Film.* Madison: University of Wisconsin Press, 1985.

Bouchard, Louise. "Lear." *Cahiers de théâtre jeu* 5 (1977): 107–110.

Boulanger, Luc. "Sexepeare au TNM." *Montréal Campus*, March 30, 1988.

Bradley, A. C. "Coriolanus." *Proceedings of the British Academy* 5 (1911–1912): 457–473.

Braunmuller, A. R. "'To the Globe I rowed': John Holles Sees *A Game at Chess.*" *English Literary Renaissance* 20 (1990): 340–356.

Brecht, Bertolt. *Brecht on Theatre.* Trans. John Willett. London: Methuen, 1964.

———. "The Curtains." In *Bertolt Brecht, Poems 1913–1956*, ed. John Willett and Ralph Manheim, 425. New York: Methuen, 1976.

Briganti, Giuliano. *Italian Mannerism.* Trans. Margaret Kunzle. London: Thames and Hudson, 1962.

Brisset, Annie. *Sociocritique de la traduction: Théâtre et altérité au Québec (1968–1988).* Longueuil, Québec: Le Préambule, 1990.

Bristol, Michael D. *Shakespeare's America, America's Shakespeare.* London and New York: Routledge, 1990.

Brockbank, Philip. "Foreword." In Brockbank, *Players*, ix.

———. "Introduction: Abstracts and brief chronicles." In Brockbank, *Players*, 1–10.

————, ed. *Players of Shakespeare: Essays in Shakespearean Performance by Twelve Players with the Royal Shakespeare Company*. Cambridge and New York: Cambridge University Press, 1985.

Brown, John Russell. *Free Shakespeare*. London: Heinemann, 1975.

Bruster, Douglas. *Drama and the Market in the Age of Shakespeare*. Cambridge: Cambridge University Press, 1992.

Bryan, George S. *The Great American Myth*. New York: Carrick and Evans, 1940.

Buzacott, Martin. *The Death of the Actor*. London and New York: Routledge, 1991.

Camerlain, Lorraine. "Echos shakespeariens." *Cahiers du théâtre jeu* 46 (1988): 5–6.

Carlson, Marvin. "Theatre Audiences and the Reading of Performance." In Postlewait and McConachie, 82–98.

Caron, Anne. *Le Père Emile Legault et le théâtre au Québec*. Montréal: Fides, 1978.

Carson, Neil. *A Companion to Henslowe's Diary*. Cambridge: Cambridge University Press, 1988.

Cartelli, Thomas. "Ideology and Subversion in the Shakespearean Set Speech." *English Literary History* 53 (1986): 1–25.

Cavell, Stanley. " 'Who does the wolf love?': Reading *Coriolanus*." *Representations* 3 (Summer 1983): 1–20.

Chambers, E. K. *The Elizabethan Stage*. 4 vols. Oxford: Clarendon Press, 1923.

Chandler, James, Arnold I. Davidson, and Harry D. Harootunian, eds. *Questions of Evidence: Proof, Practice, and Persuasion across the Disciplines*. Chicago: University of Chicago Press, 1993.

Chapman, George. *The Plays of George Chapman: The Comedies*, gen. ed. Allan Holaday. Urbana, Chicago, and London: University of Illinois Press, 1970.

————. *The Plays of George Chapman: The Tragedies with Sir Gyles Goosecappe*, gen. ed. Allan Holaday. Cambridge: D. S. Brewer, 1987.

Choquette, Gilles. "Bouchée triple." *Voir*, March 31–April 6, 1988.

Cohen, Walter. "Political Criticism of Shakespeare." In Howard and O'Connor, *Shakespeare Reproduced*, 18–46.

Coleridge, Samuel Taylor. *Shakespearean Criticism*. Ed. Thomas Middleton Raysor. 2 vols. London: J. M. Dent, 1960.

Crews, Frederick. *Skeptical Engagements*. Oxford: Oxford University Press, 1986.

Cunningham, J. S., ed. *Tamburlaine the Great*. Revels Plays. Manchester:

Manchester University Press, 1981.

Daly, Joseph Frances. *The Life of Augustin Daly*. New York: Macmillan, 1971.

Dassylva, Martial. "Ce 'Macbeth' qui est d'abord de William Shakespeare et ensuite de Michel Garneau." *La Presse*, October 23, 1978.

Davenant, William. *The Dramatic Works*. 5 vols. Edinburgh, 1872–1874. Rpt. New York: Russell and Russell, 1964.

Davenport, Robert. *The Works*. In *A Collection of Old English Plays*, ed. A. H. Bullen, vol. III. 4 vols. London, 1882–1889. Rpt. New York: B. Blom, 1964.

David, Gilbert. "D'une saison l'autre: Le facteur mise en scène." *Parachute* 55 (1988): 56–60.

Davis, Dorothy. *The History of Shopping*. London and New York: Routledge, 1986.

Davis, Tracy C. *Actresses as Working Women: Their Social Identity in Victorian Culture*. London and New York: Routledge, 1991.

Debord, Guy. *Society of the Spectacle*. Exeter: Rebel Press, 1987.

de Certeau, Michel. *The Writing of History*. New York: Columbia University Press, 1988.

de Grazia, Margreta. *Shakespeare Verbatim: The Reproduction of Authenticity and the 1790 Apparatus*. Oxford: Clarendon Press, 1991.

de Grazia, Margreta, and Peter Stallybrass. "The Materiality of the Shakespearean Text." *Shakespeare Quarterly* 44 (1993): 255–284.

Dekker, Thomas. *The Dramatic Works*. Ed. Fredson Bowers. 4 vols. Cambridge: Cambridge University Press, 1953–1961.

———. *The Guls Horne-booke*. London, 1609. Rpt. Menston: Scolar Press, 1969.

Denham, Sir John. *The Sophy*. Wing D-1009. 1642.

Dessen, Alan C. *Elizabethan Stage Conventions and Modern Interpreters*. Cambridge: Cambridge University Press, 1984.

———. *Recovering Shakespeare's Theatrical Vocabulary*. Cambridge: Cambridge University Press, 1995.

de Vries, Jan. "Purchasing Power and the World of Goods." In *Consumption and the World of Goods*, ed. John Brewer and R. Porter, 85–132. London and New York: Routledge, 1993.

Didion, Joan. "The White Album." In *The White Album*, 11–48. New York: Simon and Schuster, 1979.

Dillon, Janette. "Is There a Performance in This Text?" *Shakespeare Quarterly* 45 (1994): 74–86.

Dodsley, Robert. *A Select Collection of Old English Plays*. 1874. 15 vols.

Rpt. New York: B. Blom, 1964.

Dollimore, Jonathan, and Alan Sinfield, eds. *Political Shakespeare: New Essays in Cultural Materialism*. Manchester: Manchester University Press, 1985.

Donaldson, Peter S. "Books in Bits: Images of Print Culture in Shakespearean Films from Olivier's *Henry V* to *Prospero's Books*." Multimedia essay presented at the Center for Literary and Cultural Studies, Harvard University, February 1994.

———. "Ghostly Texts and Virtual Performances: Old Hamlet in New Media." Presented at the Shakespeare Association of America, April 1993.

Donnelly, Pat. "Brilliant Tempête Defies Tradition." *Gazette*, March 23, 1988.

———. "Shakespeare Cycle Rings with Iron." *Gazette*, April 2, 1988.

———. "Songe's Mix of Oz and Cats Makes Dizzying Theatrical Potion." *Gazette*, April 15, 1988.

Donohue, Joseph. "Evidence and Documentation." In Postlewait and McConachie, 177–197.

Dupuis, Josée. "Ici Montréal." *Télé-Métropole*, April 15, 1988.

Dyer, Richard. *Heavenly Bodies: Film Stars and Society*. London: BFI Publishing, 1987.

———. *Stars*. London: BFI Publishing, 1982.

Eccles, Mark. *Christopher Marlowe in London*. Harvard Studies in English 10 (1934). Rpt. New York: Octagon Books, 1967.

Eliot, T. S. "Tradition and the Individual Talent." In *The Sacred Wood: Essays on Poetry and Criticism*, 47–59. 1920. Rpt. London: Methuen, 1976.

Elster, John. "Belief, Bias and Rationality." In *Rationality and Relativism*, ed. Martin Hollis and Steven Lukes, 123–148. Cambridge, Mass.: MIT Press, 1982.

Empson, William. *Some Versions of Pastoral*. London: Chatto and Windus, 1935.

Fahnestock, Jeanne, and Marie Secor. "The Rhetoric of Literary Criticism." In *Textual Dynamics of the Professions: Historical and Contemporary Studies of Writing in Professional Communities*, ed. Charles Bazerman and James Paradis, 76–96. Madison: University of Wisconsin Press, 1991.

Fair Em. Ed. W. W. Greg. Malone Society. Oxford: Oxford University Press, 1928.

Fehrenbacher, Don E. *Lincoln in Text and Context*. Stanford: Stanford University Press, 1987.

Feldman, R., and E. Conee. "Evidentialism." *Philosophical Studies* 48 (1985): 15–34.

Ferber, Michael. "The Ideology of *The Merchant of Venice*." *English Literary Renaissance* 20 (1990): 431–464.

Festival du Théâtre des Amériques du 27 mai au 12 juin 1993. Publicity brochure.

Feuillerat, Albert, ed. *The Prose Works of Sir Philip Sidney*. 4 vols. 1912–1926. Rpt. Cambridge: Cambridge University Press, 1965.

Field, Nathan. *The Plays*. Ed. William Peery. Austin: University of Texas Press, 1950.

Fletcher, John, and Francis Beaumont. *The Works*. Ed. Arnold Glover and A. R. Waller. 10 vols. Cambridge: Cambridge University Press, 1905–1912.

Fletcher, John, and Philip Massinger. *Sir John Van Olden Barnavelt*. Ed. T. H. Howard-Hill. Malone Society. Oxford: Oxford University Press, 1980.

Foucault, Michel. *The Archaeology of Knowledge*. Trans. A. M. Sheridan Smith. New York: Harper and Row, 1976.

———. *Foucault Live (Interviews, 1966–84)*. Trans. John Johnston, ed. Sylvère Lotringer. Semiotext(e) Foreign Accent Series. New York: Columbia University Press, 1989.

———. "What Is an Author?" In *Language, Counter-Memory, Practice: Selected Essays and Interviews*, ed. Donald F. Bouchard, 113–138. Ithaca: Cornell University Press, 1977.

Fraser, Matthew. "Fops, Firebrands and Fair Ladies." *Globe and Mail*, April 6, 1988.

Fried, Michael. *Absorption and Theatricality: Painting and Beholder in the Age of Diderot*. Berkeley: University of California Press, 1980.

Friedman, Winifred. "Introduction." In *Boydell's Shakespeare Gallery*. New York: Garland, 1976.

Gaines, Jane. "Dead Ringer: Jacqueline Onassis and the Look-Alike." *South Atlantic Quarterly* 88 (1989): 461–486.

Gallion, Sally Marie. "*Coriolanus* on the Restoration and Eighteenth-Century Stage: Does Virtue 'Lie in th'Interpretation of the Time?'" Diss. University of Missouri–Columbia, 1979.

Garneau, Michel, trans. *Coriolan de William Shakespeare*. Montreal: VLB, 1989.

———, trans. *Macbeth de William Shakespeare*. Montreal: VLB, 1978.

———, trans. *La Tempête de William Shakespeare*. Montreal: VLB, 1989.

Gélinas. Aline. "La Fête des rois." *Voir*, May 5–11, 1988.

———. "Françoise Faucher: L'Aventure, c'est l'aventure." *Voir*, March

17–23, 1988, 7.

George a Greene. Ed. F. W. Clarke. Malone Society. Oxford: Oxford University Press, 1911.

Gervinus, G. G. *Shakespeare* (1849–1850). Rev. edition. *Shakespeare Commentaries.* Trans. F. E. Bunnett. London: Smith, Elder, 1877.

Giroux, Henry, and Roger I. Simon. "Pedagogy and the Critical Practice of Photography." In *Disturbing Pleasures: Learning Popular Culture,* ed. Henry Giroux and Roger I. Simon, 93–103. London and New York: Routledge, 1994.

Glapthorne, Henry. *The Plays and Poems.* 2 vols. London: J. Pearson, 1874.

Glymour, Clark. *Theory and Evidence.* Princeton: Princeton University Press, 1980.

Greenblatt, Stephen. "Introduction." In *The Power of Forms in the English Renaissance,* ed. Stephen Greenblatt, 3–6. Norman: University of Oklahoma Press, 1982.

———. *Shakespearean Negotiations: The Circulation of Social Energy in Renaissance England.* Berkeley and Los Angeles: University of California Press, 1988.

Greenblatt, Stephen, and Giles Gunn. *Redrawing the Boundaries: The Transformation of English and American Literary Studies.* New York: Modern Language Association of America, 1992.

Greenfield, Peter H. "Touring." In *A New History of English Drama,* ed. John D. Cox and David Kastan. New York: Columbia University Press, forthcoming.

Greenwood, John. *Shifting Perspectives and the Stylish Style: Mannerism in Shakespeare and His Jacobean Contemporaries.* Toronto: University of Toronto Press, 1988.

Greg, W. W. *Dramatic Documents from the Elizabethan Playhouses.* 2 vols. Oxford: Clarendon Press, 1931.

Grossmann, Edwina Booth. *Recollections by His Daughter and Letters to Her and His Friends.* New York: Century Company, 1894.

Guérard, Daniel. "Bon Dimanche," *CFTM,* March 27, 1988.

Gurik, Robert. *Hamlet, prince du Québec.* N.p.: Leméac, 1977.

Gurr, Andrew. *Playgoing in Shakespeare's London.* Cambridge: Cambridge University Press, 1987.

———. *The Shakespearean Stage 1574–1642.* 3d edition. Cambridge: Cambridge University Press, 1991.

———, ed. *King Richard II.* Cambridge and New York: Cambridge University Press, 1984.

Hall, Joseph. *The Works.* Ed. Philip Wynter. 1863. Rpt. New York: AMS Press, 1969.

Halperin, Richard. *The Poetics of Primitive Accumulation: English Renaissance Culture and the Genealogy of Capital.* Ithaca and London: Cornell University Press, 1991.

Hammond, Antony, ed. *Richard III.* Arden edition. London: Methuen, 1981.

Hapgood, Robert. *Shakespeare the Theatre-Poet.* Oxford: Clarendon Press, 1988.

Harrison, Richard Clarence. "Walt Whitman and Shakespeare." *PMLA* 44 (1929): 1201–1238.

Hart, Henry M., and John T. McNaughton. "Some Aspects of Evidence and Inference in the Law." In *Evidence and Inference,* ed. Daniel Lerner, 48–72. Glencoe, Ill.: Free Press, 1958.

Hauser, Arnold. *Mannerism: The Crisis of the Renaissance and the Origin of Modern Art.* 2 vols. London: Routledge and Kegan Paul, 1965.

Hazlitt, William. *The Complete Works.* Ed. P. P. Howe. 21 vols. London: J. M. Dent, 1930–1934.

Heinemann, Margo. "How Brecht Read Shakespeare." In Dollimore and Sinfield, 202–230.

Heywood, Thomas. *The Dramatic Works.* Ed. J. Pearson. 6 vols. 1874. Rpt. New York: Russell and Russell, 1964.

Hilton, Julian. *Performances.* London: Macmillan, 1987.

Hodgdon, Barbara. "The Critic, the Poor Player, Prince Hamlet, and the Lady in the Dark." In *Shakespeare Reread: The Text in New Contexts,* ed. Russ McDonald, 259–293. Ithaca: Cornell University Press, 1994.

———. *The End Crowns All: Closure and Contradiction in Shakespeare's History.* Princeton: Princeton University Press, 1991.

———. *Henry IV Part Two.* Manchester: Manchester University Press, 1993.

———. "Splish Splash and the Other: Lepage's Intercultural *Dream* Machine." *Essays in Theatre/Etudes théâtrales* 12:1 (November 1993): 29–40.

Hofstadter, Richard. *The American Political Tradition and the Men Who Made It.* New York: Alfred A. Knopf, 1959.

Holderness, Graham, ed. *The Shakespeare Myth.* Manchester: Manchester University Press, 1988.

Holderness, Graham, Bryan Loughrey, and Andrew Murphy. "What's the Matter? Shakespeare and Textual Theory." *Textual Practice* 9 (1995): 93–120.

Homier Roy, René. "Touche-à-tout." *CKAC*, April 15, 1988.

Hook, Judith. *The Baroque Age in England*. London: Thames and Hudson, 1976.

Hook, Lucyle. "Shakespeare Improv'd, or a Case for the Affirmative." *Shakespeare Quarterly* 4 (1953): 289–299.

Hosley, Richard. "The Gallery over the Stage in the Public Playhouse of Shakespeare's Time." *Shakespeare Quarterly* 8 (1957): 15–31.

Howard, Jean E. "The New Historicism in Literary Studies." In *Renaissance Historicism: Selections from "English Literary Renaissance,"* ed. Arthur F. Kinney and Dan S. Collins, 3–33. Amherst: University of Massachusetts Press, 1987.

Howard, Jean E., and Marion F. O'Connor. "Introduction." In Howard and O'Connor, 1–17.

———, eds. *Shakespeare Reproduced: The Text in History and Ideology*. New York and London: Methuen, 1987.

Hudson, H. N. *Lectures on Shakespeare*. New York: Baker and Scribner, 1848.

Hunt, Leigh. *Leigh Hunt's Dramatic Criticism: 1808–1831*. Ed. Lawrence Huston Houtchens and Carolyn Washburn Houtchens. New York: Columbia University Press, 1949.

Hunter, G. K. "The Beginnings of English Drama: Resolution and Continuity." In *Renaissance Drama as Cultural History: Essays from "Renaissance Drama" 1977–1987*, ed. Mary Beth Rose, 287–310. Evanston: Northwestern University Press, 1990.

Hunter, Jefferson. *Image and Word: The Interaction of Twentieth-Century Photographs and Texts*. Cambridge, Mass.: Harvard University Press, 1987.

Inchbald, Elizabeth. *Inchbald's British Theatre*. London: Longman, Hurst, Rees, and Orm, 1808.

Iser, Wolfgang. *Shakespeares Historien: Genesis und Geltung*. Konstanz: Universitätsverlag, 1988.

Jackson, Russell, and Robert Smallwood, eds. *Players of Shakespeare 2: Further Essays in Shakespearean Performance by Players with the Royal Shakespeare Company*. Cambridge and New York: Cambridge University Press, 1989.

———. *Players of Shakespeare 3: Further Essays in Shakespearean Performance by Players with the Royal Shakespeare Company*. Cambridge and New York: Cambridge University Press, 1993.

Jameson, Fredric. *Postmodernism, or, The Cultural Logic of Late Capitalism*. Durham: Duke University Press, 1991.

Jones, Virgil L. "Methods of Satire in the Political Drama of the Restoration." *Journal of English and Germanic Philology* 21 (1922): 662–669.

Jonson, Ben. *Ben Jonson*. Ed. C. H. Herford and Percy and Evelyn Simpson. 11 vols. Oxford: Clarendon Press, 1925–1952.

Kennedy, Dennis. *Looking at Shakespeare*. Cambridge: Cambridge University Press, 1993.

Kimball, Roger. *Tenured Radicals: How Politics Has Corrupted Our Higher Education*. New York: Harper and Row, 1990.

Knutson, Roslyn L. *The Repertory of Shakespeare's Company 1594–1613*. Fayetteville: University of Arkansas Press, 1991.

Kott, Jan. *Shakespeare Our Contemporary*. New York: Norton, 1974.

Krauss, Rosalind E. *The Optical Unconscious*. Cambridge: Massachusetts Institute of Technology, 1993.

Kyd, Thomas. *The First Part of Hieronimo* and *The Spanish Tragedy*. Ed. Andrew S. Cairncross. Regents Renaissance Drama. Lincoln: University of Nebraska Press, 1967.

Larue-Langlois, Jacques. "Les Théâtres de Michel Garneau." *Le Devoir*, October 28, 1978.

Leacroft, Richard. *The Development of the English Playhouse*. London: Eyre Methuen, 1973.

Lecomte, Anne-Marie. "Shakespeare aux mains des femmes." *Montréal Campus*, March 16, 1988.

Lefebvre, Paul. "Shakespeare en jupons." *MTL*, March 1988.

Leinwand, Theodore B. "Shakespeare and the Middling Sort." *Shakespeare Quarterly* 44 (1993): 295–302.

Lennep, William Van, ed. *The London Stage 1600–1800, Part 1: 1660–1700*. Carbondale: Southern Illinois University Press, 1965.

Lévesque, Robert. "A Montréal, ce printemps, c'est Shakespeare partout." *Le Devoir*, April 16, 1988.

———. "Asselin et Gaudin s'accaparent bellement William Shakespeare." *Le Devoir*, April 8, 1988.

———. "Françoise Faucher: De la race des grandes interprètes." *Le Devoir*, March 12, 1988.

———. "Le Prix du CACUM au 'Printemps Shakespeare.'" *Le Devoir*, April 9, 1988.

———. "Quand Shakespeare s'habille dans l'Est." *Le Devoir*, March 14, 1989.

———. "Robert Lepage: La route semée de théâtres." *Le Devoir*, April 18, 1988.

Levine, Lawrence. *High Brow, Low Brow: The Emergence of Cultural Hier-*

archy in America. Cambridge, Mass., and London: Harvard University Press, 1988.

Locrine. Ed. Ronald B. McKerrow. Malone Society. Oxford: Oxford University Press, 1908.

Lodge, Thomas. *The Wounds of Civil War*. Ed. J. Dover Wilson. Malone Society. Oxford: Oxford University Press, 1910.

Long, William B. "'A bed / for woodstock': A Warning for the Unwary." *Medieval and Renaissance Drama in England* 2 (1985): 91–118.

———. "*John a Kent and John a Cumber*: An Elizabethan Playbook and Its Implications." In *Shakespeare and Dramatic Tradition: Essays in Honor of S. F. Johnson*, ed. W. R. Elton and William B. Long, 125–143. Newark: University of Delaware Press, 1989.

———. "Stage Directions: A Misinterpreted Factor in Determining Textual Provenance." *Text* 2 (1985): 121–137.

Lounsbury, Thomas R. *Shakespeare as a Dramatic Artist*. 1901. Rpt. New York: Ungar, 1965.

Macbeth—Coriolan—La Tempête. Dir. Robert Lepage. Prod. Théâtre Repère. Festival d'Automne, Paris, 1992. Press Release.

Mann, D. *The Elizabethan Player: Contemporary Stage Representations*. London and New York: Routledge, 1991.

Marlowe, Christopher. *Marlowe's "Doctor Faustus" 1604–1616*. Ed. W. W. Greg. Oxford: Clarendon Press, 1950.

Marsden, Jean. "'Modesty Unshackled': Dorothy Jordan and the Dangers of Cross-dressing." *Studies in Eighteenth-Century Culture* 22 (1992): 21–35.

Massinger, Philip. *Believe as You List*. Ed. Charles J. Sisson. Malone Society. Oxford: Oxford University Press, 1928.

———. *The Plays and Poems*. Ed. Philip Edwards and Colin Gibson. 5 vols. Oxford: Oxford University Press, 1976.

Mayne, Jasper. *The Amorous War*. Wing M-1463. 1648.

McGugan, Ruth Ella. "Nahum Tate and the Coriolanus Tradition in English Drama with a Critical Edition of Tate's *The Ingratitude of a Commonwealth*." Diss. University of Illinois, 1965.

McKendrick, Neil, John Brewer, and J. H. Plumb. *The Birth of a Consumer Society: The Commercialization of Eighteenth-Century England*. London: Hutchinson, 1982.

McKenzie, Stanley D. "'Unshout the noise that banish'd Martius': Structural Paradox and Dissembling in *Coriolanus*." *Shakespeare Studies* 18 (1986): 189–204.

McLuskie, Kathleen. "'Lawless Desires Well Tempered.'" In *Erotic Politics:*

Desire on the Renaissance Stage, ed. Susan Zimmerman, 103–126. London and New York: Routledge, 1992.

———. "The Poets Royal Exchange: Patronage and Commerce in Early Modern Drama." *Yearbook of English Studies* 21 (1991): 53–62.

McMillin, Scott. *The Elizabethan Theatre and "The Book of Sir Thomas More."* Ithaca and London: Cornell University Press, 1987.

Melchiori, Barbara Arnett. "Undercurrents in Victorian Illustrations of Shakespeare." In *Images of Shakespeare: Proceedings of the Third Congress of the ISA, 1986*, ed. Werner Habicht, et al., 120–128. Newark: University of Delaware Press, 1988.

Middleton, Thomas. *The Family of Love.* London, 1608.

Middleton, Thomas, and Thomas Dekker. *The Roaring Girl.* Ed. Andor Gomme. New Mermaids. London: Ernest Benn, 1976.

Mitchell, W. J. T. *Picture Theory: Essays on Verbal and Visual Representation.* Chicago and London: University of Chicago Press, 1994.

Montrose, Louis. "Professing the Renaissance: The Poetics and Politics of Culture." In Veeser, *The New Historicism*, 15–36.

Morrison, Ken. "Back to the Future." *Montreal Mirror*, April 1, 1988.

Munday, Anthony. *The Death of Robert Earl of Huntingdon.* Ed. John C. Meagher. Malone Society. Oxford: Oxford University Press, 1967.

———. *Sir Thomas More.* Ed. Vittorio Gabrieli and Giorgio Melchiori. Revels Plays. Manchester: Manchester University Press, 1990.

Nabbes, Thomas. *The Works of Thomas Nabbes.* In *A Collection of Old English Plays.* Ed. A. H. Bullen. 4 vols. London, 1882–1889. Rpt. New York: B. Blom, 1964.

Nardocchio, Elaine F. *Theatre and Politics in Modern Québec.* Edmonton: University of Alberta Press, 1986.

Nashe, Thomas. *The Works.* Ed. Ronald B. McKerrow. 5 vols. London, 1904–1911. Rpt. with corrections and supplementary notes. Ed. F. P. Wilson. Oxford: B. Blackwell, 1958.

Nicoll, Allardyce. "Political Plays of the Restoration." *Modern Language Review* 16 (1921): 224–242.

Nunn, Trevor. "Shakespeare as Shakespeare Intended?" In theatre program for *Timon of Athens*. London: Proscenium Publications, 1991.

Odell, George C. D. *Shakespeare from Betterton to Irving.* 2 vols. 1920. Rpt. New York: Dover Publications, 1966.

Orgel, Stephen. "The Authentic Shakespeare." *Representations* 21 (1988): 1–25.

———. "What Is a Text?" *Research Opportunities in Renaissance Drama* 24 (1981): 3–6.

Ornstein, Robert. *A Kingdom for a Stage: The Achievement of Shakespeare's History Plays*. Cambridge, Mass.: Harvard University Press, 1972.

Osborne, Laurie. "The Texts of *Twelfth Night*." *English Literary History* 57 (1990): 37–61.

Ouaknine, Serge. "La Dialectique du pouvoir dans sa jouissance." *Vice Versa* 25 (1988): 28.

Oxberry, William. "Memoir of Miss Ann Maria Tree." In *Oxberry's Dramatic Biography*, III: 198–213. London: G. Virtue, 1825.

Patterson, Annabel. *Censorship and Interpretation: The Conditions of Writing and Reading in Early Modern England*. Madison: University of Wisconsin Press, 1984.

Peele, George. *The Dramatic Works*. Ed. Frank S. Hook, John Yoklavich, R. Mark Benbow, and Elmer Blistein. 2 vols. New Haven and London: Yale University Press, 1961–1970.

Pettigrew, John, and Jamie Portman. *Stratford: The First Thirty Years*. 2 vols. Toronto: Macmillan, 1985.

Phelan, Peggy. *Unmarked: The Politics of Performance*. London and New York: Routledge, 1993.

Pontaut, Alain. "Jean Boilard rend un inoubliable *Richard II*." *Le Devoir*, September 24, 1988.

Postlewait, Thomas. "Autobiography and Theatre History." In Postlewait and McConachie, 248–272.

———. "Historiography and the Theatrical Event: A Primer with Twelve Cruxes." *Theatre Journal* 43 (1991): 157–178.

Postlewait, Thomas, and Bruce A. McConachie, eds. *Interpreting the Theatrical Past: Essays in the Historiography of Performance*. Iowa City: University of Iowa Press, 1989.

The P. R. B. Journal: William Michael Rossetti's Diary of the Pre-Raphaelite Brotherhood: 1849–1853. Ed. William E. Fredeman. Oxford: Clarendon Press, 1975.

"Un Printemps Shakespeare." *Châtelaine*, July 1988, 18.

Prosser, David. "The Education of the Audience." *Canadian Theatre Review* 57 (Winter 1988): 17–21.

The Puritan. Ed. John S. Farmer. Amersham, England: Tudor Facsimile Series, 1911.

Rappaport, Steve Lee. *Worlds within Worlds: Structures of Life in Sixteenth-Century London*. Cambridge: Cambridge University Press, 1989.

"The Revenger's Tragedy" Attributed to Thomas Middleton: A Facsimile of the 1607/8 Quarto. Ed. MacD. P. Jackson. Rutherford, Madison, Teaneck: Fairleigh Dickinson Press, 1983.

Ronalds, Francis S. *The Attempted Whig Revolution of 1678–1681*. Totowa, N.J.: Rowman and Littlefield, 1974.

Rosler, Martha. "In, Around, and Afterthoughts (on Documentary Photography)." In *The Contest of Meaning: Critical Histories of Photography*, ed. Richard Bolton, 303–342. Cambridge: Massachusetts Institute of Technology Press, 1989.

Rowley, William. *All's Lost by Lust* and *A Shoemaker, a Gentleman*. Ed. Charles Wharton Stork. Philadelphia: University of Pennsylvania Press, 1910.

Rutter, Carol, with Sinead Cusack, Paola Dionisotti, Fiona Shaw, Juliet Stevenson, and Harriet Walter. *Clamorous Voices: Shakespeare's Women Today*. London and New York: Routledge/Theatre Arts, 1989.

Saddlemyer, Ann. "On the Necessity of Criticising Criticism." *Theatre History in Canada* 8 (1987): 135–140.

Salter, Denis. "Actorly Reading in (Post)colonial Space." Unpublished paper contributed to 1993 Shakespeare Association of America seminar.

Schoenbaum, Samuel. *Shakespeare: A Documentary Life*. Oxford: Clarendon Press, 1975.

Sedgwick, Eve Kosofsky. "Against Epistemology." In Chandler et al., 132–136.

"Sex, Lies and Kung Fu." *Maclean's*, May 10, 1993, 51–52.

Shakespeare, William. *The Norton Facsimile: The First Folio of Shakespeare*. Ed. Charlton Hinman. New York and London: Paul Hamlyn, 1968.

———. *Shakespeare's Plays in Quarto*. Ed. Michael J. B. Allen and Kenneth Muir. Berkeley and Los Angeles: University of California Press, 1982.

———. *Twelfth Night: The Arden Shakespeare*. Ed. J. M. Lothian and T. W. Craik. New York: Routledge, 1975, rpt. 1988.

———. *Twelfth Night: Inchbald's British Theatre*, vol. 4. London: Longman, Hurst, Rees, and Orm, 1808.

———. *William Shakespeare: The Complete Works*. Gen. ed. Stanley Wells and Gary Taylor. Oxford: Oxford University Press, 1986.

———. *William Shakespeare: Works*. Gen. ed. Alfred Harbage. Baltimore: Penguin, 1969.

———. *Works: The Riverside Shakespeare*. Ed. G. B. Evans et al. Boston: Houghton Mifflin, 1974.

Shakespeare, William, and John Fletcher. *The Two Noble Kinsmen*. Ed. G. R. Proudfoot. Regents Renaissance Drama. Lincoln: University of Nebraska Press, 1970.

Sharpham, Edward. *A Critical Old Spelling Edition of the Works of Edward*

Sharpham. Ed. Christopher Gordon Petter. New York and London: Garland, 1986.

Shattuck, Charles. "Introduction." In Shattuck, *The Shakespeare Promptbooks,* x–xx.

———. *Shakespeare on the American Stage from the Hallams to Edwin Booth.* Washington, D.C.: Folger Shakespeare Library, 1976.

———. *The Shakespeare Promptbooks: A Descriptive Catalogue.* Urbana: University of Illinois Press, 1965.

Shirley, Henry. *The Martyred Soldier.* In *A Collection of Old English Plays,* ed. A. H. Bullen, I: 165–256. 4 vols. London, 1882–1889.

Shirley, James. *The Cardinal.* Ed. E. M. Yearling. Revels Plays. Manchester: Manchester University Press, 1986.

———. *The Gentleman of Venice.* Ed. Wilson F. Engel. Studies in English Literature no. 62. Salzburg: Institut für Engl. Sprache, 1976.

Sinfield, Alan. *Faultlines: Cultural Materialism and the Politics of Dissident Reading.* Berkeley and Los Angeles: University of California Press, 1992.

———. "Royal Shakespeare: Theatre and the Making of Ideology." In Dollimore and Sinfield, 158–181.

Skura, Meredith Anne. *Shakespeare the Actor and the Purposes of Playing.* Chicago and London: University of Chicago Press, 1993.

Solomon-Godeau, Abigail. *Photography at the Dock.* Minneapolis: University of Minnesota Press, 1991.

Songe d'une nuit d'été. Dir. Robert Lepage. Prod. Théâtre du Nouveau Monde, 1988. Press release and program.

Sontag, Susan. *On Photography.* New York: Dell Publishing Company, 1973.

Sorge, Thomas. *Gespielte Geschichte: Die ausgestellte Fiktion in Morus' "Utopia" und in Shakespeares englischen Historienspielen.* Frankfurt am Main: Peter Lang, 1992.

Spencer, Christopher. *Nahum Tate.* New York: Twayne Publishers, 1972.

Spencer, Hazelton. *Shakespeare Improved.* Cambridge, Mass.: Harvard University Press, 1927.

Stanislavski, Konstantin. "From the Production Plan of *Othello.*" In *Acting: A Handbook of the Stanislavski Method,* comp. Toby Cole, 130–138. New York: Crown, 1975.

Stevenson, Laura. *Praise and Paradox: Merchants and Craftsmen in Elizabethan Popular Literature.* Cambridge: Cambridge University Press, 1984.

St-Hilaire, Jean. "Le Printemps Shakespearien de Montréal." *Le Soleil,* April 30, 1988.

————. "'Songe d'une nuit d'été.' Lepage crée une mise en scène ensorcelante." *Le Soleil*, April 29, 1988.

Strode, Hudson. *Jefferson Davis*. 3 vols. New York: Harcourt, Brace, 1964.

Styan, J. L. *The Shakespeare Revolution*. Cambridge: Cambridge University Press, 1977.

Talbot, Michelle. "'Macbeth'. . . une grimace à l'impossible." *Dimanche-Matin*, November 5, 1978.

Tate, Nahum. "Preface." In *The Ingratitude of a Common-Wealth*. London, 1682. Rpt. London: Cornmarket Press, 1969.

Taylor, Gary. "General Introduction." In *William Shakespeare: A Textual Companion*, ed. Stanley Wells and Gary Taylor, 1–68. Oxford: Clarendon Press, 1987.

The Telltale. Ed. R. A. Foakes and J. C. Gibson. Malone Society. Oxford: Oxford University Press, 1960.

La Tempête de William Shakespeare. Dir. Alice Ronfard. Prod. Théâtre Expérimental des Femmes, 1988. Press release.

Tennenhouse, Leonard. *Power on Display: The Politics of Shakespeare's Genres*. London and New York: Routledge, 1988.

"Le Testament d'un auteur éternel." *La Presse*, March 12, 1988.

Thaon, Brenda. "Michel Garneau's Macbeth: An Experiment in Translating." In *La Traduction: L'Universitaire et le practicien*, ed. Arlette Thomas and Jacques Flamand, 207–212. Ottawa: University of Ottawa Press, 1984.

Thirsk, Joan. *Economic Policies and Projects: The Development of a Consumer Society in Early Modern England*. Oxford: Clarendon Press, 1978.

Thompson, Kristin, and David Bordwell. *Film History: An Introduction*. New York: McGraw-Hill, 1994.

Thomson, Leslie. "A Quarto 'Marked for Performance': Evidence of What?" *Medieval and Renaissance Drama in England* 8 (1995): 176–210.

Thomson, Peter. *Shakespeare's Professional Career*. Cambridge: Cambridge University Press, 1992.

Tillyard, E. M. W. *Shakespeare's History Plays*. New York: Macmillan, 1947.

Traubel, Horace. *With Walt Whitman at Camden*. 5 vols. New York: Rowman and Littlefield, 1961.

Tropea, Silvana. "Ron Daniels Finds the Space inside Shakespeare." *American Theatre* 11 (1994): 40–41.

Tupper, John Lucas. "Viola and Olivia." In *Art and Poetry: Being Thoughts towards Nature Conducted Principally by Artists*. London: Dickinson and Company, 1850.

Turner, Thomas Reed. *Beware the People Weeping: Public Opinion and the*

Assassination of Abraham Lincoln. Baton Rouge and London: Louisiana State University Press, 1982.

The Two Merry Milkmaids. Ed. John S. Farmer. Tudor Facsimile Texts. Amersham, 1914.

Tynan, Kenneth. *Curtains*. New York: Atheneum, 1961.

Ubersfeld, Anne. *L'Ecole du spectateur*. Paris: Editions sociales, 1981.

Usherwood, Stephen. *Shakespeare Play by Play*. Illus. Raymond Piper. New York: Hill and Wang, 1967.

Veeser, H. Aram. "Introduction." In Veeser, *The New Historicism*, ix–xvi.

————. *The New Historicism*. New York and London: Routledge, 1989.

Wapull, George. *The Tide Tarrieth No Man*. Ed. Ernest Rühl. *Shakespeare-Jahrbuch* 43 (1907): 1–52.

Wardle, Irving. *Theatre Criticism*. London and New York: Routledge, 1992.

A Warning for Fair Women. Ed. John S. Farmer. Amersham, England: Tudor Facsimile Series, 1912.

Watermeier, Daniel. *Between Actor and Critic, Selected Letters of Edwin Booth and William Winter*. Princeton: Princeton University Press, 1971.

Webster, John. *The Devil's Law-Case*. Ed. Frances A. Shirley. Regents Renaissance Drama. Lincoln: University of Nebraska Press, 1972.

Weimann, Robert. "Bifold Authority in Shakespeare's Theatre." *Shakespeare Quarterly* 39 (1988): 401–417.

————. "'Moralize Two Meanings' in One Play: Divided Authority on the Morality Stage." In *Medieval and Early Renaissance Drama: Reconsiderations*, ed. Milla Riggio and Martin Stevens. Special issue of *Mediaevalia* 18 (1995): 427–450.

————. "Representation and Performance: Authority in Shakespeare's Theater." *PMLA* 107 (1992): 497–510.

————. *Shakespeare and the Popular Tradition in the Theater: Studies in the Social Dimension of Dramatic Form and Function*. Ed. Robert Schwarts. Baltimore: Johns Hopkins University Press, 1987.

————. "Textual Authority and Performative Agency: The Uses of Disguise in Shakespeare's Theatre." *New Literary History* 25 (1994): 789–808.

Welsh, Alexander. *Strong Representations: Narrative and Circumstantial Evidence in England*. Baltimore: Johns Hopkins University Press, 1992.

Whetstone, George. *Promos and Cassandra*. Ed. John S. Farmer. Amersham, England: Tudor Facsimile Series, 1910.

Whigham, Frank. "Ideology and Class Conduct in *The Merchant of Venice*." *Renaissance Drama* n.s. 10 (1979): 93–115.

White, Hayden. *The Content of the Form: Narrative Discourse and Histori-*

cal Representation. Baltimore: Johns Hopkins University Press, 1987.

———. Metahistory: The Historical Imagination in Nineteenth-Century Europe. Baltimore: Johns Hopkins University Press, 1973.

———. "New Historicism: A Comment." In Veeser, The New Historicism, 293–302.

———. Tropics of Discourse: Essays in Cultural Criticism. Baltimore: Johns Hopkins University Press, 1978.

Whiting, George W. "Political Satire in London Stage Plays, 1680–83." Modern Philology 18 (1930–1931): 29–43.

Whitman, Walt. The Complete Writings. New York and London: P. G. Putnam's Sons, 1902.

Wikander, Matthew H. "The Spitted Infant: Scenic Emblem and Exclusionist Politics in Restoration Adaptations of Shakespeare." Shakespeare Quarterly 37 (1986): 340–358.

Wiles, David. Shakespeare's Clown: Actor and Text in the Elizabethan Playhouse. Cambridge: Cambridge University Press, 1987.

Williams, Raymond. Keywords: A Vocabulary of Culture and Society. London: Fontana/Croom Helm, 1976.

Wilson, Ann. "Deadpan." Canadian Theatre Review 57 (Winter 1988): 11–16.

———. "Starters: A Theatre Program and Its Audience." Canadian Theatre Review 71 (Summer 1992): 49–54.

Wilson, Francis. John Wilkes Booth: Fact and Fiction of Lincoln's Assassination. New York: Benjamin Blom, 1972.

Wilson, J. Dover, and T. C. Worsley. Shakespeare's Histories at Stratford 1951. London: Max Reinhardt, 1952.

Wilson, Richard. Will Power: Essays on Shakespearean Authority. London: Harvester Wheatsheaf, 1993.

Wilstach, Paul. Richard Mansfield: The Man and the Actor. New York: Scribner, 1908.

Winter, William. The Life and Art of Edwin Booth. New York: Greenwood Press, 1893.

Woodhouse, Adrian. Angus McBean. London: Quartet Books, 1982.

Worthen, W. B. "Deeper Meanings and Theatrical Technique: The Rhetoric of Performance Criticism." Shakespeare Quarterly 40 (1989): 440–455.

———. "Staging 'Shakespeare': Acting, Authority, and the Rhetoric of Performance." In Shakespeare, Theory, and Performance, ed. James Bulman, 12–28. London and New York: Routledge, 1996.

Yachnin, Paul. "The Powerless Theater." English Literary Renaissance 21 (1991): 49–74.

Index

STUDIES IN THEATRE HISTORY AND CULTURE

Marginal Sights: Staging the Chinese in America
  By James S. Moy

Melodramatic Formations: American Theatre
and Society, 1820–1870
  By Bruce A. McConachie

Meyerhold: A Revolution in Theatre
  By Edward Braun

Modern Hamlets and Their Soliloquies
  By Mary Z. Maher

The Performance of Power: Theatrical Discourse
and Politics
  Edited by Sue-Ellen Case and Janelle Reinelt

The Recurrence of Fate: Theatre and Memory in
Twentieth-Century Russia
  By Spencer Golub

Textual and Theatrical Shakespeare: Questions
of Evidence
  Edited by Edward Pechter

The Trick of Singularity: *Twelfth Night* and the
Performance Editions
  By Laurie E. Osborne

Wandering Stars: Russian Emigré Theatre,
1905–1940
  Edited by Laurence Senelick